BELIEF SYSTEMS AND THE PERCEPTION OF REALITY

This book focuses on the social psychology of belief systems and how they influence perceptions of reality. These belief systems, from politics to religion to science, not only shape one's thoughts and views but also can be the cause of conflict and disagreement over values, particularly when they are enacted in political policies.

In *Belief Systems and the Perception of Reality*, editors Bastiaan T. Rutjens and Mark J. Brandt examine the social psychological effects at the heart of the conflict by bringing together contributions under five themes: motivated reasoning, inequality, threat, scientists interpreting science, and people interpreting science. This book aims to create a more integrated understanding of reality perception and its connection with belief systems, viewed through the lens of social psychology.

The synthesis of expert contributors as well as the literature around social psychology and belief systems makes this a unique resource for students, researchers, and academics in behavioral and social sciences, as well as activists and journalists working in this political field.

Bastiaan T. Rutjens is an Assistant Professor in the Social Psychology Program of the Psychology Department at the University of Amsterdam. His research interests are in social and cultural psychology, with a particular focus on the psychological functionings of religious and secular belief systems and worldviews.

Mark J. Brandt is an Associate Professor in the Department of Social Psychology at Tilburg University. He aims to understand ideological and moral beliefs – such as political ideology, religious fundamentalism, and moral conviction – and how they structure attitudes and behaviors, how they provide people with meaning, and why people adopt them in the first place.

Current Issues in Social Psychology

Johan Karremans

Current Issues in Social Psychology is a series of edited books that reflect the state-of-the-art of current and emerging topics of interest in basic and applied social psychology.

Each volume is tightly focused on a particular topic and consists of seven to ten chapters contributed by international experts. The editors of individual volumes are leading figures in their areas and provide an introductory overview.

Example topics include: self-esteem, evolutionary social psychology, minority groups, social neuroscience, cyberbullying and social stigma.

Power and Identity
Edited by Denis Sindic, Manuela Barret and Rui Costa-Lopes

Cyberbullying
From theory to intervention
Edited by Trijntje Völlink, Francine Dehue and Conor Mc Guckin

Coping with Lack of Control in a Social World
Edited by Marcin Bukowski, Immo Fritsche, Ana Guinote & Mirosław Kofta

Intergroup Contact Theory
Recent Developments and Future Directions
Edited by Loris Vezzali & Sofia Stathi

Majority and Minority Influence
Societal Meaning and Cognitive Elaboration
Edited by Stamos Papastamou, Antonis Gardikiotis & Gerasimos Prodromitis

Mindfulness in Social Psychology
Edited by Johan C. Karremans and Esther K. Papies

Belief Systems and the Perception of Reality
Edited by Bastiaan T. Rutjens and Mark J. Brandt

BELIEF SYSTEMS AND THE PERCEPTION OF REALITY

Edited by Bastiaan T. Rutjens and Mark J. Brandt

LONDON AND NEW YORK

First published 2019
by Routledge
2 Park Square, Milton Park, Abingdon, Oxon OX14 4RN

and by Routledge
711 Third Avenue, New York, NY 10017

Routledge is an imprint of the Taylor & Francis Group, an informa business

British Library Cataloguing-in-Publication Data
A catalogue record for this book is available from the British Library

Library of Congress Cataloging-in-Publication Data
Names: Rutjens, Bastiaan T., editor. | Brandt, Mark J., editor.
Title: Belief systems and the perception of reality / edited by
Bastiaan Rutjens and Mark Brandt.
Description: New York: Taylor and Francis, [2019] |
Series: Current issues in social psychology
Identifiers: LCCN 2018016970 | ISBN 9781138070806
(hardback: alk. paper) | ISBN 9781138070813 (pbk.: alk. paper) |
ISBN 9781315114903 (ebook)
Subjects: LCSH: Belief and doubt. | Ideology—Social aspects. |
Ideology—Political aspects. | Perception (Philosophy)
Classification: LCC BF773 .B435 2018 | DDC 303.3/72—dc23
LC record available at https://lccn.loc.gov/2018016970

ISBN: 978-1-138-07080-6 (hbk)
ISBN: 978-1-138-07081-3 (pbk)
ISBN: 978-1-315-11490-3 (ebk)

Typeset in Bembo
by codeMantra

Printed and bound in Great Britain by
TJ International Ltd, Padstow, Cornwall

CONTENTS

List of contributors   *vii*

Introduction   1
Bastiaan T. Rutjens and Mark J. Brandt

THEME 1
Motivated reasoning   **7**

1 What is right is right: a three-part account of how ideology
   shapes factual belief   9
   Megan M. Ringel, Cristian G. Rodriguez, and Peter H. Ditto

2 System-level biases in the production and consumption
   of information: implications for system resilience and
   radical change   29
   *Erin P. Hennes, Adam J. Hampton, Ezgi Ozgumus, and
   Thomas J. Hamori*

THEME 2
Inequality   **45**

3 Ideology and perceptions of inequality   47
   Denise Baron, Jennifer Sheehy-Skeffington, and Nour Kteily

4 Perceptions of gender inequality in academia: reluctance to let go of individual merit ideology 63
Romy van der Lee and Naomi Ellemers

THEME 3
Threat **79**

5 Populism as political mentality underlying conspiracy theories 81
Jan-Willem van Prooijen

6 The role of cultural beliefs and existential motivation in suffering perceptions 97
Daniel Sullivan, Roman Palitsky, and Isaac F. Young

THEME 4
Scientists interpreting science **115**

7 Direct and indirect influences of political ideology on perceptions of scientific findings 117
Sean T. Stevens, Lee Jussim, Stephanie M. Anglin, and Nathan Honeycutt

8 Strategies for promoting strong inferences in political psychology research 134
Anthony N. Washburn and Linda J. Skitka

THEME 5
People interpreting science **147**

9 In genes we trust: on the consequences of genetic essentialism 149
Anita Schmalor and Steven J. Heine

10 Post-truth, anti-truth, and can't-handle-the-truth: how responses to science are shaped by concerns about its impact 164
Robbie M. Sutton, Aino Petterson, and Bastiaan T. Rutjens

Index 179

CONTRIBUTORS

Stephanie M. Anglin, Postdoc, Carnegie Mellon University

Denise Baron, PhD Student, London School of Economics and Political Science

Mark J. Brandt, Associate Professor, Tilburg University

Peter H. Ditto, Full Professor, University of California, Irvine

Naomi Ellemers, Full Professor, Utrecht University

Thomas J. Hamori, BS Student, Purdue University

Adam J. Hampton, PhD Student, Purdue University

Steven J. Heine, Full Professor, University of British Columbia

Erin P. Hennes, Assistant Professor, Purdue University

Nathan Honeycutt, PhD Student, Rutgers University

Lee Jussim, Full Professor, Rutgers University

Nour Kteily, Assistant Professor, Northwestern University

Romy van der Lee, Assistant Professor, Vrije Universiteit Amsterdam

Ezgi Ozgumus, Lab Manager, Purdue University

Roman Palitsky, PhD Student, University of Arizona

Aino Petterson, MSc Student, University of Kent

Jan-Willem van Prooijen, Associate Professor, Vrije Universiteit Amsterdam

Megan M. Ringel, PhD Student, University of California, Irvine

Cristian G. Rodriguez, PhD Student, University of California, Irvine

Bastiaan T. Rutjens, Assistant Professor, University of Amsterdam

Anita Schmalor, PhD Student, University of British Columbia

Jennifer Sheehy-Skeffington, Assistant Professor, London School of Economics and Political Science

Linda J. Skitka, Full Professor, University of Illinois at Chicago

Sean T. Stevens, Research Director, NYU–Stern School of Business

Daniel Sullivan, Assistant Professor, University of Arizona

Robbie M. Sutton, Full Professor, University of Kent

Anthony N. Washburn, PhD Student, University of Illinois at Chicago

Isaac F. Young, PhD Student, University of Arizona

INTRODUCTION

Bastiaan T. Rutjens and Mark J. Brandt

When we started working on this volume, the Brexit referendum had just taken place and President Obama was finishing the final months of his presidency. By the time the first chapters came in, Brexit negotiations had started to sour as campaign promises met economic reality, and the United States had a new president with a unique relationship with the truth. Of course, these are not necessarily new phenomena. The ideas that politicians lie, or at least bend the truth, to fit their political goals and that political campaigns make promises untethered from reality are not unique to this political age. However, the distance between reality and rhetoric might be.

Social psychology has long been concerned with people's perceptions of reality. This might concern relatively everyday perceptions, such as how we perceive the strengths and weakness of our romantic partners (Murray, Holmes, & Giffin, 1996), the detection of sarcasm in email (Kruger, Epley, Parker, & Ng, 2005), and whether wearing our lucky underwear will help us on the football field (Damisch, Stoberock, & Mussweiler, 2010). Humans have a complicated relationship with these perceptions (e.g. Ross & Ward, 1996). We think that we see the world objectively and that other rational people with the same information will see the world in the same way. And so, those people who do not share our views are irrational, ignorant, or worse. This can lead to simple, and sometimes funny, misunderstandings, but it can also play a role in escalating conflict (Kennedy & Pronin, 2008).

The current volume takes a step back. Rather than focusing on how perceptions of reality can lead to misunderstanding and conflict, we focus on how belief systems (i.e. ideological beliefs and worldviews) bias people's view on reality and the facts relevant in that reality in the first place (e.g. Flynn et al., 2017; Ringel, Rodriguez, & Ditto, 2019; Roussos & Dovidio, 2018; Van Bavel & Pereira, in press). Many of the ideas that are covered in this volume, such as biased information processing, perceptions of social inequality, conspiracy beliefs, trust in science, and ideological polarization, have been hot topics in both academia and public discourse. Nevertheless, in a time when it is necessary to add "fake news" and "post-truth" to our vocabulary, investigating how beliefs shape perceptions of reality seems to be more relevant than ever. The timing of the volume could (unfortunately) not be better.

The goal of this volume is to provide an overview of recent social psychological theorizing and research that examines how belief systems influence perceptions of reality. Belief systems, ranging from the political to the religious and even to the scientific, provide people with a lens to view the world and the events that take place in it. This harbors the potential for conflict and disagreement over values, and how those values are enacted in political policies. These types of conflicts are often studied in social and political psychology, and are at the heart of large literatures related to attitudes, morality, stereotypes, and prejudice.

Value differences and value conflicts per se are, however, not the focus of this volume. These differences and conflicts tend to spring from disagreement about how to solve a certain problem and oftentimes involve a trade-off between diverging priorities. However, people's ideological beliefs can bias how they view reality and lead them to have different perceptions of the actual facts on the ground (e.g. Baron, Sheehy-Skeffington, & Kteily, 2019; van der Lee & Ellemers, 2019) and if those facts should even be distributed to the rest of the population (Sutton, Petterson, & Rutjens, 2019). In other words, there is disagreement not so much about how to solve a certain problem but about whether there is a problem to begin with.

Let us take poverty as an example. Many people agree that poverty exists and is a bad thing that should be alleviated. Value differences, then, create conflict over *how* poverty should be reduced. Should the government reduce taxes so that businesses can hire more motivated people and, as a consequence, poverty is reduced? Or should the government provide cash grants to people in poverty to help them get by? Although this is a contentious debate, it is a debate that agrees on the basic fact: Poverty exists and is bad. However, other debates are less clear-cut. For many topics, people do not only differ on what is the best method to solve the problem, but they also differ on whether there is a problem *to begin with*. These biases in perceptions of reality emerge in a number of domains, such as the perception and interpretation of climate patterns, the ostensible danger of immigrants, the existence of structural social inequality, the interpretation of scientific data, or whether or not political elections are legitimate.

The current volume focuses on these latter questions. How is it that people disagree about the facts on the ground? Why do people perceive reality in diametrical opposite ways? Can these different construals of reality be overcome? The main goal is to bring together social psychologists who examine how people's belief systems affect their perceptions of reality across diverse domains. We hope that the volume helps to create a more integrated understanding of reality perception and its connection with beliefs and worldviews.

Book contents

Figure I.1 is a word cloud based on the chapters in this volume. As can be seen, how we see things and how this is biased by moral and political belief systems is the key overarching theme. We have organized the volume around five interconnected subthemes that illuminate the processes and domains where belief systems influence perceptions of reality. The themes are as follows: motivated reasoning, inequality, threat, scientists interpreting science, and people interpreting science.

The first theme, *motivated reasoning*, discusses motivated ideological and moral reasoning in the context of various societal issues. In Chapter 1, Ringel, Rodriguez, and Ditto start from the observation that a key contributor to partisan conflict in the United States is that liberals and conservatives hold different factual beliefs about various important policy-relevant matters such as taxes, guns, and climate change. These authors propose a three-part account of how such differential beliefs arise, by showing how ideologically and morally based beliefs (i.e. how the world *should* be) shape perceptions of reality (i.e. how the world really *is*). The three important contributors they identify are moralization, factualization, and socialization. Chapter 2, by Hennes, Hampton, Ozgumus, and Hamori, focuses on how system justification impacts on perceptions of reality. These authors highlight the specific influence of system-level motivations on biased information production and consumption, particularly in ideological contexts. When are people motivated to protect existing states of affairs and when are they biased toward motives to facilitate system rejection or social change?

Having laid the groundwork by looking at how ideology shapes perceptions of reality via various processes of motivated reasoning, we next turn to one specific contentious topic of ideological clashes: *Inequality*. Two manifestations of inequality are discussed: social and economic inequality, and gender inequality. In Chapter 3, Baron, Sheehy-Skeffington, and Kteily provide an overview of recent research on how ideology shapes perceptions of social and economic inequality.

FIGURE I.1 Word cloud created with text of all the chapters included.

Drawing from research on motivated cognition, their chapter reviews research on whether and when ideologies such as egalitarianism and conservatism are associated with biased perceptions of the degree and nature of social and economic inequality. They also investigate the consequences for support for social change. In Chapter 4, van der Lee and Ellemers focus on perceptions of gender inequality in organizations, with a particular focus on academia. The authors discuss how evidence for gender inequality is often met with skepticism and resistance, and discuss how this relates to individual-merit ideology.

The third theme focuses on how *threat* has a motivational impact on reality perceptions. First, van Prooijen (Chapter 5) discusses how some belief systems create the right environment for conspiracies to flourish, and that populism plays an important role in the creation of conspiracy theories. Populism is argued to consist of three underlying dimensions: anti-elitism, anti-pluralism, and threatened nationalism. Populism causes endorsement of alternative portrayals of reality, often in the form of conspiracy theories. Moreover, these conspiracy theories can in turn further reinforce populist sentiments. The aforementioned political changes of late feature some prominent examples of such conspiracy theories. In Chapter 6, Sullivan, Palitsky, and Young discuss perceptions of reality in the context of suffering. Suffering warrants explanation: why do I or my loved ones suffer? The authors argue that although painful experiences pertaining to suffering may sometimes pressure people toward more accurate accounts of reality, but more often it will be construed in motivated and culturally constructed ways, which are variable and potentially quite detached from reality. In other words, the ideology that goes with one's culture shapes how suffering is construed.

The fourth and fifth themes of the volume focus on how science and scientific evidence is interpreted. First, two chapters discuss how a special kind of people, namely *scientists*, interpret – and conduct – science. Scientists are humans, and so they are prone to ideologically and morally motivated reasoning just like everyone else. There has been much debate about ideological heterogeneity within the scientific community, for example, in the social sciences, and how this can shape the interpretation of scientific evidence. In Chapter 7, Stevens, Jussim, Anglin, and Honeycutt describe how political ideology can direct the processes that produce scientific facts, by influencing what topic should be studied, how to study them, and by shunning researchers and ideas that conflict with the scientists' own political values. It is one thing that ideology makes people more skeptical about certain scientific facts, but it is another (potentially more serious) thing if these facts are themselves partially products of ideology. Washburn and Skitka (Chapter 8) take up the task to come up with ways to minimize the potentially deleterious ways in which ideology shapes social and political psychology research. Building on the classic and influential ideas of Platt (1964) on strong inference, they argue that employing alternative hypotheses to prevent confirmation bias makes for better science. Competing hypotheses about ideological differences in psychological functioning should consider both flattering and less flattering explanations for human behavior, according to these authors.

The final two chapters focus on how all *other people* (i.e. members of the public) interpret science. Schmalor and Heine (Chapter 9) investigate how essentialist beliefs affect the interpretation of scientific work in genetics, more specifically how it impacts people's understanding of race, gender, and criminality, among other things. Through shaping how people construe facts about the impact of genes on behavior, genetic essentialism has important consequences for science, legislation, and ideological movements. In Chapter 10, Sutton, Petterson, and Rutjens describe how people can be motivated to dispute the truth value of scientific evidence, or even censor and obstruct science, to prevent it from having an adverse impact on society. In other words, when certain scientific findings are perceived to be threatening to collective interests and the common good, people tend to prefer to refute or dismiss the evidence. This "impact bias" has important implications for public understanding of science as well as for how debated about bias in science should be construed.

When considered as a group, the chapters in this volume show that people often differ in what they perceive to be real, or factual, and that these diverging reality perceptions stem – at least in part – from differences in ideologies and beliefs. These perceptions do not reflect anomalous beliefs, or that one side is necessarily right and the other wrong. Rather, what people (like to) believe are facts that maintain their worldview and the social systems in which they operate. To further our understanding of contemporary ideological clashes and polarization, it is important to look beyond (partisan) value conflicts (e.g. disagreements over how we should solve poverty; what is the best way to combat climate change) and acknowledge the existence of stark differences in perceptions of reality (e.g. is poverty a problem; is climate change real).

The next key step for scholars, activists, and others interested in advancing a fact-based social and political discourse is to understand how to correct inaccurate perceptions of reality. Recent work has begun to show how exposure to factual information can be effective in correcting misperceptions (Berinsky, 2017), but not always (Nyhan et al., 2014; Nyhan & Reifler, 2010). A key challenge will be to either neutralize the effects of belief systems on motivational and cognitive processes associated with perceptions of reality or to harness those effects to promote a more accurate assessment of the world. This may be done by increasing the motivational oomph of alternative motivations, such as accuracy motivations, by promoting genuine curiosity (Kahan et al., 2017) and rewarding accuracy among both the general public and the pundit class (Prior et al., 2015). We suspect that present and future work that uncovers ways to effectively neutralize the motivational power of belief systems on perceptions of reality and promote accuracy norms will be a major practical contribution of the social sciences to this pressing present-day issue.

References

Baron, D., Sheehy-Skeffington, J., & Kteily, N. (2019). Ideology and perceptions of inequality. In B. T. Rutjens & M. J. Brandt (Eds.). *Belief systems and the perception of reality.* Oxon: Routledge.

Berinsky, A. J. (2017). Rumors and health care reform: Experiments in political misinformation. *British Journal of Political Science, 47*(2), 241–262.

Damisch, L., Stoberock, B., & Mussweiler, T. (2010). Keep your fingers crossed! How superstition improves performance. *Psychological Science, 21*(7), 1014–1020.

Flynn, D. J., Nyhan, B., & Reifler, J. (2017). The nature and origins of misperceptions: Understanding false and unsupported beliefs about politics. *Political Psychology, 38*(S1), 127–150.

Kahan, D. M., Landrum, A., Carpenter, K., Helft, L., & Hall Jamieson, K. (2017). Science curiosity and political information processing. *Political Psychology, 38*(S1), 179–199.

Kennedy, K. A., & Pronin, E. (2008). When disagreement gets ugly: Perceptions of bias and the escalation of conflict. *Personality and Social Psychology Bulletin, 34*(6), 833–848.

Kruger, J., Epley, N., Parker, J., & Ng, Z. W. (2005). Egocentrism over e-mail: Can we communicate as well as we think? *Journal of Personality and Social Psychology, 89*(6), 925.

Murray, S. L., Holmes, J. G., & Griffin, D. W. (1996). The self-fulfilling nature of positive illusions in romantic relationships: Love is not blind, but prescient. *Journal of Personality and Social Psychology, 71*(6), 1155.

Nyhan, B., & Reifler, J. (2010). When corrections fail: The persistence of political misperceptions. *Political Behavior, 32*(2), 303–330.

Nyhan, B., Reifler, J., Richey, S., & Freed, G. L. (2014). Effective messages in vaccine promotion: A randomized trial. *Pediatrics, 133*(4), e835–e842.

Platt, J. R. (1964). Strong inference. *Science, 146,* 347-353.

Prior, M., Sood, G., & Khanna, K. (2015). You cannot be serious: The impact of accuracy incentives on partisan bias in reports of economic perceptions. *Quarterly Journal of Political Science, 10*(4), 489–518.

Ringel, M. M., Rodriguez, C. G., & Ditto, P. H. (2019). What is right is right: A three-part account of how ideology shapes factual belief. In B. T. Rutjens & M. J. Brandt (Eds.). *Belief systems and the perception of reality.* Oxon: Routledge.

Ross, L., & Ward, A. (1996). Naive realism in everyday life: Implications for social conflict and misunderstanding. In T. Brown, E. S. Reed, & E. Turiel (Eds.). *Values and knowledge* (pp. 103–135). Hillsdale, NJ: Erlbaum.

Roussos, G., & Dovidio, J. F. (2018). Hate speech is in the eye of the beholder: The influence of racial attitudes and freedom of speech beliefs on perceptions of racially motivated threats of violence. *Social Psychological and Personality Science, 9,* 176–185.

Sutton, R. M., Petterson, A., & Rutjens, B. T. (2019). Post-truth, anti-truth, and can't-handle-the-truth: How responses to science are shaped by concerns about its impact. In B. T. Rutjens & M. J. Brandt (Eds.). *Belief systems and the perception of reality.* Oxon: Routledge.

Van Bavel, J. J., & Pereira, A. (2019). The partisan brain: An identity-based model of political belief. *Trends in Cognitive Science.*

van der Lee, R., & Ellemers, N. (2019). Perceptions of gender inequality in academia: Reluctance to let go of individual merit ideology. In B.T. Rutjens & M.J. Brandt (Eds.). *Belief systems and the perception of reality.* Oxon: Routledge.

THEME 1
Motivated reasoning

1

WHAT IS RIGHT IS RIGHT

A three-part account of how ideology shapes factual belief

Megan M. Ringel, Cristian G. Rodriguez, and Peter H. Ditto

In the days after Congressman Steve Scalise and three others were shot and wounded while practicing for an annual charity baseball game between Republican and Democratic lawmakers, the calls to inject a more civil tone into America's increasingly toxic political discourse resounded from both sides of the aisle. The sentiment behind those calls for civility was no doubt sincere, but we suspect that many attempts at civil discussion that were initiated by those calls met a similar unfortunate fate. As liberals and conservatives sat down to discuss the issues of the day – taxes, guns, health care, and the rest – their civil intentions were almost certainly tested upon discovering that many of the basic facts underlying their political opinions were not shared by their discussion partners. Republicans citing data showing that low taxes spur economic growth, that more gun owners make communities safer, and that Obamacare is imploding in an irreversible death spiral quickly found their Democratic friends citing data supporting diametrically opposite conclusions on each of these points. As such conversations continued, frustration on both sides was likely to build as each attempt to move toward some productive mutual understanding was stymied by the inability to agree on the ground-level facts that necessarily form the foundation of any attempt at compromise or negotiation. It is tough to have a civil political discussion, let alone a productive one, when the two sides begin that discussion with different sets of facts.

The questions we explore in this chapter concern the causes and consequences of the factual divide between Red (conservative) and Blue (liberal) America. Specifically, we propose a three-part account of how such differential beliefs arise or, more precisely, an account of how prescriptive beliefs (ideologically and morally based beliefs regarding how the world *should be*) shape descriptive ones ("factual" beliefs regarding how the world really *is*). Our account identifies three important contributing processes: *moralization* (the infusion of issues and events with moral significance); *factualization* (the construction of pseudo-descriptive justifications for moral evaluations); and *socialization* (the reinforcement of morally palatable beliefs by selective exposure to ideologically sympathetic people, groups, and media sources). Our core contention is that the factual gulf between liberals and conservatives is an important contributor to the corrosive polarization that currently afflicts American national politics, not just because the inability to agree on basic ground-level "facts" makes political transactions like negotiation and compromise more difficult, but also because differences in factual belief can fuel negative perceptions and feelings across party lines. If one person believes a fact to be true that another believes just as certainly to be false, it is hard for either one not to see the other as stupid, disingenuous, or both.

Politics, morality, and facts

Politics is and in fact should be about moral vision: individuals and political parties offering their unique vision of what is right and wrong for the country and its citizens, and how to realize that vision through public policy. It is not surprising or odd that people differ in their vision of what constitutes a morally enlightened society, nor that these different moral visions form the basis of major political divisions and coalitions such as that between the left (liberals, progressives, the Democratic party in the United States) and the right (conservatives, traditionalists, the Republican party in the United States). Differences in moral sensitivity and value have the dual function of binding subgroups together in defense and celebration of the shared moral vision of their (liberal or conservative) tribe and driving a wedge between the subgroups as the differences in what each side values and fears translate into real-world conflicts over policies that are alternatively viewed as championing or defiling each side's vision of a just and moral society (Graham et al., 2013).

Politics seems particularly infused with morality of late. Many key political issues are moral ones – abortion, same-sex marriage – and even issues that are not inherently moral are often seen through a moral lens. Former House Speaker John Boehner spoke of national debt as a "moral threat" (Epstein, 2011), Senator Bernie Sanders called income inequality "the great moral issue of our time" (Schulson, 2016), and former Vice President Al Gore said of climate change that "it is indeed a single, reckless and immoral act if one fails to take his part in addressing this problem" ("Climate Change," 2010). Imbuing political issues with morality can fuel commitment and spur action in supporters (Skitka, Bauman, & Sargis, 2005), but its cost is the implication that the opposition is acting immorally. Polling data reflect this growing animosity as Democrats' and Republicans' views of each other have become increasingly negative since the 1960s (Pew Research Center, 2016).

These moral differences are accompanied by different factual beliefs. Perhaps the two most memorable phrases of 2017 were "fake news" and "alternative facts," and public opinion data confirm that the political parties show sharp differences in what they believe to be true. For example, 92% of Democrats agree that there is "solid evidence" of global warming, compared to 52% of Republicans (Pew Research Center, 2017), and 80% of Democrats, compared to 33% of Republicans, agree that the "Russian government tried to influence the outcome of last fall's U.S. presidential election" (Washington Post, 2017). In short, a factual gulf has emerged along ideological lines for many issues. The emergence and consequences of differing moral convictions, each with their associated sets of facts, are what we seek to explain in the sections that follow.

Moralization

In the last two decades, researchers have explored the role of moral attitudes (or moral convictions) in social and political behavior (Skitka et al., 2005). A moral attitude involves the evaluation of an attitude object as fundamentally right or wrong, moral or immoral, rather than a mere preference (Rozin, 1999). Moral attitudes have distinct features, including universality, objectivity, and emotion (Skitka, 2010). Moral attitudes are experienced as universal truths that should apply to everyone, regardless of circumstance or cultural differences. They are experienced as self-evident, objectively true beliefs and are strongly associated with intense emotions, such as disgust or anger, more so than strong nonmoral attitudes. Moral attitudes have unique consequences and predict behavior for which other attitude strength components cannot account (Skitka et al., 2005).

Rozin and colleagues conducted influential work on how commonplace behaviors, such as vegetarianism (Rozin, Markwith, & Stoess, 1997) and cigarette smoking (Rozin & Singh, 1999), become moralized. People may moralize eating meat because something prompts them to see the connection between a moral principle (e.g. not harming animals) and the act of eating meat. Strong affective experiences can also lead to moralization. A person may not be moved to become a vegetarian just by knowing that eating meat harms animals but may be more motivated if they were to watch an emotionally arousing video of a factory farm. Feeling strong emotions, such as disgust, is thought to be part of how cigarette smoking evolved into a moral issue (rather than a matter of taste or preference) in the United States (Rozin & Singh, 1999). The link between strong feelings of disgust and moralized attitudes has been replicated with other issues as well, such as attitudes toward homosexuality (Olatunji, 2008) and obesity (Ringel, 2016).

Political moralization

But how do political issues become moralized? We propose two types of political moralization that often have negative consequences. The first type to consider is what we call *issue moralization*. Issue moralization occurs when people connect broad moral values to specific political issues. Consider the contentious issue of abortion in the United States. Antiabortion proponents may link abortion to one or more moral principles, such as prohibitions against harming innocent life or violations related to notions of sexual purity. Those in favor of abortion rights may moralize the issue by linking it to concerns about harm to the mother's life or a woman's right to control her own body.

A person's emotions toward an issue and how much they care about it (i.e. attitude importance) are also thought to be crucial to the moralization process (Brandt, Wetherell, & Crawford, 2015; Wisneski & Skitka, 2017). Longitudinal research suggests a bidirectional influence between moralization and affect. Strong emotions lead to greater moralization over time, but moralization also predicts stronger emotions over time (Brandt, Wisneski, & Skitka, 2015). Thus, people can enter a cycle in which an emotional reaction leads to moralization, and moralization leads to a greater sense of outrage, disgust, or other strong emotions. Attitude importance also predicts greater moralization of an issue over time – the more a person cares about an issue, the more likely they are to imbue it with moral significance (Brandt, Wetherell, & Crawford, 2015). In sum, the moralization process involves both cognitive and affective components, and should occur for issues people deem personally important.

Outside influences such as politicians and media sources can encourage citizens to moralize a political issue. Marietta (2008) contends that politicians often use "sacred rhetoric," which leads people to frame issues in terms of nonnegotiable moral values rather than pragmatic assessments of costs and benefits. Morally framed messages tend to contain strong emotional language, which appeals to audiences that are likely to share the same emotional response to a given issue (Brady, Wills, Jost, Tucker, & Van Bavel, 2017; Kreps & Monin, 2011). Rhetoric invoking disgust – considered one of the most influential emotions in moral judgments (e.g. Schnall, Haidt, Clore, & Jordan, 2008) – has been found to lessen support for gay rights (Gadarian & van der Vort, 2017). People perceive the communicator of a moral message as more certain and confident in their position, thereby increasing the communicator's persuasive appeal (Kreps & Monin, 2011). Given these benefits of moral framing, it is no wonder that politicians and other skilled communicators use it to their advantage.

A second type of moralization that can shed light on political behavior is what we call *personal moralization*. Personal moralization represents the darker side of political conflict, wherein people are not focused on arguments about an issue itself but rather focused on mistrust, blame, and demonization of the other side. One reason politics becomes invested with moral significance is that people tend to *intentionalize* differences of opinion about issues. Rather than seeing a political dispute as simply a pragmatic disagreement between actors who all want the same outcome, people often ascribe nefarious intentions to those on the other side. When people feel highly involved in a political issue, they are more likely to attribute selfish and biased motives to those who disagree with their position (Reeder, Pryor, Wohl, & Griswell, 2005). When this occurs, it becomes easy to demonize the other side. With the issue of illegal immigration, for example, rather than each side framing the issue in terms of which policies work best to regulate safe immigration into the United States, it has devolved into a fight about intentions. The right accuses the left of not just being soft on illegal immigration but of intentionally encouraging immigration as a way to grow the democratic voter base. The left, in turn, sees the right's tough stance on immigration as stemming from racist motivations rather than a more noble desire to enforce existing immigration law and protect American workers from unfair competition for jobs.

Personal moralization is particularly problematic in that it involves a broader view of oneself and one's own group as morally good, while individuals on the other side are seen as morally bad. This fits with what other researchers have described as the *intergroup relations function* of morality (Ellemers & van den Bos, 2012). The in-group's morality, a crucial part of in-group identity, can be affirmed by disparaging the out-group's moral standing and establishing the moral distinctiveness of one's in-group. This may explain why former Vice President Joe Biden often spoke out eloquently against this kind of intentionalization, urging fellow politicians to question their opponents' judgment but never their motives (Singer, 2015).

Consequences of political moralization

Political moralization has troubling implications for interpersonal and political behavior. According to Tetlock and colleagues' (2000) sacred value protection model, the belief that certain values are sacred leads people to take rigid stances on issues and reject pragmatic compromises. Merely construing an attitude as moral increases its strength, leading to greater attitude-behavior correspondence, greater resistance to persuasion, and more extreme and universal evaluations of behavior than non-moralized attitudes (Luttrell, Petty, Briñol, & Wagner, 2016; Van Bavel, Packer, Haas, & Cunningham, 2012). Individuals who hold moral attitudes show greater intolerance of people with opposing viewpoints and less desire to interact with dissimilar others (Skitka et al., 2005). People who moralize a greater number of political issues hold more positive feelings about their in-group and greater animosity toward, and even dehumanization of, political out-group members (Pacilli, Roccato, Pagliaro, & Russo, 2016; Ryan, 2014). In sum, moralization may increase political gridlock both by increasing attraction and loyalty to one's own side, and by lowering willingness to interact and compromise with the other side.

Finally, experiencing a threat to one's moral values can also change how a person responds to messages related to the threatened value. When the in-group's moral image is threatened, in-group members tend to respond with defensiveness and outrage toward the out-group (Täuber & Van Zomeren, 2013). After exposure to a value-threatening news story, people who held nonviolence as an important moral value were more likely to believe disparaging claims from scientific and political sources about the effects of violent video games (Rothmund, Bender, Nauroth, & Gollwitzer, 2015). Similarly, people evaluate an attitude-congruent scientific study more favorably when they hold a relevant value as personally important and feel the value is under attack (Bender, Rothmund, Nauroth, & Gollwitzer, 2016). If an individual feels like a cherished moral value has been threatened, their motivation to protect this moral value can lead them to interpret information in a biased fashion. In fact, as we will discuss further in the next section, moralization plays a crucial role in shaping the beliefs people hold about political issues.

Factualization

If you asked the average person why they hold a certain political view, such as their opinion on same-sex marriage, most individuals would cite a number of supporting principles, factual evidence, and logical arguments that ostensibly led them to their opinion. Their story would give you the impression that they arrived at their current position only after careful consideration of all the best pieces of information. Decades of psychological research, however, suggest that the process is often less bottom up (i.e. effortful consideration of information prior to drawing a conclusion) than top down, with principles, facts, and logic flowing from intuitions, expectancies, and motivations to reach a desired conclusion (Ditto, Pizarro, & Tannenbaum, 2009). A wealth of research shows that people desire consistency or coherence between their attitudes, beliefs, and behavior (Cooper, 2007). Models of *explanatory coherence* (e.g. Simon, Krawezyk, & Holyoak, 2004) suggest that achieving such consistency requires a dynamic process in which attitudes, beliefs, and behaviors all influence one another in an iterative process. The same processes are evident in the interplay between moral-political views and factual beliefs. Through a process of *moral coherence*, moral attitudes can be influenced by, as well as exert influence on, factual beliefs (Clark, Chen, & Ditto, 2015; Liu & Ditto, 2013).

Moral judgments, in fact, may be especially susceptible to this seemingly backward reasoning process (Ditto et al., 2009). Moral judgments often arise from intuitive or emotional reactions rather than analytical thinking (Haidt, 2001). Following this intuition, people are adept at finding concrete reasons for their moral views, which can make it seem as though they had these reasons all along. This backward process can lead to *factualization* or the construction of pseudo-descriptive justifications for moral evaluations.

Turning moral opinions into moral facts

There are two main logics that people rely on to factualize moral beliefs: deontological and consequentialist. Both are affected by motivated reasoning in ways that lead us to feel our moral intuitions are grounded in something deeper, more real, and objective. Deontological reasoning grounds moral judgments in inviolate principles that make certain actions morally right or wrong, regardless of the consequences. A person who believes that abortion is wrong, no matter the circumstances, is employing deontological logic by adhering to a broad moral principle that prohibits harming a fetus. An individual relying on deontological logic is often characterized as believing that even morally good ends (e.g. relieving a rape victim of the unfair trauma of carrying her rapist's baby) cannot justify morally bad means (e.g. ending the fetus' life via abortion). In contrast, people can also rely on consequentialist logic to justify moral positions. Consequentialist (also often referred to as utilitarian) reasoning is based on an analysis of the costs and benefits of moral actions, and can thus conclude that in some cases, the morality of ends can justify even morally questionable means. In this sense, a consequentialist may recognize the moral implications of ending the life of a healthy human fetus but still feel it is morally justified because of the profound moral unfairness of asking a victimized woman to carry to term the offspring of her abuser.

Although deontological and consequentialist logics are often at odds, either can support moral intuitions in a way that makes prescriptive opinions resemble descriptive facts. Consider a typical justification for a descriptive belief, such as "sugary drinks are bad for a person's health *because* they increase the risk of developing diabetes and obesity." Deontological and consequentialist justifications produce the same type of justification for moral beliefs, one serving to ground moral intuitions in broad principles ("Capital punishment is wrong *because* it is wrong to kill another human being") and the other in advantageous cost-benefit analyses ("Capital punishment is wrong *because* the costs associated with keeping an inmate on death row outweigh the benefits"). Either kind of justification, deontological or consequentialist, can make moral positions feel like factual ones, and there is evidence that both kinds of justifications are shaped by ideologically based motivations.

Motivated deontology

Politicians, like many other public figures, work hard to portray themselves as people of principle as we admire people who steadfastly adhere to moral standards no matter the cost (e.g. Everett, Pizarro, & Crockett, 2016). But that is precisely the problem with principles; their power flows from their generality, the willingness to stick with them even when they are costly or lead to morally questionable outcomes. The generality of principles is what makes adhering to them so hard, which explains why principled judgment is both so admired and so often violated. Instead, people tend to apply their principles selectively, touting them when they lead to favorable judgment outcomes and abandoning them when they do not.

This tendency to invoke principles in a post hoc fashion to support desired outcomes is well illustrated in an experiment involving a modified version of the classic footbridge dilemma (Uhlmann, Pizarro, Tannenbaum, & Ditto, 2009). Participants were asked to choose whether they would sacrifice one man's life in order to save 100 others. The scenarios entailed either sacrificing a Black man to save "100 members of the New York Philharmonic" or sacrificing a White man to save "100 members of the Harlem Jazz Orchestra." Liberals faced with a decision about sacrificing a Black man to save 100 (ostensibly White) people chose to save his life, citing deontological reasons (i.e. it is never justified to kill a person) to support their choice. Liberals, however, were significantly more willing to sacrifice the White man to save 100 (ostensibly Black) people, rejecting deontological reasoning when justifying their choice. In other words, liberals grounded their choice in deontological principles when it helped them achieve a desired outcome but rejected those same principles when they did not support their preferred outcome. Although conservative participants tended to be more evenhanded in their decisions in this race-relevant scenario, they showed the same selective use of deontological principles in another study reported by Uhlmann et al. (2009), examining judgments about the morality of civilian collateral damage caused by the actions of either the American or the Iraqi military. In this case, the judgments of political liberals were unaffected by the nationality of the perpetrators, whereas conservatives were significantly more forgiving when American actions led to unintended civilian deaths than when Iraqi actions did.

US politics is replete with examples of motivated deontology, resulting in hypocritical principle-switching. Consider the recent issue of filibuster rules in the US Senate. In 2013, when the Senate was under Democratic control, Democrats changed filibuster rules so that judicial nominees (with the exception of Supreme Court Justices) could be confirmed with a simple majority, ensuring that the minority party could not delay or obstruct future nominations (Savage, 2017). At the time, Republicans balked at the rule change, arguing that it is the fundamental right of the minority party to exercise their voice and to oppose undesirable judicial nominees. When Republicans gained control of the Senate in 2015, however, they kept the rules in place and, in 2017, even adjusted the rules to include Supreme Court nominees, to the ire of Democrats, who then comprised the minority party. Both parties have eloquently defended the Senate filibuster when it has suited their goals and maligned it just as eloquently when it hasn't. In each case, their position is framed in terms of their faithfulness to broad principles, with both positions and principles switching places depending on which party is in power.

Motivated consequentialism

The other way to turn moral opinions into moral facts is to ground them in a favorable cost-benefit analysis. Consequentialism can be thought of as a "rational" form of moral evaluation in which the quality of a moral act is determined by an analysis of whether its benefits outweigh its costs. In politics, policy positions are most typically justified with arguments, not about their inherent morality but about how they are likely to produce beneficial consequences for those involved. In the legal debate over same-sex marriage, for example, a great deal of time was spent presenting data on whether it was good or bad for the well-being of children. Although, to many of us, whether a policy produces beneficial outcomes for children seems an appropriate yardstick by which to evaluate its morality, problems arise when both sides produce evidence that the policy position they favor morally also produces the greater good. This tendency to regard actions perceived as moral as also being beneficial is a process Liu and Ditto (2013) termed *motivated consequentialism*.

In one study, Liu and Ditto (2013) examined views on four political issues (forceful interrogations, condom promotion, capital punishment, and stem cell research) and found moderate-to-strong positive correlations between people's moral opinions and their factual beliefs about the effectiveness of their preferred policies. For instance, the more participants believed that stem cell research is immoral, the more undesirable costs (and fewer benefits) they believed were associated with stem cell research. This pattern would occur, of course, if people were simply making judgments using consequentialist logic such that their evaluation of whether a given policy was morally desirable was based on their analysis of whether or not it was effective. Challenging this rational explanation, Liu and Ditto (2013) conducted an experiment manipulating moral evaluation of the policy and examining whether moral evaluations shaped beliefs about its costs and benefits. Participants read moral arguments either in favor of or against capital punishment. Importantly, these arguments focused only on the inherent morality or immorality of capital punishment, with no mention at all of its potential costs (e.g. its likelihood of resulting in wrongful executions) or benefits (e.g. its likelihood of deterring future crime). Although no "facts" about its costs or benefits were mentioned, people led to view the morality of capital punishment more positively endorsed more benefits and fewer costs of capital punishment compared to their pre-essay judgments, while those led to view its morality more negatively showed the opposite pattern. That is, both groups factualized their attitudes about capital punishment by aligning their descriptive beliefs about its costs and benefits to fit their prescriptive evaluations of its inherent morality.

Ideological reasoning

Google "conservative logic 101," and click on images. You will see pages of what look like dorm room posters mocking conservatives for their faulty reasoning. Now do the same with "liberal logic 101," and you will see pages of virtually identical images strategically rewritten to ridicule the quality of liberal rather than conservative logic. These dueling internet memes are a wonderfully tangible example of a mirror image perception held by Red and Blue America, the shared belief that the other side's arguments just don't make sense. These mutual perceptions suggest that logical reasoning itself can be affected by ideological commitments.

Psychologists studying people's capacity for logical reasoning have for years noted a phenomenon called "belief bias" (Evans, Barston, & Pollard, 1983; Feather, 1964; Oakhill & Johnson-Laird, 1985). When evaluating the validity of logical syllogisms (arguments containing two premises and a conclusion), people are biased to see arguments as logical when the conclusion is plausible. For example, the following two syllogisms have the same logical structure:

> All cold-blooded animals like water
> Fish are cold-blooded animals
> Fish like water

> All things made of plants are healthy
> Cigarettes are made of plants
> Cigarettes are healthy

Both arguments are logically valid (examples of modus ponens reasoning for those of you who remember your own logic 101 class from college). But research participants asked to evaluate them (while told to ignore the truth value of all statements) are much more likely to see the first syllogism as logically sound than the second one. The fact that cigarettes are not actually healthy makes it difficult for people to accept that the logic leading up to that implausible conclusion can be solid.

This leads to interesting effects when two groups have different beliefs about what conclusions are plausible. Gampa, Wojcik, Motyl, Nosek, and Ditto (2017) presented thousands of liberals and conservatives with both valid and invalid logical syllogisms across a range of political topics but manipulated whether the conclusions were consistent with liberal or conservative beliefs. So, for example, both groups saw the following two arguments:

> Things that harm the economy burden job creators
> Tax increases burden job creators
> Tax increases harm the economy

> Programs that help the economy help unemployed find jobs
> Welfare programs help unemployed find jobs
> Welfare programs help the economy

Both arguments have an identical logical structure, which, in this case, is actually invalid (logicians refer to this fallacy as "affirming the consequent"; both syllogisms actually become valid if the conclusion and second premise are swapped). However, Gampa et al. found that liberals are more likely than conservatives to catch the logical flaw in the first syllogism, whereas conservatives are more likely than liberals to catch the flaw in the second. A similar pattern occurs with valid syllogisms, where each side shows inappropriate skepticism of sound logic when it syields a conclusion that challenges their side's political beliefs. The subjective believability of the arguments mediated the relationship between participant political ideology and accuracy in argument ratings, and these results were replicated across three studies, including a nationally representative sample. The upshot of this pattern of partisan belief bias is clear: my side's moral arguments seem logical, and your side's don't.

To summarize, motivated reasoning processes can convert moral opinions into moral facts by grounding them in principles and logic – both formal logic and the logic of cost-benefit analysis. In this way, factualization adds fuel to the fire that moralization starts. Moralization infuses issues with emotion and energy, which, in turn, shapes the way information is processed and reinforces moral intuitions by grounding them in principles, facts, and logic. Ironically, factualization processes can be seen as demoralizing moral judgments by making them seem more like descriptive judgments, but this process makes political disagreements that much more volatile. Indeed, the more a person perceives a moral belief to be objectively true, the more uncomfortable they feel about interacting with someone who disagrees with their view (Goodwin & Darley, 2008). Matters of opinion can tolerate disagreement, but disagreement about facts implies something more problematic. And once this battle is joined by others – when the disagreement is no longer between me and you but rather between us and them – the temperature goes up more still. As we will discuss in the next section, people's tendency to selectively expose themselves to ideologically sympathetic people, groups, and media sources also plays a significant role in the development of political conflict.

Socialization

The psychological processes of moralization and factualization described in the previous sections do not happen in a vacuum but embedded in social contexts. People not only moralize their beliefs and reinforce them with fact-like justifications but are also inclined to surround themselves with other people who share those beliefs and justifications. We use the term *socialization* very much how it is used classically in sociology to describe the internalization of the social norms, values, and ideologies of a society (Persell, 1990). Just as children come to learn the rules of their national, ethnic, or religious culture, a similar process occurs in which people are reinforced by their social environment to internalize the factual beliefs of their ideological culture. This requires some degree of separation between groups – such as having friends that are mostly part of your ideological group and exposure to media that reinforce your group's beliefs. This tendency to construct social environments as ideological "safe spaces" involves several group dynamics that make democratic dialogue and compromise less likely by consecrating ideologically supportive belief systems as a reflection of socially shared reality.

Similarity and group formation

Early social psychologists showed that people tend to select their social interactions and environments based on perceived similarity (Williams, 1959) and, conversely, that interpersonal closeness leads to over-perceiving similarity (Newcomb, 1963). More recent studies have shown a robust association between value similarities and interpersonal attraction (e.g. Lee et al., 2009). Social media studies have found that this effect is also present in internet communities and interpersonal relationships: people tend to have similar friends on Facebook, according to political ideology (Bakshy, Messing, & Adamic, 2015) and personal values (Lonnqvist & Itkonen, 2016).

Perceived similarity with other group members also contributes to stronger in-group identification. Perceiving higher levels of fit with one's group makes group identity more salient and tends to maximize intergroup differences and minimize intragroup differences (Blanz, 1999; Hornsey, 2008). This basic process underlying identification with the in-group and differentiation from the out-group accounts for several different phenomena in intergroup relations, such as stereotyping, prejudice, and out-group derogation (Haslam, Oakes, Reynolds, & Turner, 1999; Jetten, Spears, & Postmes, 2004). Moralization of political issues tends to magnify social identification effects as people who moralize a greater number of political issues hold more positive feelings about their in-group and greater animosity toward political out-group members (Ryan, 2014).

Selective exposure

A long research tradition on *selective exposure* (Festinger, 1957; Lazarsfeld, Berelson, & Gaudet, 1948) has shown, across multiple domains, that people systematically choose situations that support rather than challenge prior attitudes and beliefs (Frey, 1986; Hart et al., 2009). This tendency to consume ideologically friendly media and associate with homogenous, like-minded groups can reinforce moralization and factualization.

There is consistent evidence that media consumers tend to select outlets that align with their ideological views, transforming the act of watching television or clicking on a headline into an act of identity affirmation (Iyengar & Hahn, 2009; Knobloch-Westerwick & Meng, 2011). For example, in a repeated surveys study with nationally representative samples, Rodriguez, Moskowitz, Salem, and Ditto (2017) found not only that respondents systematically chose pro-attitudinal over counter-attitudinal news sources but that this tendency toward audience fragmentation increased significantly between 2000 and 2012. There is little reason to suspect that this trend is subsiding as several recent studies continue to show an association between viewers' ideology and cable and online news consumption (e.g. Barnidge et al., 2017; Feezell, 2016).

Importantly, selective exposure does not equal the total absence of counter-attitudinal information (Garrett, 2009). Evidence suggests that the draw of attitude-consistent information is stronger than the avoidance of counter-attitudinal information (Garrett, Carnahan, & Lynch, 2013), and highly ideological individuals do sometimes access crosscutting information sources, especially when it is viewed as a way to gain advantage over the other political group (Knobloch-Westerwick & Kleinman, 2012). Moreover, selective exposure may be a symptom of political polarization as much as its cause (Bennett & Iyengar, 2008, 2010; Lee & Cappella, 2001) since evidence suggests that partisan media do not persuade or reinforce already ideologized individuals but rather only influence those with little exposure and interest in political news (Arceneaux, Johnson, & Cryderman, 2013). Still, watching or reading pro-attitudinal news is linked to both greater accessibility of political identity (Knobloch-Westerwick & Meng, 2011) and increased affective polarization (Garrett et al., 2014; Iyengar, Sood, & Lelkes, 2012).

Social media, with the almost limitless variety of information and opinions it contains, have the potential to override effects of selective exposure. However, evidence points in the other direction. Internet users replicate similar patterns of media consumption to those they consume as offline media, relying heavily on like-minded news websites (Johnson, Zhang, & Bichard, 2011). People avoid crosscutting discussions online in blogs and forums (Heatherly, Lu, & Lee, 2016). Users on Facebook present patterns of ideological selectivity in friendships and selecting content (Bakshy et al., 2015). Twitter users tend to cluster by ideology, following and sharing content from pro-attitudinal partisan websites (e.g. grass-roots blogs) rather than traditional outlets (Himelboim, McCreery, & Smith, 2013). Twitter users also tend to share (i.e. retweet) content aligned with their own ideological stance during politically controversial issues but not for other issues, such as sports or entertainment events (Barberá, Jost, Nagler, Tucker, & Bonneau, 2015). This body of research is consistent with the tenet that in their everyday media consumption – whether on paper, television, or social media – people are disproportionately likely to read, see, and hear arguments aligned with their prior beliefs.

Even if people's media consumption habits serve to surround them with ideologically congenial information, perhaps this bubble is burst during their everyday interactions with friends and neighbors who do not share their political views. To the contrary, research suggests that Americans increasingly live in places populated mostly with their ideological brethren. The publication of "The Big Sort" (Bishop, 2009) introduced the hypothesis that political polarization in America is associated with geographical patterns of ideological clustering (see also Gimpel & Hui, 2015; Sussel, 2013). Increasingly, liberals choose to live in places (often cities) disproportionately populated with liberals, while conservatives reside in places (often suburban or rural) disproportionately populated by conservatives. According to this account, people are motivated (albeit often implicitly) to select neighborhoods where crosscutting ideological contact is minimized. Decreased ideological fit predicts lower neighborhood satisfaction (Hui, 2013), worse interpersonal relations (Chopik & Motyl, 2016), and higher motivation to migrate (Motyl, 2014; Motyl, Iyer, Oishi, Trawalter, & Nosek, 2014). Experimental studies confirm that most people are reluctant to personally discuss political issues with a cross-ideological partner, considering it less preferable than taking out the trash (Frimer, Skitka, & Motyl, 2017) and will even refuse to comply with an experimenter's instructions when asked to write counter-attitudinal essays extoling the positive qualities of a president of the opposite party (Collins, Crawford, & Brandt, 2017; Nam, Jost, & Van Bavel, 2013).

In other words, living near like-minded others is psychologically satisfying and may have such a significant effect on perceived well-being that people are motivated to move to ideologically congenial areas.

In summary, socialization processes are a crucial last step in the construction of Red and Blue America's alternative factual worlds. A wealth of evidence suggests that people actively seek exposure to ideologically supportive information and like-minded people, and to a lesser extent avoid exposure to ideologically challenging information and political opponents. In this way, people place themselves in information and social environments that reinforce and amplify the effects of moralization and factualization. Holding a belief by oneself, even one grounded in moral commitment and intellectual justification, is a challenge if those around you feel and believe otherwise. But when surrounded by people, both real and virtual, who share your beliefs, that perceived consensus makes those views subjectively more plausible.

The expanding political divide

Our argument in a nutshell is this. Moralization *turns teams into tribes*. It contributes to an "us versus them" mentality, inciting intense emotions, unwillingness to compromise, and the desire to see the views of one's own side as righteous and the other's side as sacrilege. Factualization *turns opinions into facts*. Selective appeals to principles, logic, and favorable cost-benefit analyses justify preferred conclusions and create the impression that one's position is grounded in reason and objectively true. Socialization *turns beliefs into socially shared truth*. It further reifies moral opinions into moral facts as people become more confident in the validity of their beliefs when they believe more people share those beliefs.

These three processes converge to create the divergent factual worlds of liberals and conservatives, and have far-reaching implications for beliefs, policy preferences, and political conflict. First, these processes make it more likely that people will acquire and vigorously defend inaccurate beliefs. Erroneous beliefs may, in turn, lead to bad public policy as partisans can successfully push policies that appear sufficiently evidence based to their supporters, even if such policies are built on inaccurate reasoning or information. Importantly, nearly everyone is vulnerable to these processes. A recent meta-analysis of political bias revealed that partisans of all stripes show similar degrees of bias when exposed to belief-confirming or -disconfirming information (Ditto et al., in press). Experts and highly educated people are likewise susceptible (at times even more so than the less educated) to political biases (e.g. Kahan et al., 2012).

Perhaps the most troubling result of these processes, though, is the corrosive political conflict that ensues. When people begin to see themselves as occupying the moral high ground and believe their views to be objectively true, constructive dialogue or compromise can become nearly impossible. Once an issue is moralized, people are more likely to turn a blind eye to the flaws of their own reasoning but will keenly seize on any flaw in their opponents' arguments. When a moral opinion becomes factualized, it is easy for people to feel like their view is the obviously correct one; as a result, anyone who disagrees seems stupid (or outright immoral). Simply put, we feel anger toward people when they firmly believe something that we just as firmly disbelieve. Choosing sides is also an important social process. Identifying strongly with one side leads to reinforcement of one's group-based beliefs and greater perceived moral distance between the in-group and out-group. Ultimately, these processes can feed into one another and breed the kind of political environment in which people no longer disagree over specific policies but rather distrust and despise the political out-group and anything with which it is associated.

Conclusion

"In these circumstances they did what most of us do, and, being ignorant of the truth, persuaded themselves into believing what they wished to believe" (Arrian, First Century AD).

One of the casualties of factualization of beliefs across political groups is scientific data. Scientific reasoning is often considered the last resort to resolve differences in terms of public debate, public policy, and social progress. In the bare-knuckle competition that is modern politics, scientific data is seen by many as the sole referee available to fairly and objectively adjudicate the truth. Yet, as literature shows, scientific data and its claims of objectivity are entangled in a web of moral outrage, motivated confabulation, and ideological isolation. We direct disproportionate skepticism toward scientific findings that threaten our own worldviews and complacent acceptance of data that confirm what we already believe (Ditto & Lopez, 1992). These dynamics undermine the bright line distinguishing facts and values that was championed by Enlightenment scholars and that forms the foundation of positivistic views of science and progress. In politics, as in other realms of human experience, what is taken for reality is not based on a clean slate of indisputable evidence but on a complex fabric of motivations and intuitions about the world, the good, and the truth. As a society, we will have to decide whether a functional political system can be sustained in a world of fake news and alternative facts, where politics defines reality rather than the other way around.

References

Arceneaux, K., Johnson, M., & Cryderman, J. (2013). Communication, persuasion, and the conditioning value of selective exposure: Like minds may unite and divide but they mostly tune out. *Political Communication, 30*(2), 213–231. doi:10.1080/10584609. 2012.737424.

Bakshy, E., Messing, S., & Adamic, L. (2015). Exposure to ideologically diverse news and opinion on Facebook. *Science, 348*(6239), 1130–1132. doi:10.1111/j.1460-2466. 2008.00410.x.

Barberá, P., Jost, J. T., Nagler, J., Tucker, J. A., & Bonneau, R. (2015). Tweeting from left to right: Is online political communication more than an echo chamber? *Psychological Science, 26*(10), 1531–1542. doi:10.1177/0956797615594620.

Barnidge, M., Gunther, A. C., Kim, J., Hong, Y., Perryman, M., Tay, S. K., & Knisely, S. (2017). Politically motivated selective exposure and perceived media bias. *Communication Research*, 1–22. doi:10.1177/0093650217713066.

Bender, J., Rothmund, T., Nauroth, P., & Gollwitzer, M. (2016). How moral threat shapes laypersons' engagement with science. *Personality and Social Psychology Bulletin*, *42*(12), 1723–1735. doi:10.1177/0146167216671518.

Bennett, W. L., & Iyengar, S. (2008). A new era of minimal effects? The changing foundations of political communication. *Journal of Communication*, *58*(4), 707–731. doi:10.1111/j.1460-2466.2008.00410.x.

Bennett, W. L., & Iyengar, S. (2010). The shifting foundations of political communication: Responding to a defense of the media effects paradigm. *Journal of Communication*, *60*(1), 35–39. doi:10.1111/j.1460-2466.2009.01471.x.

Bishop, B. (2009). *The big sort: Why the clustering of like-minded America is tearing us apart*. New York, NY: Houghton Mifflin Harcourt.

Blanz, M. (1999). Accessibility and fit as determinants of the salience of social categorizations. *European Journal of Social Psychology*, *29*(1), 43–74. doi:10.1002/(SICI)1099-0992(199902)29:1<43::AID-EJSP913>3.0.CO;2-Z.

Brady, W. J., Wills, J. A., Jost, J. T., Tucker, J. A., & Van Bavel, J. J. (2017). Emotion shapes the diffusion of moralized content in social networks. *Proceedings of the National Academy of Sciences*, *114*(28), 7313–7318. doi:10.1073/pnas.1618923114.

Brandt, M. J., Wetherell, G., & Crawford, J. T. (2015). Moralization and intolerance of ideological outgroups. In J. P. Forgas, P. van Lange, & L. Jussim (Eds.), *Social psychology and morality* (pp. 1–27). New York, NY: Psychology Press.

Brandt, M. J., Wisneski, D. C., & Skitka, L. J. (2015). Moralization and the 2012 U.S. presidential election campaign. *Journal of Social and Political Psychology*, *3*(2), 211–237. doi:10.5964/jspp.v3i2.434.

Chopik, W. J., & Motyl, M. (2016). Ideological fit enhances interpersonal orientations. *Social Psychological and Personality Science*, *7*(8), 759–768. doi:10.1177/1948550616658096.

Clark, C. J., Chen, E. E., & Ditto, P. H. (2015). Moral coherence processes: Constructing culpability and consequences. *Current Opinion in Psychology*, *6*, 123–128. doi:10.1016/j.copsyc.2015.07.016.

Climate change 'a moral issue' – ex-US vice president Al Gore (2010, June 9). Retrieved from www.eco-business.com/news/climate-change-moral-issue-ex-us-vice-president-al/.

Collins, T. P., Crawford, J. T., & Brandt, M. J. (2017). No evidence for ideological asymmetry in dissonance avoidance. *Social Psychology*, *48*(3), 123–134. doi:10.1027/1864-9335/a000300.

Cooper, J. (2007). *Cognitive dissonance: Fifty years of a classic theory*. Thousand Oaks, CA: Sage.

Ditto, P. H., Liu, B. S., Clark, C. J., Wojcik, S. P., Chen, E. E., Grady, R. H., Celniker, J. B., & Zinger, J. F. (2018). At least bias is bipartisan: A meta-analytic comparison of partisan bias in liberals and conservatives. *Perspectives on Psychological Science*. Advance online publication. doi: 10.1177/1745691617746796.

Ditto, P. H., & Lopez, D. F. (1992). Motivated skepticism: Use of differential decision criteria for preferred and nonpreferred conclusions. *Journal of Personality and Social Psychology*, *63*(4), 568–584.

Ditto, P. H., Pizarro, D. A., & Tannenbaum, D. (2009). Motivated moral reasoning. In D. M. Bartels, C. W. Bauman, L. J. Skitka, & D. L. Medin (Eds.), *The psychology of learning and motivation* (Vol. 50, pp. 307–338). Burlington, MA: Academic Press.

Ellemers, N., & van den Bos, K. (2012). Morality in groups: On the social-regulatory functions of right and wrong. *Social and Personality Psychology Compass*, *6*(12), 878–889. doi:10.1111/spc3.12001.

Epstein, J. (2011, February 28). Boehner: Debt a 'moral threat' to U.S. Retrieved from www.politico.com/story/2011/02/boehner-debt-a-moral-threat-to-us-050313.

Evans, J. St. B. T., Barston, J. L., & Pollard, P. (1983). On the conflict between logic and belief in syllogistic reasoning. *Memory and Cognition, 11*(3), 295–306.

Everett, J. A., Pizarro, D. A., & Crockett, M. J. (2016). Inference of trustworthiness from intuitive moral judgments. *Journal of Experimental Psychology: General, 145*(6), 772–787. doi:10.1037/xge0000165.

Feather, N. T. (1964). Acceptance and rejection of arguments in relation to attitude strength, critical ability, and intolerance of inconsistency. *The Journal of Abnormal and Social Psychology, 69*(2), 127–136. doi:10.1037/h0046290.

Feezell, J. T. (2016). Predicting online political participation: The importance of selection bias and selective exposure in the online setting. *Political Research Quarterly, 69*(3), 495–509. doi:10.1177/1065912916652503.

Festinger, L. (1957). *A theory of cognitive dissonance*. Stanford, CA: Stanford University Press.

Frey, D. (1986). Recent research on selective exposure to information. *Advances in Experimental Social Psychology, 19*, 41–80. doi:10.1016/S0065-2601(08)60212-9.

Frimer, J. A., Skitka, L. J., & Motyl, M. (2017). Liberals and conservatives are similarly motivated to avoid exposure to one another's opinions. *Journal of Experimental Social Psychology, 72*, 1–12. doi:10.1016/j.jesp.2017.04.003.

Gâdarian, S. K., & van der Vort, E. (2017). The gag reflex: Disgust rhetoric and gay rights in American politics. *Political Behavior*. Advance online publication. doi:10.1007/s11109-017-9412-x.

Gampa, A., Wojcik, S. P., Motyl, M., Nosek, B. A., & Ditto, P. H. (under review). (Ideo)logical reasoning: Ideology impairs sound reasoning.

Garrett, R. K. (2009). Echo chambers online?: Politically motivated selective exposure among Internet news users. *Journal of Computer-Mediated Communication, 14*(2), 265–285. doi:10.1111/j.1083-6101.2009.01440.x.

Garrett, R. K., Carnahan, D., & Lynch, E. K. (2013). A turn toward avoidance? Selective exposure to online political information, 2004–2008. *Political Behavior, 35*(1), 113–134. doi: 10.1007/s11109-011-9185-6.

Garrett, R. K., Dvir-Gvirsman, S., Johnson, B. K., Tsfati, Y., Neo, R., & Dal, A. (2014). Implications of pro- and counterattitudinal information exposure for affective polarization. *Human Communication Research, 40*(3), 309–332. doi:10.1111/hcre.12028.

Gimpel, J. G., & Hui, I. S. (2015). Seeking politically compatible neighbors? The role of neighborhood partisan composition in residential sorting. *Political Geography, 48*, 130–142. doi:10.1016/j.polgeo.2014.11.003.

Goodwin, G. P., & Darley, J. M. (2008). The psychology of meta-ethics: Exploring objectivism. *Cognition, 106*, 1339–1366. doi:10.1016/j.cognition.2007.06.007.

Graham, J., Haidt, J., Koleva, S., Motyl, M., Iyer, R., Wojcik, S. P., & Ditto, P. H. (2013). Moral foundations theory: The pragmatic validity of moral pluralism. *Advances in Experimental Social Psychology* (Vol. 47, 1st ed.). doi:10.1016/B978-0-12-407236-7.00002-4.

Haidt, J. (2001). The emotional dog and its rational tail. *Psychological Review, 108*(4), 814–834. doi:10.1037//0033-295X.

Hart, W., Albarracín, D., Eagly, A. H., Brechan, I., Lindberg, M. J., & Merrill, L. (2009). Feeling validated versus being correct: A meta-analysis of selective exposure to information. *Psychological Bulletin, 135*(4), 555–588. doi:10.1037/a0015701.

Haslam, S. A., Oakes, P. J., Reynolds, K. J., & Turner, J. C. (1999). Social identity salience and the emergence of stereotype consensus. *Personality and Social Psychology Bulletin, 25*(7), 809–818. doi:10.1177/0146167299025007004.

Heatherly, K. A., Lu, Y., & Lee, J. K. (2016). Filtering out the other side? Cross-cutting and like-minded discussions on social networking sites. *New Media & Society*, 1–19. doi:10.1177/1461444816634677.

Himelboim, I., McCreery, S., & Smith, M. (2013). Birds of a feather tweet together: Integrating network and content analyses to examine cross-ideology exposure on twitter. *Journal of Computer-Mediated Communication*, *18*(2), 40–60. doi:10.1111/jcc4.12001.

Hornsey, M. J. (2008). Social identity theory and self-categorization theory: A historical review. *Social and Personality Psychology Compass*, *2*, 204–222. doi:10.1111/j.1751-9004.2007.00066.x.

Hui, I. (2013). Who is your preferred neighbor? Partisan residential preferences and neighborhood satisfaction. *American Politics Research*, *41*(6), 997–1021. doi:10.1177/1532673X13482573.

Iyengar, S., & Hahn, K. S. (2009). Red media, blue media: Evidence of ideological selectivity in media use. *Journal of Communication*, *59*(1), 19–39. doi:10.1111/j.1460-2466.2008.01402.x.

Iyengar, S., Sood, G., & Lelkes, Y. (2012). Affect, not ideology: A social identity perspective on polarization. *Public Opinion Quarterly*, *76*(3), 405–431. doi:10.1093/poq/nfs038.

Jetten, J., Spears, R., & Postmes, T. (2004). Intergroup distinctiveness and differentiation: A meta-analytic integration. *Journal of Personality and Social Psychology*, *86*(6), 862–879. doi:10.1037/0022-3514.86.6.862.

Johnson, T. J., Zhang, W., & Bichard, S. L. (2011). Voices of convergence or conflict? A path analysis investigation of selective exposure to political websites. *Social Science Computer Review*, *29*(4), 449–469. doi:10.1177/0894439310379962.

Kahan, D. M., Peters, E., Wittlin, M., Slovic, P., Ouellette, L. L., Braman, D., & Mandel, G. (2012). The polarizing impact of science literacy and numeracy on perceived climate change risks. *Nature Climate Change*, *2*(10), 732–735. doi:10.1038/nclimate1547.

Knobloch-Westerwick, S., & Kleinman, S. B. (2012). Preelection selective exposure: Confirmation bias versus informational utility. *Communication Research*, *39*(2), 170–193. doi:10.1177/0093650211400597.

Knobloch-Westerwick, S., & Meng, J. (2011). Reinforcement of the political self through selective exposure to political messages. *Journal of Communication*, *61*(2), 349–368. doi:10.1111/j.1460-2466.2011.01543.x.

Kreps, T. A., & Monin, B. (2011). "Doing well by doing good"? Ambivalent moral framing in organizations. *Research in Organizational Behavior*, *31*, 99–123. doi:10.1016/j.riob.2011.09.008.

Lazarsfeld, P. F., Berelson, B., & Gaudet, H. (1948). *The people's choice: How the voter makes up his mind in a presidential campaign*. New York, NY: Columbia University Press.

Lee, G., & Cappella, J. N. (2001). The effects of political talk radio on political attitude formation: Exposure versus knowledge. *Political Communication*, *18*(4), 369–394. doi:10.1080/10584600152647092.

Lee, K., Ashton, M. C., Pozzebon, J. A., Visser, B. A, Bourdage, J. S., & Ogunfowora, B. (2009). Similarity and assumed similarity in personality reports of well-acquainted persons. *Journal of Personality and Social Psychology*, *96*(2), 460–472. doi:10.1037/a0014059.

Liu, B. S., & Ditto, P. H. (2013). What dilemma? Moral evaluation shapes factual belief. *Social Psychological and Personality Science*, *4*(3), 316–323. doi:10.1177/1948550612456045.

Lonnqvist, J. E., & Itkonen, J. V. A. (2016 February). Homogeneity of personal values and personality traits in Facebook social networks. *Journal of Research in Personality*, *60*, 24–35. doi:10.1016/j.jrp.2015.11.001.

Luttrell, A., Petty, R. E., Briñol, P., & Wagner, B. C. (2016). Making it moral: Merely labeling an attitude as moral increases its strength. *Journal of Experimental Social Psychology*, *65*, 82–93. doi:10.1016/j.jesp.2016.04.003.

Marietta, M. (2008). From my cold, dead hands: Democratic consequences of sacred rhetoric. *The Journal of Politics, 70*(3), 767–779. doi:10.1017/S0022381608080742.

Motyl, M. (2014). "If he wins, I'm moving to Canada": Ideological migration threats following the 2012 U.S. presidential election. *Analyses of Social Issues and Public Policy, 14*(1), 123–136. doi:10.1111/asap.12044.

Motyl, M., Iyer, R., Oishi, S., Trawalter, S., & Nosek, B. A. (2014). How ideological migration geographically segregates groups. *Journal of Experimental Social Psychology, 51*, 1–14. doi:10.1016/j.jesp.2013.10.010.

Nam, H. H., Jost, J. T., & Van Bavel, J. J. (2013). "Not for all the tea in China!" Political ideology and the avoidance of dissonance-arousing situations. *PLoS One, 8*(4), e59837. doi:10.1371/journal.pone.0059837.

Newcomb, T. M. (1963). Stabilities underlying changes in interpersonal attraction. *The Journal of Abnormal and Social Psychology, 66*(4), 376–386. doi:10.1037/h0041059.

Oakhill, J., & Johnson-Laird, P. N. (1985). The effects of belief on the spontaneous production of syllogistic conclusions. *Quarterly Journal of Experimental Psychology Section A, 37*(4), 553–569. doi:10.1080/14640748508400919.

Olatunji, B. O. (2008). Disgust, scrupulosity and conservative attitudes about sex: Evidence for a mediational model of homophobia. *Journal of Research in Personality, 42*(5), 1364–1369.

Pacilli, M. G., Roccato, M., Pagliaro, S., & Russo, S. (2016). From political opponents to enemies? The role of perceived moral distance in the animalistic dehumanization of the political outgroup. *Group Processes & Intergroup Relations, 19*(3), 360–373. doi:10.1177/1368430215590490.

Persell, C. H. (1990). *Understanding society: An introduction to sociology*, 3rd ed. New York, NY: Harper & Row.

Pew Research Center (2016, June). Partisanship and political animosity in 2016. Retrieved from www.people-press.org/2016/06/22/1-feelings-about-partisans-and-the-parties/.

Pew Research Center (2017, October). Global warming and environmental regulation, personal environmentalism. Retrieved from www.people-press.org/2017/10/05/7-global-warming-and-environmental-regulation-personal-environmentalism/7_02/.

Reeder, G. D., Pryor, J. B., Wohl, M. J., & Griswell, M. L. (2005). On attributing negative motives to others who disagree with our opinions. *Personality & Social Psychology Bulletin, 31*(11), 1498–1510. doi:10.1177/0146167205277093.

Ringel, M. M. (2016). *The moralization of obesity: Exploring control attributions and disgust as predictors of judgments about obesity* (Master's thesis). University of California, Irvine.

Rodriguez, C. G., Moskowitz, J. P., Salem, R. M., & Ditto, P. H. (2017). Partisan selective exposure: The role of party, ideology and ideological extremity over time. *Translational Issues in Psychological Science.* doi:10.1037/tps000121.

Rothmund, T., Bender, J., Nauroth, P., & Gollwitzer, M. (2015). Public concerns about violent video games are moral concerns – How moral threat can make pacifists susceptible to scientific and political claims against violent video games. *European Journal of Social Psychology, 45*(6), 769–783. doi:10.1002/ejsp.2125.

Rozin, P. (1999). The process of moralization. *Psychological Science, 10*(3), 218–221. doi:10.1111/1467-9280.00139.

Rozin, P., Markwith, M., & Stoess, C. (1997). Moralization and becoming a vegetarian: The transformation of preferences into values and the recruitment of disgust. *Psychological Science, 8*(2), 67–73.

Rozin, P., & Singh, L. (1999). The moralization of cigarette smoking in the United States. *Journal of Consumer Psychology, 8*(3), 321–337. doi:10.1207/s15327663jcp0803_07.

Ryan, T. J. (2014). Reconsidering moral issues in politics. *The Journal of Politics, 76*(2), 380–397. doi:10.1017/S0022381613001357.

Savage, C. (2017, April 3). The senate filibuster, explained. *The New York Times*. Retrieved from www.nytimes.com/2017/04/03/us/politics/filibuster-supreme-court-neil-gorsuch. html?_r=0.

Schnall, S., Haidt, J., Clore, G. L., & Jordan, A. H. (2008). Disgust as embodied moral judgment. *Personality and Social Psychology Bulletin, 34*(8), 1096–1109. doi:10.1177/ 0146167208317771.

Schulson, M. (2016, March 15). The moral vision of Bernie Sanders. Retrieved from http://religionandpolitics.org/2016/03/15/the-moral-vision-of-bernie-sanders/.

Simon, D., Krawezyk, D. C., & Holyoak, K. J. (2004). Construction of preferences by constraint satisfaction. *Psychological Science, 15*, 331–336. doi:10.1111/j.0956-7976. 2004.00678.x.

Singer, S. (2015, May 17). Biden urges Yale grads to question judgment, not motives. Retrieved from http://www.sandiegouniontribune.com/sdut-biden-urges-yale-grads-to-question-judgment-not-2015may17-story.html.

Skitka, L. J. (2010). The psychology of moral conviction. *Social and Personality Psychology Compass, 4*(4), 267–281. doi:10.1111/j.1751-9004.2010.00254.x.

Skitka, L. J., Bauman, C. W., & Sargis, E. G. (2005). Moral conviction: Another contributor to attitude strength or something more? *Journal of Personality and Social Psychology, 88*(6), 895–917. doi:10.1037/0022-3514.88.6.895.

Sussel, J. (2013). New support for the big sort hypothesis: An assessment of Partisan geographic sorting in California, 1992–2010. *Political Science and Politics, 46*(4), 768–773. doi:10.1057/pol.2009.6.

Täuber, S., & Van Zomeren, M. (2013). Outrage towards whom? Threats to moral group status impede striving to improve via out-group-directed outrage. *European Journal of Social Psychology, 43*, 149–159. doi:10.1002/ejsp.1930.

Tetlock, P. E., Kristel, O. V., Elson, S. B., Green, M. C., & Lerner, J. S. (2000). The psychology of the unthinkable: Taboo trade-offs, forbidden base rates, and heretical counterfactuals. *Journal of Personality and Social Psychology, 78*(5), 853–870. doi:10.1037/ 0022-3514.78.5.853.

Uhlmann, E. L., Pizarro, D. A., Tannenbaum, D., & Ditto, P. H. (2009). The motivated use of moral principles. *Judgment and Decision Making, 4*(6), 476–491.

Van Bavel, J. J., Packer, D. J., Haas, I. J., & Cunningham, W. A. (2012). The importance of moral construal: Moral versus non-moral construal elicits faster, more extreme, universal evaluations of the same actions. *PLoS ONE, 7*(11), 1–14. doi:10.1371/journal. pone.0048693.

Washington Post (2017, July 16). *Washington Post-ABC News Poll*. Retrieved from www. washingtonpost.com/page/2010-2019/WashingtonPost/2017/07/16/National-Politics/Polling/question_18943.xml?uuid=YUEe3mnbEeeUq1sfD_RZ3w.

Williams, R. M. (1959). Friendship and social values in a suburban community: An exploratory study. *The Pacific Sociological Review, 2*(1), 3–10.

Wisneski, D. C., & Skitka, L. J. (2017). Moralization through moral shock: Exploring emotional antecedents to moral conviction. *Personality and Social Psychology Bulletin, 43*(2), 139–150. doi:10.1177/0146167216676479.

2

SYSTEM-LEVEL BIASES IN THE PRODUCTION AND CONSUMPTION OF INFORMATION

Implications for system resilience and radical change

Erin P. Hennes, Adam J. Hampton, Ezgi Ozgumus, and Thomas J. Hamori

Misperceptions of reality have long been studied in the psychological sciences. Although dramatic departures from reality are indicative of mental illness (e.g., Jahoda, 1958), more subtle distortions are often associated with mental health and goal achievement (e.g., Taylor & Brown, 1988). Individuals' positive illusions about their romantic partners (e.g., Murray, Holmes, & Griffin, 1996) and members of their in-groups (e.g., Bullock, Gerber, Hill, & Huber, 2015) are also often associated with adaptive outcomes such as relationship persistence (e.g., Murray, Griffin, Derrick, Harris, Aloni, & Leder, 2011) and group cohesion (Huddy, 2003). In this chapter, we examine emerging evidence that individuals sometimes also hold positive illusions about current states of affairs more broadly, even in contexts in which the status quo does not advantage them or their social groups (i.e., system justification; Jost, Hennes, & Lavine, 2013). We examine the role of system justification and related constructs in both information production (i.e., misinformation) and consumption (i.e., motivated reasoning). Consistent with the majority of the literature, we focus primarily on instances in which system *justification* biases reasoning. However, we also suggest several directions for future research, including the possibility of bias emerging from system *rejection*. We conclude by considering whether accurate or biased perceptions of the status quo facilitate optimal societal functioning.

Production and consumption of factual claims

According to contemporary dynamic models of cognition, the way in which a stimulus is processed is impacted by both *bottom-up* (features of the stimulus itself, such as its color or shape) and *top-down* influences (aspects of the perceiver or the context; see Kosslyn & Koenig, 1992 for a review). Information processing is frequently veridical – if it were not, humans would be unable to successfully navigate their surroundings (e.g., Jussim, 1991). However, extensive research has demonstrated that information processing frequently departs from outcomes predicted by models of accuracy or rational choice (see, e.g., Griffin, Gonzalez, Koehler, & Gilovich, 2012; Kunda, 1990). For the purpose of this review, we refer to *bottom-up* influences on cognition as those resulting from information producers (e.g., the characteristics of the information itself) and *top-down influences* on cognition as those resulting from the information consumers (e.g., motivated reasoning).

The specific *bottom-up* influences on cognition that are the focus of this chapter regard the production of "alternative facts" or "fake news." The aim of such information is to intentionally deceive and is distinct from constructs such as partisan news, in which information is framed to persuade but is not factually inaccurate (Allcott & Gentzkow, 2017). *Top-down* influences on cognition are external to the stimulus itself such that the same object (such as a piece of scientific information about climate change) can be experienced differently (a) by different people or (b) by the same person in different situations. In turn, the same object can elicit variable downstream judgments, decisions, and behaviors. Psychologists have accumulated an impressive collection of findings that suggest that an individual's needs and desires can shape perceptual and cognitive processes at many stages, such as visual perception (e.g., Balcetis & Dunning, 2006), information gathering (e.g., Hart, Albarracín, Eagly, Brechan, Lindberg, & Merrill, 2009), recall (e.g., Story, 1998), and evaluation of information (e.g., Ditto, Scepansky, Munro, Apanovitch, & Lockhart, 1998).

Information consumption has important consequences for downstream attitude formation, decision making, and behavior. Presumably, high-quality evidence from reliable sources is often more persuasive than weak evidence (e.g., Eagly & Chaiken, 1993). Individuals are usually motivated to hold accurate beliefs (Festinger, 1950) and to believe that their attitudes are the result of careful examination of factual information (e.g., Ross & Ward, 1996). Inaccurate but ostensibly strong factual claims are often especially problematic for individuals who are (or perceive themselves to be) well educated about an issue or in which the issue is personally important (Petty & Cacioppo, 1986; Taber & Lodge, 2006). Kunda (1990) noted that accuracy motivation can even *increase* bias when paired with directional goals to reach a desired conclusion. Humans are generally unaware of their biases and experience *bias blind spots* in which they are more skilled in recognizing the biases of others than of themselves (Pronin, Lin, & Ross, 2002). Humans' conviction of their own impartiality implies a parallel conviction that dissenting views are ignorant or biased (e.g., Ross & Ward, 1996). These tendencies are not helped by the fact that individuals are often drawn to "echo chambers" that reinforce their ideological worldview and dismiss contradictory information (e.g., Barberá, Jost, Nagler, Tucker, & Bonneau, 2015).

Together, the literature suggests that individuals are generally accurate but tend to be unaware of departures from reality, either due to their own biased processing or because the information itself is distorted. Distorted information production and consumption can work in tandem such that bottom-up misinformation might be integrated and further distorted via top-down processes. As discussed later and throughout this volume, misperceptions of reality can have critical negative and positive consequences across a variety of domains (e.g., Jost et al., 2013; Taylor & Brown, 1988).

System justification motivation

We adopt the taxonomy introduced by Jost et al. (2013) in distinguishing between self-, group-, and system-serving motivations. At each level, both dispositional and situational factors influence the prevalence and persistence of biases in information production and consumption. Self-serving biases, such as self-enhancement, predominantly operate to protect and augment one's self-concept and status in society (e.g., Ditto, 2009). Group-serving biases, such as partisan bias, frequently serve to bolster the favorable perception and status of the in-group (e.g., Taber & Lodge, 2006). Following from these well-established literatures, we examine recent work that suggests that bias may also result from system-level phenomena. According to system justification theory, people are compelled – often at a nonconscious level – to defend and legitimize the social, economic, and political arrangements in which they live (Jost, Banaji, & Nosek, 2004). This motivation is believed to exist for most people, but varies due to dispositional (e.g., need for closure; Hennes, Nam, Stern, & Jost, 2012) and situational factors (e.g., terrorist attacks; Ullrich & Cohrs, 2007).

Those who benefit from the existing social structure are likely to be motivated to protect it for self- and group-level reasons. However, instances in which the disadvantaged also defend an oppressive status quo have historically been more difficult to explain (see Jost & van der Toorn, 2012 for a review). Jost (1995) proposed that the oppressed carry "*false or inaccurate beliefs* that are contrary to their own social interest and which thereby contribute to the maintenance of the disadvantaged position of the self or the group" (p. 400, emphasis added). It is likely distressing to believe that one exists within an unjust reality, so "lower status people generally find it less punishing to think of themselves as correctly placed by a just society than to think of themselves as exploited, or victimized by an unjust society" (Lane, 1959, p. 49). This concept of *false consciousness* (see also Marx & Engels, 1846/1970) was central to the original arguments of system justification theory (Jost & Banaji, 1994). Since that time, the theory has been broadened to explain the defense of status quo positions on a number of outcomes (e.g., support for the Tea Party and Occupy Wall Street movements, Hennes et al., 2012; consumer behavior, Cutright, Wu, Banfield, Kay, & Fitzsimons, 2011) by *both* low and high status group members. Thus, we argue that system justification can motivate the maintenance of "false or inaccurate beliefs" to arrive at system-justifying conclusions.

Consumption of system-level distortions of reality

In many cases, research examining false beliefs in the context of status quo defense has focused on scientific information about climate change. This example is interesting because of evidence that capitalist economic systems and reliance on fossil fuels are partially responsible for skepticism about climate change (e.g., CO_2 emissions by country are correlated, $r = -0.54$, with citizens' climate change concern; Wike, 2016). Skepticism in the United States became even more pronounced during the recession (a period of economic system threat) and has declined as the economy has recovered (Scruggs & Benegal, 2012; see also, Hennes, Ruisch, Feygina, Monteiro, & Jost, 2016). Indeed, system justification (particularly economic system justification) is a robust and proximal predictor of climate change attitudes, even over and above partisanship and political ideology (Hennes et al., 2016; see also, Hennes et al., 2012; cf., Feygina, Jost, & Goldsmith, 2010; Leviston & Walker, 2014).

In one example of motivated reasoning in the context of climate change, individuals who were led to feel dependent on the governmental system reported a greater desire to avoid learning new information about the economy and the environment, apparently to avoid encountering information that might threaten system legitimacy (Shepherd & Kay, 2012). Similarly, skepticism about climate change is associated with "solution aversion" or resistance to changes to the status quo that would be necessary to alleviate environmental problems (Campbell & Kay, 2014). Finally, messages about the dire consequences of global warming decreased belief in global warming's existence among individuals with higher belief in a just world (Lerner, 1980), presumably because such messages threaten individuals' conviction that the world is predictable and fair (Feinberg & Willer, 2011).

System-level motives also appear to impact selective exposure to and evaluation of scientific information in domains beyond climate change. For instance, individuals evaluate scientific data as more persuasive when it supports the meritocratic ideology that hard work leads to success, especially after they have been experimentally induced to feel increased system threat (Ledgerwood, Mandisodza, Jost, & Pohl, 2011). Individuals also resist the publication and funding of scientific research when the studies' implications are perceived to be threatening to the common good (Chapter 8).

Disregard of scientific evidence that threatens status quo arrangements can also be observed throughout the legal system. For instance, the death penalty is still enforced in much of the United States (Death Penalty Information Center, 2018) despite evidence suggesting that it does little to deter crime (Radelet & Lacock, 2009), and polygraph tests continue to be used despite major questions of their validity (see Iacono, 2008 for a review). Psychiatrists are still called in to predict future violence, even though they have been found to be wrong more often than they are right (see Lion et al., 1974 for an early review), and limiting instructions regarding prior convictions are still given to juries despite evidence that jurors often use this information to decide on guilt (and 98% of attorneys and 43% of judges admit that they recognize this; Note, 1968).

In one fascinating example, expert testimony was disregarded because it did not support traditional ideals. *Paris Adult Theater I v. Slaton* (413 U.S. 49 (1973)) involved the state of Georgia's injunction against showing obscene films in an adults-only movie theatre. In delivering the opinion of the court, Chief Justice Burger wrote:

> [B]ut, it is argued, there are no scientific data which conclusively demonstrate that exposure to obscene material adversely affects men and women or their society....We reject this argument. It is not for us to resolve empirical uncertainties underlying state legislation...Although there is no conclusive proof of a connection between antisocial behavior and obscene material, the legislature of Georgia could quite reasonably determine that such a connection does or might exist.

Just as evidence regarding the effectiveness of capital punishment was disregarded by participants in Lord, Ross, and Lepper's (1979) classic study because it was inconsistent with their attitudes, similar processes appeared to have occurred in *Paris Adult Theatre v. Slaton* because of the Court's perceived concern about the degradation of society (see also Blasi & Jost, 2006).

In addition to evaluations of scientific evidence, system-level motives may also influence perceptual processes. During times of perceived governmental stability, individuals visually represented racially ambiguous political candidates in group-serving ways (e.g., Whites tended to see the candidate as lighter skinned, and Blacks tended to see the candidate as darker skinned). However, when the government was perceived to be unstable, both Blacks and Whites judged the candidate to be lighter skinned (Stern, Balcetis, Cole, West, & Caruso, 2016). Consistent with studies illustrating that social judgments of interpersonal warmth influence physiological judgments of ambient warmth (e.g., IJzerman & Semin, 2010; Zhong & Leonardelli, 2008) and that judgments of temperature affect belief in global warming (e.g., Egan & Mullin, 2012; Li, Johnson, & Zaval, 2011), evidence also suggests that system justification may impact the degree to which individuals "feel" global warming. In experiments conducted in public parks during the summer, system justification (either dispositionally measured or experimentally induced) was associated with reporting the temperature to be cooler, which was itself associated with greater skepticism about climate change. These findings did not replicate in a windowless, temperature-controlled room, where the ambient temperature would ostensibly provide limited information about climate (Hennes, Feygina, & Jost, 2018).

Several studies indicate that system-level motives also influence recall. Haines and Jost (2000) found that individuals tended to remember reasons for their own (experimentally manipulated) lower status as legitimate, even if they were actually given no explanation or even an illegitimate explanation for the power differential. Individuals higher in social dominance recalled having been exposed to evidence of less inequality, even when they were explicitly incentivized to be accurate (Kteily, Sheehy-Skeffington, & Ho, 2017). When system justification was experimentally heightened, individuals in both the United States and France recalled evidence of their academic competence in ways that were more consistent with complementary gender stereotypes. Women recalled having earned higher Scholastic Assessment Test (SAT) scores and had more positive autobiographical memories in verbal domains compared to math domains, whereas men reported the opposite pattern (Bonnot & Jost, 2014; Bonnot & Krauth-Gruber, 2018). In both correlational and experimental studies, system justification led individuals to misremember information in a way that was indicative of less severe environmental problems, which was then associated with a reduction in belief in climate change (Hennes et al., 2016). Finally, individuals misremembered undeserving people as having experienced less good fortune (e.g., in a lottery) compared to deserving people. These effects extended to the self, such that those who randomly experienced bad fortune were more likely to remember their own prior bad deeds than participants who experienced good fortune (Callan, Kay, Davidenko, & Ellard, 2009). In sum, we argue that evidence is more likely to be attended to, accepted as factual, veridically perceived, accurately remembered, and acted upon when it protects the belief that the status quo is just, fair, and stable.

Production of system-level distortions of reality

Although the majority of the misinformation literature has not specifically invoked system justification theory, several examples indicate that information *producers* are also often motivated to maintain the status quo (for either self-, group-, or system-serving reasons). In the context of climate change, 92% of environmentally skeptical books published between 1972 and 2005 were linked to conservative think tanks (Jacques, Dunlap, & Freeman, 2008). In 2006, two reporters for ABC News revealed that an electric cooperative had paid an academic scientist $100,000 to cast doubt on the science surrounding anthropogenic climate change (Boykoff, 2013; Sandell & Blakemore, 2006). The media also often endeavor to report "balanced" information such that both experts who assert and experts who deny the existence of climate change are given equivalent airtime. This is despite the fact that only approximately 3% of climate scientists report skepticism regarding human's role in changing climates (e.g., Anderegg, Prall, Harold, & Schneider, 2010). In an analysis of reports about the Kyoto Protocol, Dispensa and Brulle (2003) found that 40% of American reporting presented climate science as conclusive compared to 89%–100% in New Zealand and Finland. Such imbalance of perspectives can promote the illusion that expert opinion on this topic is mixed (Boykoff & Boykoff, 2004).

Because these examples were not constructed to isolate the level of motivation, misinformation may have also been the result of mere self-interest motivations or group-level cues. However, recent work has controlled for the impact of at least one group-level motivation – partisanship – on susceptibility to misinformation. Hennes, Ruisch, Jagel, and Jost (2018) examined data from focus group interviews of registered Republicans in which the subject of the interviews was not disclosed in advance. They found that the frequency with which participants made system-justifying statements, such as those that framed sustainability as threatening to the economic status quo, was associated with greater skepticism about climate change (e.g., "I mean, being good stewards of the planet is something that we all should strive for. But destroying our way of life or our economy just because, isn't something we should do"). More importantly, higher system justifiers were more likely to make false factual claims (e.g., "One volcano eruption emits more toxic chemicals into our environment than all the cars put together"), which was associated with the belief that climate change is a hoax. In contrast, those who believed in climate change were more likely to make true factual claims. Although the sources of the factual claims in this study are unclear and are likely to be the result of both bottom-up and top-down processes, it is notable that exposure to conservative media (but not liberal media) was also associated with greater use of factually inaccurate claims. Together, this qualitative data suggests that Republicans vary in their level of system justification motivation and their attitudes and factual beliefs about climate change. Republicans who were higher in system justification and who viewed more conservative media appeared to have more factually inaccurate views about climate change.

Correcting misperceptions of reality

How might practitioners intervene on misperceptions of reality resulting from system justification motivation? Interestingly, one of the most effective strategies for encouraging individuals to reject the status quo is simply to change it. In one oft-cited example, African-American students were surveyed 3 days before and 1 day after the decision in *Brown v. Board of Education* (347 U.S. 483 (1954)), in which race-based school segregation was declared unconstitutional. Students more strongly opposed all-Black colleges the day after the decision than they had merely a few days before (Kelman, 2001; see also, Laurin, 2018). Individuals even adjust their attitudes in anticipation of a new status quo, such as by rating possible futures as more desirable when led to believe that the outcome is more likely (e.g., the impending election of either Bush vs. Gore; a tuition increase vs. decrease; Kay, Jimenez, & Jost, 2002).

Interestingly, Tankard and Paluck (2017) reported more mixed evidence about the effect of system change in provoking attitude change. They found that providing participants with information suggesting that a Supreme Court ruling in support of marriage equality was more likely increased participants' perception of Americans' support for marriage equality as well as their own support for it. However, a natural pre-post experiment found that when the Supreme Court actually ruled in favor of marriage equality, participants again increased their belief that others supported marriage equality but did not change their own attitudes. At the same time, support for same-sex marriage grew by 10% from 2014 to 2017, compared to an average of 1% per year for the previous years (2001–2014) for which data was available (Pew Research Center, 2017). Although there are many possible explanations for this surge, this data is at least broadly consistent with the perspective that the public has increasingly come to accept the new status quo. This suggests that simply implementing new policies may be an effective strategy for garnering support for system change.

Although these examples suggest that, in at least some cases, system change can provoke attitude change, evidence of the effectiveness of bias reduction strategies is more limited. For instance, factual inaccuracies about weapons of mass destruction (WMDs) disseminated by the George W. Bush administration were widely persuasive in garnering public support for the war on Iraq. Correcting the misinformation was effective for Germans (who did not support the war and were not directly involved), but not for Americans (who were largely supportive of the war in its early stages in 2003) or Australians (who supported the war but were not directly involved). Furthermore, Americans were the only group who held fast to their confidence in the misinformation after it was retracted (Lewandowsky, Stritzke, Oberauer, & Morales, 2005). Similarly, many participants in another set of studies who received a correction explaining that Iraq did not have WMDs failed to change their misperceptions, and some subgroups became even more likely to believe in their existence than did those who did not receive a correction. This was particularly pronounced among ideologically committed conservatives (who tend to be higher in system justification motivation; Nyhan & Reifler, 2010).

At the same time, various lines of research have found some success in reducing the negative influence of misinformation. For instance, Ecker, Lewandowsky, and Tang (2010) found that informing an audience that information they would later consume may be erroneous successfully increased the amount of correct answers that participants gave in a recall task. Other research has reduced the influence of misinformation by having influential celebrity figures frame truthful information in a way that resonates with the public. However, this method can backfire if the public figure is polarizing (e.g., Barack Obama) or discredited for not being an expert (Nisbet, 2009). Each of these methods is also limited in that they require an outside party to inform individuals that the information they consumed was false. In many real-world cases, individuals are not exposed to a counter-message.

As a third alternative, if high system justifiers are indeed *motivated* to distort system-threatening information in order to defend the status quo, it should be possible to satisfy or circumvent this motivation to facilitate more objective information processing. Indeed, several experiments have sought to satisfy system justification motivations through another outlet, such as by affirming the strength of the country (Kay, Jost, & Young, 2005). Consistent with this possibility, Liviatan and Jost (2014) found that system affirmation inhibited nonconscious goal pursuit to legitimate the status quo among participants under system threat.

Feygina, Jost, and Goldsmith increased support for pro-environmental policy by framing pro-environmental efforts as system-sanctioned (2010). Finally, leading high system justifiers to believe that the economy was in recovery (rather than recession) eliminated motivated misremembering of anthropogenic climate change information among high system justifiers (Hennes et al., 2016). In sum, these findings suggest that addressing the specific motivation(s) underlying biased production and consumption of information may be key to increasing veridical representations of reality.

System rejection and directions for future research

Future research should continue to examine opportunities for satiating system justification motivation and alleviating biases in perceptions of reality. At the same time, because the extant literature has primarily endeavored to alleviate real-world problems such as climate change, income inequality, and race- and sex-based discrimination (e.g., Hennes et al., 2016; Kteily et al., 2017; Payne, 2001), the predominant focus has been on high system justifiers and biases that perpetuate a dysfunctional status quo. However, it is not clear that those who fail to justify the status quo lack system justification motivation. Indeed, several scholars have posited the existence of a countervailing system rejection motivation in favor of system improvement and change (Hennes et al., 2016; Johnson & Fujita, 2012; Jost, Chaikalis-Petritsis, Abrams, Sidanius, van der Toorn, & Bratt, 2012; Kay & Friesen, 2011).

Hennes et al. (2016) propose that system change may also be implicated in biased information processing, leading social problems to be perceived to be more *severe* than they actually are. This proposition is consistent with work suggesting that motivated information processing may be useful in spurring goal-directed action (Cole, Balcetis, Alter, & Trope, 2018). Many social justice scholars have lamented the pervasiveness of apathy and inertia when it comes to protest and support for social progress (e.g., Jost, Becker, Osborne, & Badaan, 2017; Moore, 1978). Therefore, it may be that individuals highly motivated to change the system nonconsciously exaggerate structural problems (both via top-down and bottom-up methods) to mobilize the necessary resources to take effective action. A lay perspective might assume that veridical perceptions of reality are a necessary precondition for ensuring functional social systems (Jost et al., 2013). However, it may be that effective social progress is more likely if problems are exaggerated in order to overcome human's general tendency toward inaction. Indeed, motivated perceptions of the self and one's close others are often associated with better health outcomes and relationship persistence than accuracy in those domains (e.g., Murray et al., 1996; Taylor & Brown, 1988).

Scholars must also address the possibility of motivated reasoning resulting from system justification on the left (see also Banaji, 2017). System justification theory argues that individuals are motivated to perceive societal institutions as legitimate, over and above concerns about the self and the group. However, in practice, many of the domains in which system justification has been tested have made it difficult to distinguish between self-, group-, and system-level processes, particularly in distinguishing between "conservative" biases driven by social identity considerations and those driven by defense of the status quo. Although some studies demonstrate that system justification effects are robust after controlling for partisanship and ideology (e.g., Hennes et al., 2016; Hennes et al., 2018) and international research demonstrates justification of leftist social systems (e.g., Cichocka & Jost, 2014), future work should continue to examine cases in which political liberals also system justify.

In sum, the evidence summarized here suggests that some individuals sometimes don rose-colored glasses when evaluating the state of existing societal arrangements. We encourage scholars to continue to examine the implications of such misperceptions of reality for both individual and societal well-being.

Acknowledgments

Portions of this chapter are adapted from the doctoral dissertation of the first author. The authors thank Mark J. Brandt and Bastiaan T. Rutjens for their insightful feedback, and the members of the Social Cognition of Social Justice Lab, particularly Zachary Chacko, Hayley Green, Zehan Li, Xiyao Ge, Matthew Caldwell, and Stefanie Walsh for their assistance and feedback on the preparation of this chapter.

References

Allcott, H., & Gentzkow, M. (2017). Social media and fake news in the 2016 election. *Journal of Economic Perspectives, 31*, 211–236. doi:10.3386/w23089.

Anderegg, W. R. L., Prall, J. W., Harold, J., & Schneider, S. H. (2010). Expert credibility in climate change. *Proceedings of the National Academy of Sciences of the United States of America, 107*, 12107–12109. doi:10.1073/pnas.1003187107.

Balcetis, E., & Dunning, D. (2006). See what you want to see: Motivational influences on visual perception. *Journal of Personality and Social Psychology, 91*, 612–625. doi:10.1037/0022-3514.91.4.612.

Banaji, M. R. (2017, May). Discussant comments. In J. T. Jost (Chair), *New directions in system justification theory.* Symposium conducted at the 29th annual meeting of the Association for Psychological Science, Boston, MA.

Barberá, P., Jost, J. T., Nagler, J., Tucker, J. A., & Bonneau, R. (2015). Tweeting from left to right: Is online political communication more than an echo chamber? *Psychological Science, 26*, 1531–1542. doi:10.1177/0956797615594620.

Blasi, G., & Jost, J. T. (2006). System justification theory and research: Implications for law, legal advocacy, and social justice. *California Law Review, 94*, 1119–1168. doi:10.2307/20439060.

Bonnot, V., & Jost, J. T. (2014). Divergent effects of system justification salience on the academic self-assessments of men and women. *Group Processes & Intergroup Relations, 17*, 453–464. doi:10.1177/1368430213512008.

Bonnot, V., & Krauth-Gruber, S. (2018). Gender stereotype-consistent memories: How system justification motivation distorts the recollection of information related to the self. *The Journal of Social Psychology, 158*, 125–136. doi:10.1080/00224545.2017.1317232.

Boykoff, M. T. (2013). Public enemy no. 1? Understanding media representations of outlier views on climate change. *American Behavioral Scientist, 57,* 796–817. doi:10.1177/0002764213476846.

Boykoff, M. T., & Boykoff, J. M. (2004). Balance as bias: Global warming and the US prestige press. *Global Environmental Change, 14,* 124–136. doi:10.1016/j.gloenvcha.2003.10.001.

Bullock, J. G., Gerber, A. S., Hill, S. J., & Huber, G. A. (2015). Partisan bias in factual beliefs about politics. *Quarterly Journal of Political Science, 10,* 519–578. doi:10.3386/w19080.

Callan, M. J., Kay, A. C., Davidenko, N., & Ellard, J. H. (2009). The effects of justice motivation on memory for self-and other-relevant events. *Journal of Experimental Social Psychology, 45,* 614–623. doi:10.1016/j.jesp.2009.02.013.

Campbell, T. H., & Kay, A. C. (2014). Solution aversion: On the relation between ideology and motivated disbelief. *Journal of Personality and Social Psychology, 107,* 809–824. doi:10.1037/a0037963.

Cichocka, A., & Jost, J. T. (2014). Stripped of illusions? Exploring system justification processes in capitalist and post-communist societies. *International Journal of Psychology, 49,* 6–29. doi:10.1002/ijop.12011.

Cole, S., Balcetis, E., Alter, A., & Trope, Y. (2018). *Seeing is for self-regulating: Motivated visual processing in the service of goal pursuit.* Unpublished manuscript.

Cutright, K. M., Wu, E. C., Banfield, J. C., Kay, A. C., & Fitzsimons, G. J. (2011). When your world must be defended: Choosing products to justify the system. *Advances in Consumer Research, 37,* 254–258. doi:10.1086/658469.

Death Penalty Information Center (2018). Facts about the death penalty. Retrieved from http://deathpenaltyinfo.org/documents/FactSheet.pdf.

Dispensa, J. M., & Brulle, R. J. (2003). Media's social construction of environmental issues: Focus on global warming – A comparative study. *International Journal of Sociology and Social Policy, 23,* 74–105. doi:10.1108/01443330310790327.

Ditto, P. H. (2009). Passion, reason, and necessity: A quantity-of-processing view of motivated reasoning. In T. Bayne, & J. Fernández (Eds.), *Delusion and self-deception: Affective and motivational influences on belief formation.* New York, NY: Psychology Press. doi:10.1037/0022-3514.75.1.53.

Ditto, P. H., Scepansky, J. A., Munro, G. D., Apanovitch, A. M., & Lockhart, L. K. (1998). Motivated sensitivity to preference-inconsistent information. *Journal of Personality and Social Psychology, 75,* 53–69. doi:10.1037/0022-3514.75.1.53.

Eagly, A. H., & Chaiken, S. (1993). *The psychology of attitudes.* Orlando, FL: Harcourt Brace Jovanovich College.

Ecker, U. K., Lewandowsky, S., & Tang, D. T. (2010). Explicit warnings reduce but do not eliminate the continued influence of misinformation. *Memory & Cognition, 38,* 1087–1100. doi:10.3758/MC.38.8.1087.

Egan, P. J., & Mullin, M. (2012). Turning personal experience into political attitudes: The effect of local weather on American's perceptions about global warming. *Journal of Politics, 74,* 796–809. doi:10.1017/s0022381612000448.

Feinberg, M., & Willer, R. (2011). Apocalypse soon? Dire messages reduce belief in global warming by contradicting just world beliefs. *Psychological Science, 22,* 34–38. doi:10.1177/0956797610391911.

Festinger, L. (1950). Informal social communication. *Psychological Review, 57,* 271–282. doi:10.1037/h0056932.

Feygina, I., Jost, J. T., & Goldsmith, R. E. (2010). System justification, the denial of global warming, and the possibility of "system-sanctioned change." *Personality and Social Psychology Bulletin, 36,* 326–338. doi:10.1177/0146167209351435.

Griffin, D. W., Gonzalez, R., Koehler, D. J., & Gilovich, T. (2012). Judgmental heuristics: A historical overview. In K. Holyoak, & R. G. Morrison (Eds.), *The Oxford handbook of thinking and reasoning* (pp. 322–345). Oxford: Oxford University Press.

Haines, E. L., & Jost, J. T. (2000). Placating the powerless: Effects of legitimate and illegitimate explanations on affect, memory, and stereotyping. *Social Justice Research, 13,* 219–236. doi:10.1023/A:1026481205719.

Hart, W., Albarracín, D., Eagly, A. H., Brechan, I., Lindberg, M. J., & Merrill, L. (2009). Feeling validated versus being correct: A meta-analysis of selective exposure to information. *Psychological Bulletin, 135,* 555–588. doi:10.1037/a0015701.

Hennes, E. P., Feygina, I., & Jost, J. T. (2018). *Feels like global warming: System justification and the judgment of ambient temperature.* Unpublished manuscript.

Hennes, E. P., Nam, H. H., Stern, C., & Jost, J. T. (2012). Not all ideologies are created equal: Epistemic, existential, and relational needs predict system-justifying attitudes. *Social Cognition, 30,* 669–688. doi:10.1521/soco.2012.30.6.669.

Hennes, E. P., Ruisch, B. C., Feygina, I., Monteiro, C. A., & Jost, J. T. (2016). Motivated recall in the service of the economic system: The case of anthropogenic climate change. *Journal of Experimental Psychology: General, 145,* 755–771. doi:10.1037/xge0000148.supp.

Hennes, E. P., Ruisch, B. C., Jagel, K., & Jost, J. T. (2018). *Two paths to misinformation: System justification and conservative media exposure each predict misinformation about climate change.* Unpublished manuscript.

Huddy, L. (2003). Group membership, ingroup loyalty, and political cohesion. In D. O. Sears, L. Huddy, & R. Jervis (Eds.), *Oxford handbook of political psychology* (pp. 511–558). New York, NY: Oxford University Press. doi:10.1093/oxfordhb/9780199760107.013.0023.

Iacono, W. G. (2008). Polygraph testing. In E. Borgida, & S. T. Fiske (Eds.), *Beyond common sense: Psychological science in the courtroom* (pp. 219–236). Malden, MA: Blackwell Publishing.

IJzerman, H., & Semin, G. R. (2010). Temperature perceptions as a ground for social proximity. *Journal of Experimental Social Psychology, 46,* 867–873. doi:10.1016/j.jesp.2010.07.015.

Jacques, P. J., Dunlap, R. E., & Freeman, M. (2008). The organization of denial: Conservative think tanks and environmental skepticism. *Environmental Politics, 17,* 349–385. doi:10.1080/09644010802055576.

Jahoda, M. (1958). *Current concepts of positive mental health.* New York, NY: Basic Books.

Johnson, I. R., & Fujita, K. (2012). Change we can believe in: Using perceptions of changeability to promote system-change motives over system-justification motives in information search. *Psychological Science, 23,* 133–140. doi:10.1177/0956797611423670.

Jost, J. T. (1995). Negative illusions: Conceptual clarification and psychological evidence concerning false consciousness. *Political Psychology, 16,* 397–424. doi:10.2307/3791837.

Jost, J. T., & Banaji, M. R. (1994). The role of stereotyping in system–justification and the production of false consciousness. *British Journal of Social Psychology, 33,* 1–27. doi:10.1111/j.2044–8309.1994.tb01008.x.

Jost, J. T., Banaji, M. R., & Nosek, B. A. (2004). A decade of system justification theory: Accumulated evidence of conscious and unconscious bolstering of the status quo. *Political Psychology, 25,* 881–919. doi:10.1111/j.1467–9221.2004.00402.x.

Jost, J. T., Becker, J., Osborne, D., & Badaan, V. (2017). Missing in (collective) action: Ideology, system justification, and the motivational antecedents of two types of protest behavior. *Current Directions in Psychological Science, 26,* 99–108. doi:10.1177/0963721417690633.

Jost, J. T., Chaikalis-Petritsis, V., Abrams, D., Sidanius, J., van der Toorn, J., & Bratt, C. (2012). Why men (and women) do and don't rebel: Effects of system justification on willingness to protest. *Personality and Social Psychology Bulletin, 38*, 197–208. doi:10.1177/0146167211422544.

Jost, J. T., Hennes, E. P., & Lavine, H. (2013). "Hot" political cognition: Its self-, group-, and system serving purposes. In D. Carlston (Ed.), *Oxford handbook of social cognition* (pp. 851–875), Oxford: Oxford University Press.

Jost, J. T., & van der Toorn, J. (2012). System justification theory. In P. A. M. van Lange, A. W. Kruglanski, & E. T. Higgins (Eds.), *Handbook of theories of social psychology* (Vol. 2, pp. 313–343). London: Sage.

Jussim, L. (1991). Social perception and social reality: A reflection-construction model. *Psychological Review, 98*, 54–73. doi:10.1037/0033–295X.98.1.54.

Kay, A. C., & Friesen, J. (2011). On social stability and social change: Understanding when system justification does and does not occur. *Current Directions in Psychological Science, 20*, 360–364. doi:10.1177/0963721411422059.

Kay, A. C., Jimenez, M. C., & Jost, J. T. (2002). Sour grapes, sweet lemons, and the anticipatory rationalization of the status quo. *Personality and Social Psychology Bulletin, 28*, 1300–1312. doi:10.1177/01461672022812014.

Kay, A. C., Jost, J. T., & Young, S. (2005). Victim derogation and victim enhancement as alternate routes to system justification. *Psychological Science, 16*, 240–246. doi:10.1111/j.0956-7976.2005.00810.x.

Kelman, H. C. (2001). Reflections on social and psychological processes of legitimization and delegitimization. In J. T. Jost, & B. Major (Eds.), *The psychology of legitimacy: Emerging perspectives on ideology, justice, and intergroup relations*. Cambridge: Cambridge University Press.

Kosslyn, S. M., & Koenig, O. (1992). *Wet mind: The new cognitive. Neuroscience.* New York, NY: The Free Press.

Kteily, N. S., Sheehy-Skeffington, J., & Ho, A. K. (2017). Hierarchy in the eye of the beholder: (Anti-) egalitarianism shapes perceived levels of social inequality. *Journal of Personality and Social Psychology, 112*, 136–159. doi:10.1037/pspp0000097.

Kunda, Z. (1990). The case for motivated reasoning. *Psychological Bulletin, 108*, 480–498. doi:10.1037/0033–2909.108.3.480.

Lane, R. E. (1959). The fear of equality. *The American Political Science Review, 53*, 35–51. doi:10.2307/1951729.

Laurin, K. (2018). Inaugurating rationalization: Three field studies find increased rationalization when anticipated realities become current. *Psychological Science, 29*, 483–494. doi:10.1177/0956797617738814.

Ledgerwood, A., Mandisodza, A., Jost, J. T., & Pohl, M. (2011). Working for the system: Motivated defense of meritocratic beliefs. *Social Cognition, 29*, 322–340. doi:10.1521/soco.2011.29.3.322.

Lerner, M. J. (1980). *The belief in a just world: A fundamental delusion.* New York, NY: Plenum Press.

Leviston, Z., & Walker, I. (2014). *System legitimacy and support for climate change policy in Australia.* Paper presented at the International Society of Justice Research 15th Biennial Conference, New York, NY.

Lewandowsky, S., Stritzke, W. G., Oberauer, K., & Morales, M. (2005). Memory for fact, fiction, and misinformation: The Iraq War 2003. *Psychological Science, 16*, 190–195. doi:10.1111/j.0956-7976.2005.00802.x.

Li, Y., Johnson, E. J., & Zaval, L. (2011). Local warming: Daily temperature change influences belief in global warming. *Psychological Science, 22*, 454–459. doi:10.1177/0956797611400913.

Lion, J. R., Kenefick, D. P., Albert, J., Bach-y-Rita, G., Blumer, D., Monroe, R. R., Roth, L. H., & Tupin, J. P. (1974). *Clinical aspects of the violent individual. Task Force Report #8.* American Psychiatric Association, Washington, DC.

Liviatan, I., & Jost, J. T. (2014). A social-cognitive analysis of system justification goal striving. *Social Cognition, 32*, 95–129. doi:10.1521/soco.2014.32.2.95.

Lord, C. G., Ross, L., & Lepper, M. R. (1979). Biased assimilation and attitude polarization: The effects of prior theories on subsequently considered evidence. *Journal of Personality and Social Psychology, 37*, 2098–2109. doi:10.1037/0022-3514.37.11.2098.

Marx, K., & Engels, F. (1846/1970). *The German ideology.* C. J. Arthur (Ed.). New York, NY: International Publishers.

Moore, B. Jr. (1978). *Injustice: The social bases of obedience and revolt.* White Plains, NY: Sharpe.

Murray, S. L., Griffin, D. W., Derrick, J. L., Harris, B., Aloni, M., & Leder, S. (2011). Tempting fate or inviting happiness? Unrealistic idealization prevents the decline of marital satisfaction. *Psychological Science, 22*, 619–626. doi:10.1177/0956797611403155.

Murray, S. L., Holmes, J. G., & Griffin, D. W. (1996). The benefits of positive illusions: Idealization and the construction of satisfaction in close relationships. *Journal of Personality and Social Psychology Bulletin, 70*, 79–98. doi:10.1037/0022-3514.70.1.79.

Nisbet, M. C. (2009). Communicating climate change: Why frames matter for public engagement. *Environment: Science and Policy for Sustainable Development, 51*, 12–23. doi:10.3200/ENVT.51.2.12–23.

Note (1968). To take the stand or not to take the stand: The dilemma of the defendant with a criminal record. *Columbia Journal of Law & Social Problems, 4*, 215–229.

Nyhan, B., & Reifler, J. (2010). When corrections fail: The persistence of political misperceptions. *Political Behavior, 32*, 303–330. doi:10.1007/s11109-010-9112-2.

Paris Adult Theater I v. Slaton, 413 U.S. 49 (1973).

Pashler, H., & Wagenmakers, E. J. (2012). Editors' introduction to the special section on replicability in psychological science: A crisis of confidence? *Perspectives on Psychological Science, 7*, 528–530. doi:10.1177/1745691612465253.

Payne, B. K. (2001). Prejudice and perception: The role of automatic and controlled processes in misperceiving a weapon. *Journal of Personality and Social Psychology, 81*, 181–192. doi:10.1037/0022-3514.81.2.181.

Petty, R. E., & Cacioppo, J. A. (1986). The elaboration likelihood model of persuasion. *Advances in Experimental Social Psychology, 19*, 123–205. doi:10.1016/S0065-2601(08)60214-2.

Pew Research Center. (2017). Support for same-sex marriage grows, even among groups that had been skeptical. Retrieved from www.people-press.org/2017/06/26/support-for-same-sex-marriage-grows-even-among-groups-that-had-been-skeptical/.

Pronin, E., Lin, D. Y., & Ross, L. (2002). The bias blind spot: Perceptions of bias in self versus others. *Personality and Social Psychology Bulletin, 28*, 369–381. doi:10.1177/0146167202286008.

Radelet, M. L., & Lacock, T. L. (2009). Recent developments: Do executions lower homicide rates? The views of leading criminologists. *The Journal of Criminal Law and Criminology*, 489–508. www.jstor.org/stable/20685045.

Ross, L., & Ward, A. (1996). Naive realism in everyday life: Implications for social conflict and misunderstanding. In E. S. Reed, & E. Turiel (Eds.), *Values and knowledge* (pp. 103–135). Hillsdale, NJ: Lawrence Erlbaum.

Sandell, C., & Blakemore, B. (2006, July 27). ABC News reporting cited as evidence in congressional hearing on global warming. Retrieved from http://abcnews.go.com/Technology/GlobalWarming/story?id=2242565&page=1.

Scruggs, L., & Benegal, S. (2012). Declining public concern about climate change: Can we blame the great recession? *Global Environmental Change, 22*, 505–515. doi:10.1016/j.gloenvcha.2012.01.002.

Shepherd, S., & Kay, A. C. (2012). On the perpetuation of ignorance: System dependence, system justification, and the motivated avoidance of sociopolitical information. *Journal of Personality and Social Psychology, 102*, 264–280. doi:10.1037/a0026272.

Stern, C., Balcetis, E., Cole, S., West, T. V., & Caruso, E. M. (2016). Government instability shifts skin tone representations of and intentions to vote for political candidates. *Journal of Personality and Social Psychology, 110*, 76–95. doi:10.1037/pspi0000040.

Story, A. L. (1998). Self-esteem and memory for favorable and unfavorable personality feedback. *Personality and Social Psychology Bulletin, 24*, 51–64. doi:10.1177/0146167298241004.

Sutton, R. M., Petterson, A., & Rutjens, B. T. (2018). Impact bias in the motivated rejection – and opposition – to science. In M. Brandt, & B. Rutjens (Eds.), *Belief systems and the perception of reality*. London and New York, NY: Routledge.

Taber, C. S., & Lodge, M. (2006). Motivated skepticism in the evaluation of political beliefs. *American Journal of Political Science, 50*, 755–769. doi:10.1111/j.1540–5907.2006.00214.x.

Tankard, M. E., & Paluck, E. L. (2017). The effect of a supreme court decision regarding gay marriage on social norms and personal attitudes. *Psychological Science, 28*, 1334–1344. doi:10.1177/0956797617709594.

Taylor, S. E., & Brown, J. D. (1988). Illusion and well-being: A social psychological perspective on mental health. *Psychological Bulletin, 103*, 193–210. doi:10.1037/0033-2909.103.2.193.

Ullrich, J., & Cohrs, J. C. (2007). Terrorism salience increases system justification: Experimental evidence. *Social Justice Research, 20*, 117–139. doi:10.1007/s11211-007-0035-y.

Wike, R. (2016, April 18). What the world thinks about climate change in 7 charts. Pew Research Center. Retrieved from www.pewresearch.org/fact-tank/2016/04/18/what-the-world-thinks-about-climate-change-in-7-charts/.

Zhong, C.-B., & Leonardelli, G. J. (2008). Cold and lonely: Does social exclusion literally feel cold? *Psychological Science, 19*, 838–842. doi:10.1111/j.1467-9280.2008.02165.x.

THEME 2
Inequality

3

IDEOLOGY AND PERCEPTIONS OF INEQUALITY

Denise Baron, Jennifer Sheehy-Skeffington, and Nour Kteily

Introduction

Contemporary issues of social inequality continue to attract attention and debate in theatres of public opinion and policy. There is increasing disagreement between political parties, decision-makers, and segments of the population on whether inequality between social groups is a problem, and how it should be addressed (Baker & Fausset, 2015; Blow, 2013; Elliott, 2017; Grant & Sandberg, 2014; Ratcliffe, 2015; Williams & Ceci, 2015). Indeed, one need look no further than the recent rise of populism to see how perceived divergence between the 'haves' and the 'have-nots' animates political action on both the left and the right (Andrain, 2014; Cassidy, 2016; Goodwin & Heath, 2016; Gray, 2017; Inglehart & Norris, 2016; Chapter 5).

Opinions diverge not only on the desirability and causes of inequality but also on its very nature and functioning. Individuals from across the political spectrum have different perceptions of how much inequality exists between economic, racial, gender, and other social groups, and how much mobility is available within intergroup hierarchies (Chambers, Swan, & Heesacker, 2015; Cohn, 2014; Kraus, Rucker, & Richeson, 2017; Kraus & Tan, 2015; Kteily, Sheehy-Skeffington, & Ho, 2017; Porter, 2014). If people perceive inequality at varying levels and in conflicting ways, their perceived need for public policy interventions may differ as well. Recent research has thus started to consider the inputs that shape individuals' perceptions of inequality (Dawtry, Sutton, & Sibley, 2015; see also Sheehy-Skeffington, Kteily, & Hauser, 2016).

Foremost among these inputs, and our current focus, is ideology. This chapter will first outline our understanding of both ideology and perceptions of inequality, before considering a range of origins of people's inequality perceptions. It will then consider evidence for how ideology may influence perceptions of inequality, and what that could mean for contemporary political debates. This analysis will focus primarily on the potential influence ideology exerts on perceptions of inequality, but we will also touch on the reflexive nature of these two constructs by highlighting the implications of varied and biased perceptions of inequality in public debate.

Ideology

Ideology in its most general form refers to a system of ideas and ideals about how power, status, and other resources should be distributed in society (see e.g. Eagleton, 1991). It is conventionally discussed in the social sciences as political orientation, an aggregation of attitudes about personal and collective liberties, law and order, the role of government, appropriate social behaviour, and other elements that organise society. When analysing contemporary Western democracies, this spectrum of political orientation typically runs from conservative or right-wing to liberal or left-wing (see Knapp & Wright, 2006; Ruypers, 2005; though see Malka, Lelkes, & Soto, 2017).

Digging deeper than policy preferences, research in political psychology has examined the mechanisms underlying political orientation in terms of two attitudinal dimensions: support for or opposition to change (linked with social liberalism vs. conservatism, respectively) and support for or opposition to equality (linked with economic liberalism and conservatism, respectively; see Jost, Federico, & Napier, 2009; Kandler, Bleidorn, & Riemann, 2012; Treier & Hillygus, 2009; though see Malka et al., 2017). Given its explicit link to inequality, this chapter focuses on the second of these two dimensions. Anti-egalitarianism specifically indexes the extent to which one supports a hierarchical structure of society in which valued goods are distributed unevenly between individuals and social groups.

Perceptions of inequality

Social inequality refers to the unequal distribution of resources, such as power, wealth, opportunities, and rewards, between individuals or groups in society, as well as the resulting status hierarchy formed by these differential resource allocations.

In this chapter, we use the term 'inequality perceptions' to refer to how large or small we perceive the difference in resources between individuals or groups to be, and our perception of how fixed it is. That is, we are concerned with perceptions of the *extent* of inequality or hierarchy in any given society, and *mobility* within that hierarchy. These features of inequality are distinct from value judgements such as whether inequality is just or beneficial. Whereas ideology is inherently linked to evaluations of the *desirability* of inequality, its relationship with perceptions of the *extent* of inequality and social mobility is not self-evident. It is thus worth considering whether ideological beliefs play a role even in shaping these more 'objective' aspects of inequality perception.

Origins of inequality perceptions

One's understanding of the nature and extent of inequality between social groups is not merely a case of 'reading' information easily accessible from societal observation. Rather, as with most judgements of political realities, it is the product of multiple inputs, from personal experience to media consumption and social influence.

The most intuitive source of inequality perceptions is personal exposure to signals of inequality, such as through interactions and encounters in everyday life. Perceiving resource disparities depends in part on whether one has had the opportunity to observe extreme cases of advantage and disadvantage, as indexed through differences in clothing, housing quality, and neighbourhood appearance across the socio-economic spectrum (see Dawtry et al., 2015; Kraus, Park, & Tan, 2017; Sheehy-Skeffington et al., 2016).

A similarly straightforward source of influence on the perceived degree of inequality is the news media one consumes. Whereas classically liberal or left-wing news outlets are likely to report on the existence of extreme poverty or group-based discrimination, conservative or right-wing television channels and newspapers spend less time reporting on such topics (see e.g. McKendrick et al., 2008; McNair, 2009), leading to very different pictures across their audiences of the nature and functioning of inequality in their society (e.g. Diermeier, Goecke, Niehues, & Thomas, 2017; Kraus & Tan, 2015).

Other sources of information on perceptions of inequality arise from the social context: through communication among one's family, friends, and political groups. Given that one's ideological orientation is heavily influenced by upbringing and socialisation (e.g. Duriez & Soenens, 2009; Guimond & Palmer, 1996; see Sears & Levy, 2003), it is likely that one's perception about how society is structured reflects discussions with parents and peers. At a broader level, political parties and elites send cues to their followers about what they would like them to believe are the most important societal concerns, inequality being one among many competing issues (see Dettrey & Campbell, 2013; Kuklinski & Hurley, 1994).

In sum, individual perceptions of societal inequality and intergroup hierarchy originate, in part, from the same sources as do ideological attitudes: experience, media framing, and social context. The next question is whether ideological motivation itself – and specifically, egalitarianism – might be another important source of inequality perceptions.

The role of motivation

In order to understand the possibility that inequality perceptions may be sensitive to individual motivations, we need to consider the political effect of drawing attention to inequality and its functioning. In liberal democracies, there is a pervasive norm of egalitarianism and in particular of equality of opportunity. Where resource inequalities do exist, public consensus is that they should not be extreme, and should involve the ability for anyone with the appropriate ability and effort to move up the social hierarchy (e.g. Fong, 2001; Inglehart, 2008; Katz, & Hass, 1988). One implication is that those who benefit from inequality, and thus stand to lose if it is addressed, might be motivated to downplay its existence, or to emphasise its fair or meritocratic nature (see Alesina & La Ferrara, 2005; Kteily et al., 2017; Piketty, 1995).

The most obvious way in which one might benefit from inequality is by being positioned at the top of a power or resource hierarchy. This motivation likely underpins the fact that White Americans and American males perceive the American racial and gender hierarchies to be less steep than do minorities and women, respectively (Bonilla-Silva, 2006; Kraus, Rucker, & Richeson, 2017; Kteily et al., 2017, Study 1a; Sears & Henry, 2005). Judgements of the fixedness of inequality are also related to social position, with White Americans perceiving greater advances towards racial equality than people of colour (Brodish, Brazy, & Devine, 2008; Eibach & Ehrlinger, 2006; Eibach & Keegan, 2006). Similarly, occupying a higher socio-economic position in the United States is associated with judgements of greater social mobility (Kraus & Tan, 2015).

Beyond the material benefits offered by inequality to those positioned at the top, inequality provides psychological benefits to those who, as individuals, simply have a stronger underlying preference for it. The question thus arises whether those with an ideological motivation to support inequality or the economic status quo might experience or report perceptions of inequality in line with this motivation. The next section turns to evidence for the relationship between political orientation or trait egalitarianism on the one hand, and perceptions of the extent and functioning of inequality on the other.

The relationship between ideology and perceptions of inequality

The link between ideology and inequality perceptions has primarily been studied within the context of liberals and conservatives in the United States. Looking specifically at income inequality, Chambers, Swan, and Heesacker (2014) found that political liberals overestimated the increase in inequality that has occurred in the United States in comparison with political conservatives. This link between political orientation and inequality perceptions extends beyond judgements of the degree of or changes in inequality, to its functioning in the form of social mobility. The same paper reported that the underestimation of trends in social mobility was greatest among politically liberal participants in comparison with moderates and conservative participants (Chambers et al., 2015).

Looking at deeper ideological motivations, the link between egalitarianism and inequality perceptions was the topic of a recent paper by Kteily et al. (2017). These authors considered the link between perceptions of the extent of inequality and individual levels of anti-egalitarianism, the latter measured as social dominance orientation (SDO). SDO indexes support inequality between social groups

(Ho et al., 2015) and are thus an ideological orientation towards maintaining social hierarchy. High SDO individuals favour ideologies that justify the hierarchical status quo (e.g. meritocracy, belief in Karma), while low SDO individuals favour ideologies (e.g. universalism, socialism) that emphasise the need for changes of the status quo and redistributive policies (Cotterill et al., 2014; Kteily, Ho, & Sidanius, 2012; Kteily, Sheehy-Skeffington, & Ho, 2017; Sidanius & Pratto, 1999; for a review, see Sidanius, Cotterill, Sheehy-Skeffington, Kteily, & Carvacho, 2016).

Across eight studies, Kteily et al. (2017) found that the more individuals supported hierarchy between different groups, the lower the levels of inequality they perceived between groups at either end of the social hierarchy. Perceiving less inequality between groups was, in turn, associated with disapproval of policies designed to reduce inequality. This association between ideology and perceptions of the extent of inequality was observed in the case of real societal groups, fictitious scenarios, and even abstract images depicting hierarchy. The authors found that it was not clearly a case of bias on just one end of the political spectrum: in a study of memory of inequality, low SDO individuals were found to overestimate the degree of hierarchy they had previously seen, while high SDO individuals underestimated the degree of hierarchy they had seen (Kteily et al., 2017, Study 5).

There is thus emergent evidence that variation in ideological orientation predicts variation in perceptions both of the extent and of the functioning of inequality in social systems. The question remains, however, as to what mechanisms underlie the relationship. How exactly might varying ideological preferences contribute to different perceptions, observations, or reports of inequality? Below we consider the most likely candidate explanations, weighing the evidence for each.

Differential exposure

One reason that ideology and inequality perceptions are related could be ideological preferences causing us to self-select into environments and information sources offering exposure to more or less disparities in power and resources. Experimental research has demonstrated that we seek out information and news consistent with our political identities, which therefore reinforces and narrows our exposure to information from specific ideological perspectives (Hart et al., 2009; Iyengar & Hahn, 2009). Conservatives or those higher in anti-egalitarianism are thus drawn towards right-wing news sources which play down the existence of unfair inequality, while liberals or egalitarians preferentially select new sources emphasising severe inequality or discrimination. This process is likely exacerbated with increases in the consumption of online and informal news, leading to polarisation in exposure to information about inequality and how it operates (Lawrence, Sides, & Farrell, 2010; see also Bakshy, Messing, & Adamic, 2015).

Similarly, it might be that conservatism or anti-egalitarianism yields a desire to spend time with high-status people or in wealthy environments, thus diminishing one's opportunities to observe disadvantage or disparities wealth and life outcomes (see Dawtry et al., 2015; Sidanius, van Laar, Levin, & Sinclair, 2003). Conversely, we know that liberals and egalitarians are more drawn towards socio-economically diverse environments and jobs that serve the under-privileged or attenuate hierarchy (Sidanius, Pratto, Sinclair, & van Laar, 1996; Sidanius et al., 2003), giving them more exposure to inequality on a daily basis.

Although differential exposure very likely plays some role in explaining the link between ideology and perceptions of inequality, Kteily et al. (2017) present evidence that it cannot be the only explanation. When participants were pre-sented with the same stimuli depicting inequality (i.e. such as vignettes of novel intergroup conflicts or images of organisational hierarchies), the association be-tween perceptions of inequality and SDO persisted, with those higher on SDO perceiving lower levels of inequality than those lower on SDO (Kteily et al., 2017). As all participants had been given the same initial information about the fictitious societies or organisations, this association between ideology and ine-quality perceptions could not have been due to differential exposure.

Strategic reporting

A second possibility is that individuals notice the same situations and objective realities of social inequality, yet they strategically and consciously report the differences between groups in a way that either downplays or exaggerates inequal-ity, depending on their motivation to avoid or push for egalitarian social change, respectively. The perception of the degree of social hierarchy is not, according to this explanation, truly determined by ideology. Rather, everyone perceives the degree of inequality equivalently, but individuals simply report it differently to align with their strategic goals. Seen in this light, the under-reporting of in-equality by those higher in SDO is similar to the selective presentation of infor-mation consistent with partisan agendas, as observed in American media outlets (Iyengar & Hahn, 2009).

Kteily et al. (2017) directly investigated the role of strategic reporting in under-pinning their observed association between ideology and inequality perceptions. In two studies, they offered participants financial incentives for accuracy, intro-ducing a strong motivation for them to match their reports with what they had really had perceived. In both studies, those low in SDO still reported higher levels of hierarchy than those high in SDO, suggestive that ideological differ-ences brought with them differences in perceptions extending beyond strategic reporting (Kteily et al., 2017, Studies 4 and 5). It is still possible that partici-pants' motivation to bias inequality claims to fit with ideological preferences was greater than their motivation to report accurately and thus maximise monetary outcome (similar to research showing that people will forgo financial gain in order to avoid hearing information from political adversaries; Frimer, Skitka, & Motyl, 2017). Nevertheless, as such monetary incentives have been found to be powerful enough as to affect conscious motivation in other studies (see Waytz, Young, & Ginges, 2014) and also increased participants' self-reported motivation to respond with accuracy in this study, their ineffectiveness here is a sign that strategic reporting is not the sole mechanism in the link between ideology and inequality perceptions.

Motivated cognition

Rather than reporting what they observe from differential exposure or what they strategically believe will reinforce their preferences, it is possible that individuals may in fact process information in a biased manner based on their motivations to maintain or reduce social hierarchy. From this perspective, individuals' beliefs about the desirability of hierarchy (as assessed through their political orientation or more precisely via their SDO) alter their very perceptions and inferences of how much inequality exists.

This approach is in line with research on the phenomenon of motivated cognition, the tendency to conform assessments or perceptions of information to a specific goal or objective extrinsic to precision or truth (Balcetis & Dunning, 2006; Uhlmann, Pizarro, Tannenbaum, & Ditto, 2009). A growing literature has demonstrated how motivated cognition biases individuals' perceptions of reality. In five studies, Balcetis and Dunning (2006) found that individuals' motivations, such as their preferences or wishes, strongly influence their processing and assessment of visual stimuli. Their study presented participants with an ambiguous figure (e.g. one that could be interpreted as either the letter *B* or the number *13*) and found that the participants reported seeing the interpretation which produced the outcomes they favoured. The implicit measures of perception and the experimental procedures used in these studies imply that motivation influences visual information processing at the preconscious level and therefore directs which information is presented to conscious awareness (Balcetis & Dunning, 2006).

Recent research has identified motivated cognition processes in the domain of political psychology. Hulsizer, Munro, Fagerlin, and Taylor (2004) explored whether political ideology biases perceptions of historical information and events, by asking participants about the 1970 shooting of protestors by the National Guard at Kent State University. Conservative participants were less likely than liberal participants to hold the National Guard and government officials responsible for the shooting, and instead, assigned blame to the protestors (Hulsizer et al., 2004). In another paper, political ideology was shown to influence individuals' assessment and understanding of political activity such that participants with divergent political ideologies sharply disagreed about the nature and conduct of a political protest (Kahan, Hoffman, Braman, Evans, & Rachlinski, 2012). After viewing the same video of a protest, half of the participants were told that it was an anti-abortion demonstration, and the other half were told that it was a pro-gay rights demonstration. Participants of opposing political orientations in the same experimental condition disagreed about basic elements of the protest, such as whether demonstrators threatened and obstructed pedestrians. Moreover, those with shared political orientations in different experimental conditions also sharply disagreed about such elements of the protest, illustrating the influence of ideology on perceptions of the same content (Kahan, Hoffman, Bramen, Evans, & Rachlinski, 2012). Anti-egalitarian orientations, such as SDO, have also been found to predict social perceptions, particularly those associated with maintaining hierarchy. In a study on SDO and perceptions of race and status, White Americans higher in SDO judged low-status (but not high-status) mixed-race individuals as looking less White, maintaining the status difference between the two racial groups (Kteily, Cotterill, Sidanius, Sheehy-Skeffington, & Bergh, 2014; see also Ho et al., 2012). Given these links between ideology and political perceptions, it seems plausible that levels of egalitarianism might bias perceptions of social inequality through motivated reasoning processes.

In considering multiple explanations for their observed association between SDO and perceptions of the extent of inequality, Kteily et al. (2017) arrived at motivated cognition as the most likely explanation. They came to this conclusion, first, as a result of the inadequacy of differential exposure and strategic reporting in accounting for their findings, particularly in light of the effort made to financially incentivise accurate responding. Second, they observed that even the recognition of previously seen images of inequality in an incentivised memory study was coloured by ideology, implying that motivation was affecting basic cognitive processes (see Kteily et al., 2017, Study 5).

If the motivated cognition account is true, one might expect high SDO individuals to show the most biased perceptions as the objective degree of inequality they are judging increases (thereby raising the spectre of pressures for change). Conversely, egalitarians should appear most biased when the objective degree of inequality they were judging *decreases* (thereby risking that the egalitarian social change they favoured would drop from the social agenda).

In order to examine this question, Kteily et al. (2017) tested how the perceptions of inequality varied across the objective degrees of hierarchy among those high and low on SDO compared to those 'average' in SDO (placing individuals into these categories on the basis of a tertile split). True enough, as the objective hierarchy being judged became more steep, high SDO individuals' estimates of the degree of inequality lagged increasingly behind the estimates of those average and low in SDO. In contrast, when the objective hierarchy being judged became particularly flat, it was the *low* SDOs who deviated in their perceptions from high and average SDOs, continuing to see (relatively) high levels of inequality where others didn't. Taken together, these results are highly consistent with a motivated account and, in combination with the other findings, led the authors to settle on motivated cognition as the most plausible explanation for their pattern of results (see Kteily et al., 2017).

Ideologically motivated perceptions of inequality

We will now briefly consider *how* the process of motivated cognition might operate in order to ideologically colour one's perceptions of inequality. Variation in ideological motivation seems to produce different reactions to the same stimuli, influencing which information is considered and how that information is interpreted, thereby shaping judgements about overall degree of inequality.

When one first encounters information relevant to inequality, ideological motivations may act as a lens, focusing on some stimuli at the cost of others. Recent research suggests such selective attention occurs in ways that support previously held beliefs. For instance, we are more likely to view and share social media posts from other users that reinforce our political beliefs (Bakshy et al., 2015; Barberá, Jost, Nagler, Tucker, & Bonneau, 2015). Balcetis and Dunning (2006) found that motivational states impact the assessment and description of visual stimuli, while Kteily et al. (2017, Studies 3–5) demonstrated the ideological colouring of perceptions of inequality and hierarchy in images.

Motivated reasoning may also influence the manner in which information is interpreted or the inferences drawn from it. Granot and colleagues (2014) found that group identification acts as a motivation to influence the attention paid to legal evidence, the interpretation of that information, and the resulting inferences (i.e. punishment decisions). Participants were presented with videos of altercations between a civilian and a police officer, where the guilt of the (outgroup) officer was ambiguous. Participants' identification with the police was measured and their visual attention to the officer tracked through eye-tracking technology. Among those who fixated often on the officer (but not among those who rarely paid attention), participants who weakly identified with the police punished the officer more harshly than those who strongly identified with the police, an effect driven by more incriminating interpretations of the officer's actions (Granot, Balcetis, Schneider, Tyler, & Gauthier, 2014). Crawford et al. (2013) found that hierarchy-related motives have also been shown to bias information evaluation. They presented participants with newspaper articles that espoused either pro- or anti-affirmative action evidence and conclusions, followed by questions about the veracity and author bias of the articles. The researchers found that lower SDO was associated with perceiving more bias in the anti-affirmative action article and less bias in the pro-affirmative action article (Crawford et al., 2013).

Although the research reviewed earlier has made a convincing case for the ideological shaping of inequality perceptions, questions remain as to the precise mechanism through which this colouring occurs. If it is indeed the case that one's ideological motivation focuses one's attention on social stimuli that ally with that motivation, this could be illustrated through studies of visual perception. As a first attempt to address this question, Sheehy-Skeffington et al. (2016) obtained evidence indicating that individuals low in SDO were more likely to notice cues related to wealth, poverty, or inequality in a set of photographs of urban scenes than individuals high in SDO. Future studies might use methods such as eye tracking to observe this attentional bias in action, in the case of perceptions both of inequality severity and of its functioning. They could also include control conditions designed to examine whether the bias is specific to social stimuli and intergroup contexts. There is thus plenty of work to be done to illuminate the psychological processes underpinning and interacting with the ideological colouring of inequality perceptions.

Inequality perceptions shaping ideology

Before moving on from considering the processes linking ideological motivation and perceptions of inequality, it is worth considering the reverse pathway: whether perceptions of inequality might affect ideological orientation. Although this question has not been tested directly to our knowledge, it has been shown that experiences of differing levels of socio-economic status and inequality have profound psychological effects (Wilkinson & Pickett, 2017). We also know from the work of Dawtry and colleagues that neighbourhood income affects perceptions of inequality, with implications for political views (Dawtry et al., 2015). Kteily et al. (2017) provide evidence that the link between ideology and inequality perceptions is not primarily a case of the latter influencing the former, however. In four of their studies, the link between ideology and perceptions in inequality was observed with new vignettes or images depicting inequality: given that perceptions of inequality in the new scenarios were formed in the study and measured after SDO was measured, they cannot be affecting SDO in this case. In another study, longitudinal cross-lag analysis supported the conclusion that SDO affected inequality perceptions over time and not the reverse. Finally, in one study it was found that the placing of SDO before or after asking about inequality perceptions did not affect the correlations observed (Kteily et al., 2017). None of these demonstrations is definitive as one could argue that it is perceptions of inequality in general (as opposed to of the inequality in these vignettes) that influence ideology and that they do so over longer time periods than that assessed in the cross-lagged analysis (6 months) and/or earlier in life than among the adults, which Kteily et al. (2017) considered. Nevertheless, when considered in the context of the general, stable, and causally powerful nature of ideological orientations such as SDO (see, e.g. Bratt, Sidanius, & Sheehy-Skeffington, 2016; Kteily, Ho, & Sidanius, 2012; Sidanius et al., 2016), the evidence for ideology as a shaper of inequality perceptions is persuasive.

Implications of the ideological nature of inequality perceptions

That there may be ideological bias in the very perception of how much inequality exists in society and how much mobility exists within it (to say nothing of the other spheres of inequality perception, such as within organisations – see Kteily et al., 2017) has implications both theoretical and applied.

Implications for political psychology research

The work reviewed in this chapter has important theoretical implications for research in political psychology. For one, the finding that the link between SDO and perceptions of inequality seems to reflect processes operating among both anti-egalitarians and egalitarians adds to debates about whether motivated reasoning operates more on the political right than left, or, rather, extends equally across the political spectrum (Brandt, Reyna, Chambers, Crawford, & Wetherell, 2014; Jost, Glaser, Kruglanski, Sulloway, & Cooper, 2003).

This work also contributes to an emerging body of research showing how individuals' equality motives can shape their perceptions of the world around them. For example, recent work shows that individuals' SDO levels affect their perception of biracials, with anti-egalitarian Whites tending to perceive Black-White biracials as looking more Black, particularly when considering low-status Black targets (Kteily et al., 2014), or feeling a sense of threat to their group's standing (Ho et al., 2012; see also Krosch, Berntsen, Amodio, Jost, & Van Bavel, 2013). Research also suggests that individuals' equality motives predict the extent to which they perceive damaging events (e.g. having one's pay cut or home robbed) as meaningfully harmful to a given target depending on whether that target is socially advantaged or disadvantaged (Lucas & Kteily, under review), with low SDO individuals perceiving that the same act is more harmful than high SDO individuals when the target is disadvantaged (e.g. a blue-collar worker) but *less* harmful than high SDO individuals when the target is advantaged (e.g. a corporate executive).

Our work also calls for a broader examination of the inputs into perceptions of inequality. Although we have highlighted how ideology impacts perceived inequality via motivated processes, we also noted other processes that could play a role, including exposure to different media, neighbourhoods, and so on. Notably, exposure to different environments could itself be either incidental (e.g. being born and raised in one town vs. another) or motivated (e.g. explicitly seeking or avoiding certain neighbourhoods or moving to a location where others share your beliefs; Motyl, Iyer, Oishi, Trawalter, & Nosek, 2014). This review suggests that it will be important to more comprehensively examine the multitude of factors shaping how individuals come to perceive inequality in the world around them while considering the proportional contribution of motivated versus non-motivated processes.

Implications in the political sphere

The understanding of ideology and perceptions of inequality that has been reviewed in this chapter provides insight into the nature of contemporary political debate and action, as well as how it might evolve.

First, this work provides a window into the psychological processes which contribute to the extreme levels of political polarisation currently observed in many industrialised countries. To the extent that people on the political left and right perceive fundamentally different social realities (both with respect to inequality, and more broadly) as a function of their motivations, common ground between them will be elusive. When people cannot even agree on the *degree* of the problem at hand, they are doubly unlikely to converge on similar solutions (and more likely to be distrustful of and incredulous about the other side's stance).

Furthermore, divergent perceptions of inequality can be expressed as frustration with either the failure to address inequality or the excessive attention paid to it in the public sphere. These expressions can impact attitudes and beliefs of public figures, such as political leaders, thought leaders, and political pundits. As these figures themselves are in a position to shape individuals' ideological beliefs, there is the possibility of a cyclical relationship existing between ideology's influence on perceptions of inequality and vice versa.

Second, the link between ideology and inequality perceptions impacts the likelihood of implementing policies related to equal opportunity and social mobility. The very fact that inequality perceptions seem to be distorted to avoid pressures towards undesirable social change means that prospects for progress in this policy arena are slim.

Conclusion

As with other kinds of perception considered in this book, individual perceptions of the political world can be illuminated by looking at individual preferences for how society should be run. This relationship, though not surprising, has only recently been revealed empirically, and work remains to solidify our understanding of it. It is yet another case of how our apprehension of the social world is not a simple case of 'reading' objective information but is one of perceiving it through the lens of our underlying motivations, preferences, and interests.

References

Alesina, A., & La Ferrara, E. (2005). Preferences for redistribution in the land of opportunities. *Journal of Public Economics, 89*(5), 897–931.

Andrain, C. F. (2014). *Political power and economic inequality: A comparative politics approach.* Lanham, MD: Rowman & Littlefield.

Baker, P., & Fausset, R. (2015, March 7). Obama, at Selma memorial, says, "We know the march is not yet over". *New York Times.* Retrieved from www.nytimes.com/2015/03/08/us/obama-in-selma-for-edmund- pettus-bridge-attack-anniversary.html.

Bakshy, E., Messing, S., & Adamic, L. A. (2015). Political science. Exposure to ideologically diverse news and opinion on Facebook. *Science (New York, N.Y.), 348*(6239), 1130. doi:10.1126/science.aaa1160.

Balcetis, E., & Dunning, D. (2006). See what you want to see: Motivational influences on visual perception. *Journal of Personality and Social Psychology, 91*(4), 612–625. doi:10.1037/0022-3514.91.4.612.

Barberá, P., Jost, J. T., Nagler, J., Tucker, J. A., & Bonneau, R. (2015). Tweeting from left to right. *Psychological Science, 26*(10), 1531–1542. doi:10.1177/0956797615594620.

Blow, C. M. (2013, September 13). Occupy wall street legacy. *New York Times.* Retrieved from www.nytimes.com/2013/09/14/opinion/ blow-occupy-wall-street-legacy.html.

Bonilla-Silva, E. (2006). *Racism without racists: Color-blind racism and the persistence of racial inequality in the United States.* Lanham, MD: Rowman and Littlefield.

Brandt, M. J., Reyna, C., Chambers, J. R., Crawford, J. T., & Wetherell, G. (2014). The ideological-conflict hypothesis: Intolerance among both liberals and conservatives. *Current Directions in Psychological Science, 23*(1), 27–34.

Bratt, C., Sidanius, J., & Sheehy-Skeffington, J. (2016). Shaping the development of prejudice: A latent growth curve analysis of the influence of social dominance orientation on outgroup affect in youth. *Personality & Social Psychology Bulletin.*

Brodish, A. B., Brazy, P. C., & Devine, P. G. (2008). More eyes on the prize: Variability in white Americans: Perceptions of progress toward racial equality. *Personality and Social Psychology Bulletin, 34*(4), 513–527. doi:10.1177/0146167207311337.

Cassidy, J. (2016, February 10). Bernie Sanders and the new populism. *The New Yorker.* Retrieved from www.newyorker.com/news/john-cassidy/bernie-sanders-and-the-new-populism.

Chambers, J. R., Swan, L. K., & Heesacker, M. (2014). Better off than we know: Distorted perceptions of incomes and income inequality in America. *Psychological Science, 25*(2), 613. doi:10.1177/0956797613504965.

Chambers, J. R., Swan, L. K., & Heesacker, M. (2015). Perceptions of U.S. social mobility are divided (and distorted) along ideological lines. *Psychological Science, 26*(4), 413–423. doi:10.1177/0956797614566657.

Cohn, N. (2014). Polarization is dividing American society, not just politics. *New York Times.* Retrieved from www.nytimes.com/2014/06/12/upshot/polarization-is-dividing-american-society-not-just-politics.html.

Cotterill, S., Sidanius, J., Bhardwaj, A., & Kumar, V. (2014). Ideological support for the Indian caste system: Social dominance orientation, right-wing authoritarianism and karma. *Journal of Social and Political Psychology, 2,* 98–116. doi:10.5964/jspp.v2i1.171.

Crawford, J. T., Jussim, L., Cain, T. R., & Cohen, F. (2013). Right-wing authoritarianism and social dominance orientation differentially predict biased evaluations of media reports. *Journal of Applied Social Psychology, 43*(1), 163–174. doi:10.1111/j.1559-1816. 2012.00990.x.

Dawtry, R. J., Sutton, R. M., & Sibley, C. G. (2015). Why wealthier people think people are wealthier, and why it matters: From social sampling to attitudes to redistribution. *Psychological Science, 26*(9), 1389. doi:10.1177/0956797615586560.

Dettrey, B. J., & Campbell, J. E. (2013). Has growing income inequality polarized the American electorate? Class, party, and ideological polarization. *Social Science Quarterly, 94*(4), 1062–1083.

Diermeier, M., Goecke, H., Niehues, J., & Thomas, T. (2017). *Impact of inequality-related media coverage on the concerns of the citizens* (No. 258). DICE Discussion Paper.

Duriez, B., & Soenens, B. (2009). The intergenerational transmission of racism: The role of right-wing authoritarianism and social dominance orientation. *Journal of Research in Personality, 43*(5), 906–909, ISSN 0092-6566, doi:10.1016/j.jrp.2009.05.014.

Eagleton T. (1991). *Ideology: An introduction.* London: Verso.

Eibach, R. P., & Ehrlinger, J. (2006). "Keep your eyes on the prize": Reference points and racial differences in assessing progress toward equality. *Personality and Social Psychology Bulletin, 32*(1), 66–77. doi:10.1177/0146167205279585.

Eibach, R. P., & Keegan, T. (2006). Free at last? Social dominance, loss aversion, and white and black Americans; differing assessments of racial progress. *Journal of Personality and Social Psychology, 90*(3), 453–467. doi:10.1037/0022-3514.90.3.453.

Elliott, L. (2017, January 11). Rising inequality threatens world economy, says WEF. *The Guardian.* Retrieved from www.theguardian.com/business/2017/jan/11/inequality-world-economy-wef-brexit-donald-trump-world-economic-forum-risk-report.

Fong, C. (2001). Social preferences, self-interest, and the demand for redistribution. *Journal of Public Economics, 82*(2), 225–246.

Frimer, J., Skitka, L., & Motyl, M., (2017). Liberals and conservatives are similarly motivated to avoid exposure to one another's opinions. *Journal of Experimental Social Psychology, 72,* 1–12, ISSN 0022-1031, doi:10.1016/j.jesp.2017.04.003.

Goodwin, M. & Heath, O. (2016). Brexit vote explained: Poverty, low skills and lack of opportunities. Joseph Rowntree Foundation. Retrieved from www.jrf.org.uk/report/brexit-vote-explained-poverty-low-skills-and-lack-opportunities?gclid=EAIaI QobChMI0Oy5tOyF1QIVFzwbCh2IZgzMEAMYASAAEgJtsfD_BwE.

Granot, Y., Balcetis, E., Schneider, K., Tyler, T., & Gauthier, I. (2014). Justice is not blind: Visual attention exaggerates effects of group identification on legal punishment. *Journal of Experimental Psychology: General, 143*(6), 2196–2208.

Grant, A., & Sandberg, S. (2014, December 6). When talking about bias back-fires. *New York Times.* Retrieved from www.nytimes.com/2014/12/07/opinion/sunday/adam-grant-and-sheryl-sandberg-on-discrimination-at-work.html.

Gray, F. (2017, June 17). Corbyn copy: Why Jeremy and Trump are (almost) the same. *The Spectator.* Retrieved from www.spectator.co.uk/2017/06/corbyn-copy-why-jeremy-and-trump-are-almost-the-same/.

Guimond, S., & Palmer, D. L. (1996). The political socialization of commerce and social science students: Epistemic authority and attitude change. *Journal of Applied Social Psychology, 26*(22), 1985–2013.

Hart, W., Albarracín, D., Eagly, A. H., Brechan, I., Lindberg, M. J., & Merrill, L. (2009). Feeling validated versus being correct: A meta-analysis of selective exposure to information. *Psychological Bulletin, 135*(4), 555–588. doi:10.1037/a0015701.

Ho, A. K., Kteily, N., & Chen, J. M. (in press). "You're one of us": Black Americans' use of hypodescent and its association with egalitarianism. *Journal of Personality and Social Psychology.*

Ho, A. K., Sidanius, J., Kteily, N., Sheehy-Skeffington, J., Pratto, F., Henkel, K. E., … Stewart, A. L. (2015). The nature of social dominance orientation: Theorizing and measuring preferences for intergroup inequality using the new SDO 7 scale. *Journal of Personality and Social Psychology.* doi:10.1037/pspi0000033.

Ho, A. K., Sidanius, J., Pratto, F., Levin, S., Thomsen, L., Kteily, N., & Sheehy-Skeffington, J. (2012). Social dominance orientation: Revisiting the structure and function of a variable predicting social and political attitudes. *Personality and Social Psychology Bulletin, 38*(5), 583–606. doi:10.1177/0146167211432765.

Hulsizer, M., Munro, G., Fagerlin, A., & Taylor, S. (2004). Molding the past: Biased assimilation of historical information 1. *Journal of Applied Social Psychology, 34*(5), 1048–1074.

Inglehart, R. & Norris, P. (2016). "Trump, Brexit, and the rise of populism: Economic have-nots and cultural backlash." HKS Faculty Research Working Paper Series RWP16-026.

Iyengar, S., & Hahn, K. S. (2009). Red media, blue media: Evidence of ideological selectivity in media use. *Journal of Communication, 59*(1), 19–39. doi:10.1111/j.1460-2466.2008.01402.x.

Jost, J., Glaser, J., Kruglanski, A., Sulloway, F., & Cooper, H. (2003). Political conservatism as motivated social cognition. *Psychological Bulletin, 129*(3), 339–375.

Jost, J. T., Federico, C. M., & Napier, J. L. (2009). Political ideology: Its structure, functions, and elective affinities. *Annual Review of Psychology, 60*, 307–337.

Kahan, D., Hoffman, D., Braman, D., Evans, D., & Rachlinski, J. (2012). "They saw a protest": Cognitive illiberalism and the speech-conduct distinction. *Stanford Law Review, 64*(4), 851–906.

Kandler, C., Bleidorn, W., & Riemann, R. (2012). Left or right? Sources of political orientation: The roles of genetic factors, cultural transmission, assortative mating, and personality. *Journal of Personality and Social Psychology, 102*(3), 633.

Katz, I., & Hass, R. G. (1988). Racial ambivalence and American value conflict: Correlational and priming studies of dual cognitive structures. *Journal of Personality and Social Psychology, 55*(6), 893–905.

Knapp, A., & Wright, V. (2006). *The government and politics of France.* Oxon: Routledge.

Kraus, M. W., Park, J. W., & Tan, J. J. X. (2017). Signs of social class: The experience of economic inequality in everyday life. *Perspectives on Psychological Science, 12*(3), 422–435.

Kraus, M. W., Rucker, J. M., & Richeson, J. A. (2017). Americans misperceive racial economic equality. *Proceedings of the National Academy of Sciences, 114*(39), 10324–10331.

Kraus, M. W., & Tan, J. J. X. (2015). Americans overestimate social class mobility. *Journal of Experimental Social Psychology, 58*, 101–111. doi:10.1016/j.jesp.2015.01.005.

Krosch, A., Berntsen, L., Amodio, D., Jost, J., & Van Bavel, J. (2013). On the ideology of hypodescent: Political conservatism predicts categorization of racially ambiguous faces as Black. *Journal of Experimental Social Psychology, 49*(6), 1196–1203.

Kteily, N., Cotterill, S., Sidanius, J., Sheehy-Skeffington, J., & Bergh, R. (2014). "Not one of us": Predictors and consequences of denying ingroup characteristics to ambiguous targets. *Personality & Social Psychology Bulletin, 40*(10), 1231. doi:10.1177/0146167214539708.

Kteily, N. S., Ho, A. K., & Sidanius, J. (2012). Hierarchy in the mind: The predictive power of social dominance orientation across social contexts and domains. *Journal of Experimental Social Psychology, 48*, 543–549. doi:10.1016/j.jesp.2011.11.007.

Kteily, N. S., Sheehy-Skeffington, J., & Ho, A. K. (2017). Hierarchy in the eye of the beholder: (Anti-)egalitarianism shapes perceived levels of social inequality. *Journal of Personality and Social Psychology, 112*(1), 136–159.

Kuklinski, J. H., & Hurley, N. L. (1994). On hearing and interpreting political messages: A cautionary tale of citizen cue-taking. *The Journal of Politics, 56*(3), 729–751.

Lawrence, E., Sides, J., & Farrell, H. (2010). Self-segregation or deliberation? Blog readership, participation, and polarization in American politics. *Perspectives on Politics, 8*(1), 141–157.

Lucas, B., & Kteily, N. S. (Under review). (Anti-)egalitarianism differentially predicts empathy for members of advantaged versus disadvantaged groups.

Malka, A., Lelkes, Y., & Soto, C. J. (2017). Are cultural and economic conservatism positively correlated? A large-scale cross-national test. *British Journal of Political Science,* 1–25.

McKendrick, J. H., Sinclair, S., Irwin, A., O'Donnell, H., Scott, G., & Dobbie, L. (2008). The media, poverty and public opinion in the UK. *New York: Joseph Rowntree Foundation.*

McNair, B. (2009). *News and journalism in the UK.* London: Routledge.

Motyl, M., Iyer, R., Oishi, S., Trawalter, S., & Nosek, B. (2014). How ideological migration geographically segregates groups. *Journal of Experimental Social Psychology, 51*(C), 1–14.

Napier J. L., & Jost, J. T. (2008). The "antidemocratic personality" revisited: A cross-national investigation of working class authoritarianism. *Journal of Social Issues, 64*, 595–617.

Piketty, T. (1995). Social mobility and redistributive politics. *The Quarterly Journal of Economics, 110*(3), 551–584.

Porter, E. (2014, May 13). The politics of income inequality. *New York Times.* Retrieved from www.nytimes.com/2014/05/14/business/economy/the-politics-of-income-inequality.html.

Pratto, F., Sidanius, J., Stallworth, L. M., & Malle, B. F. (1994). Social dominance orientation: A personality variable predicting social and political attitudes. *Journal of Personality and Social Psychology, 67*(4), 741–763. doi:10.1037/0022-3514.67.4.741.

Ratcliffe, R. (2015, June 10). Nobel scientist Tim Hunt: Female scientists cause trouble for me in labs. *The Guardian.* Retrieved from www.theguardian.com/uk-news/2015/jun/10/nobel-scientist-tim-hunt-female-scientists-cause-trouble-for-men-in-labs.

Ruypers, J. (2005). *Canadian and world politics.* Toronto. Emond Montgomery Publication.

Sears, D. O., & Henry, P. J. (2005). Over thirty years later: A contemporary look at symbolic racism. In M. P. Zanna (Ed.), *Advances in experimental social psychology, 37,* 95–150. San Diego, CA, US: Elsevier Academic Press.

Sears, D. O., & Levy, S. (2003). Childhood and adult political development. *Oxford Handbook of political psychology.* New York, NY: Oxford University Press.

Sheehy-Skeffington, J., Kteily, N. S., & Hauser, O. (2016). *Antecedents and consequences of perceptions of economic inequality.* Paper presented at the Tobin Project Conference on Inequality and Decision-Making, Cambridge, MA.

Sidanius, J., Cotterill, S., Sheehy-Skeffington, J., Kteily, N. S., & Carvacho, H. (2016). Social dominance theory: Explorations in the psychology of oppression. In C. G. Sibley & F. K. Barlow (Eds.), *The Cambridge handbook of the psychology of prejudice.* Cambridge: Cambridge University Press. doi:10.4135/9781446249222.n47.

Sidanius, J., & Pratto, F. (1999). *Social dominance: An intergroup theory of social hierarchy and oppression.* Cambridge: Cambridge University Press.

Sidanius, J., Pratto, F., & Mitchell, M. (1994). In-group identification, social dominance orientation, and differential intergroup social allocation. *Journal of Social Psychology, 134*(2), 151. doi:10.1080/00224545.1994.9711378.

Sidanius, J., Pratto, F., Sinclair, S., & van Laar, C. (1996). Mother Teresa meets Genghis Khan: The dialectics of hierarchy-enhancing and hierarchy-attenuating career choices. *Social Justice Research, 9,* 145–170.

Sidanius, J., Van Laar, C., Levin, S., & Sinclair, S. (2003). Social hierarchy maintenance and assortment into social roles: A social dominance perspective. *Group Processes & Intergroup Relations, 6*(4), 333–352.

Treier, S., & Hillygus, D. S. (2009). The nature of political ideology in the contemporary electorate. *Public Opinion Quarterly, 73,* 679–703.

Uhlmann, E. L., Pizarro, D. A., Tannenbaum, D., & Ditto, P. H. (2009). The motivated use of moral principles. *Judgment and Decision Making, 4*(6), 479–491.

Waytz, A., Young, L. L., & Ginges, J. (2014). Motive attribution asymmetry for love vs. hate drives intractable conflict. *PNAS Proceedings of the National Academy of Sciences of the United States of America, 111,* 15687–15692. doi:10.1073/pnas.1414146111.

Wilkinson, R., & Pickett, K. (2017). The enemy between us: The psychological and social costs of inequality. *European Journal of Social Psychology, 47*(1), 11–24.

Williams, W. M., & Ceci, S. J. (2015). National hiring experiments reveal 2:1 faculty preference for women on STEM tenure track. *PNAS Proceedings of the National Academy of Sciences of the United States of America, 112,* 5360–5365. doi:10.1073/pnas.1418878112.

4

PERCEPTIONS OF GENDER INEQUALITY IN ACADEMIA

Reluctance to let go of individual merit ideology

Romy van der Lee and Naomi Ellemers

Individual merit ideology

When we think about the factors that determine career success, we tend to assume that individual-level factors are decisive. Each person who has the required competencies shows sufficient effort and persistence, and prioritizes work over other (e.g. leisure) activities should be able to succeed—or so we believe. Thus, when we observe that members of certain groups are less represented or less successful in specific job types—as is the case for women in academia—we implicitly conclude that this must be the result of valid differences in individual merit and achievement. If women are less successful than men, something must be deficient in the competencies, efforts, or priorities of these women—not in the societal or organizational systems in which they function. We refer to this as 'individual merit ideology' (see also Ellemers & Van Laar, 2010).

This resonates with a more generic tendency that people have: Believe that the world is just and fair (Lerner, 1980; see also Jost, Banaji, & Nosek, 2004). We like to think that people generally receive the outcomes they deserve, and therefore deserve the outcomes they receive. As a result, people who are successful are generally admired. Surely their success reflects some special ability or skill that they have. And when we observe others who receive ill treatment or suffer adverse outcomes, we are inclined to think they must have done something wrong to deserve this, rather than considering the possibility that this results from faulty procedures or sheer bad luck (Ellemers, 2012, 2017; Chapter 6). As a result of such just world beliefs, both members of advantaged and disadvantaged groups generally subscribe to individual merit ideology. Members of advantaged groups see their career outcomes as the result of their own performance and achievements. By doing this, they usually fail to acknowledge the impact of favourable circumstances (e.g. being offered opportunities to display one's skills) or group-level privilege (e.g. having access to relevant networks). Those who are disadvantaged may in a way realize they lack similar opportunities or social connections. Yet they mostly prefer to maintain the conviction that this is due to their own bad luck, while the system is just and fair (Jost et al., 2004). This way of thinking enables them to retain hope that over time they will be able to overcome the hurdles they face and disprove any negative expectations people may have of them because of their group membership (Ellemers, 2018).

Evidence suggests that endorsement of the individual merit ideology is strong. In fact, it persists even in cases where very concrete and unequivocal evidence is available to show that group memberships—*not* individual merit—are a decisive factor in career success. Over the years, research has consistently shown that men and women are quite reluctant to seek out, consider, or accept the possibility that gender bias plays a role in the career opportunities offered to men and women (for overviews see Barreto & Ellemers, 2015; Major & Kaiser, 2017; Stroebe, Barreto, & Ellemers, 2010).

When we consider how people view academic careers, there are several reasons why individual merit ideology is likely to be even stronger. First, academia is a context par excellence where we assume that rational decisions are made based on objective evidence. The people sitting on the committees that evaluate, hire, and promote other academics generally are trained to be objective and independent in their research. Hence, they have a strong belief in their overall ability to make accurate and unbiased judgements—also when evaluating candidate track records (Kaatz, Gutierrez, & Carnes, 2014). This reinforces the individual merit ideology, causing academic achievement and personal choices to be considered as preferred explanations for different career outcomes of men and women. Consequently, the conviction that one is able to make decisions in an objective way in itself makes people *more vulnerable* to displaying bias and, at the same time, *less likely to acknowledge* the occurrence of bias (Uhlmann & Cohen, 2007).

Second, the academic context of 'excellence' is one in which the quality of ideas and actual performance is believed to be a more important determinant of people's reputation and career success than their network connections, formal status or fit (O'Connor et al., 2017). Again, this reinforces the notion that differential success reflects differential merit. Yet academia is a highly competitive environment, where many highly talented and accomplished individuals vie with each other for very few opportunities to get hired or funded. In such a context, individuals who succeed are often perceived as deserving of the resources and outcomes they receive. However, those who fail to obtain these coveted outcomes might be perceived as having insufficient merit but may not actually be less deserving. Indeed, when considering a pool of candidates in which individual performance differences are very small or non-existent, a comparison in terms of merit is no longer informative. This is the situation where chance or subtle biases can become decisive for differential outcomes (Kaatz et al., 2014; Van Arensbergen, Van der Weijden, & Van den Besselaar, 2012).

In sum, the conviction that different outcomes must reflect differences in individual merit is highly pervasive and seems to constitute the dominant ideology in academia. This forms the backdrop for studies documenting different outcomes for men and women, and examining possible reasons for such differences in academia.

Documenting gender inequality in academia

From an historical perspective, the presence of female students and professors is relatively recent. In the Netherlands for instance, the first female student (Aletta Jacobs) who graduated from university was admitted in 1871, and the first female professor (Johanna Westerdijk) was appointed in 1917—only 100 years ago. Yet, during the past decades, in universities across the world women have begun to outnumber men at the lower academic levels and to outperform them in terms of study rate and grades acquired (e.g. European Commission, 2016; UCAS, 2016). Not surprisingly then, increasing numbers of women have been pursuing academic careers in all areas of science. However, women remain disadvantaged in all facets of academia (e.g. Shen, 2013). Studies monitoring these developments over many years clearly demonstrate that time (either at the individual level—number of years into career—or at the population level—historical cohort) is not the decisive factor in explaining this. In fact, over the years proportions of women in top academic positions have at times gone down instead of up. For instance, in the Netherlands in the 1980s, the representation of women in senior academic positions actually decreased despite increasing numbers of female candidates available, as female academics were disproportionately affected by budget cuts and organizational restructuring (Ellemers, 1993).

In fact, even after correcting for all legitimate factors that might explain differential career success (such as age, work experience, performance records, or area of expertise), there is overwhelming evidence that the academic efforts and achievement of women are valued less than those of men. This is evident from studies tracing the actual careers of large groups of academics over time, as well as from experimental studies that allow for the comparison of fictitious male and female candidates with identical achievement records (Ellemers, 2018). It also shows up in the personal narratives of transgendered scientists (e.g. Deirde/Donald McCloskey; www.deirdremccloskey.com/gender/crossing.php), who experienced a shift in the valuation of their intellectual ideas and scientific work after changing their gender appearance. For instance, despite equal performance, female academics are rated as less effective teachers (Wagner, Rieger, & Voorvelt, 2016), are less likely to receive research funding (van der Lee & Ellemers, 2015a), have lower chances of being offered tenure and being promoted (Sarsons, 2017; Sheltzer & Smith, 2014), or honoured with an endowed chair (Treviño, Gomez-Mejia, Balkin, & Mixon, 2015). They are also paid less than their male colleagues at every career stage (De Goede, Van Veelen, & Derks, 2016; Shen, 2013; see also Joshi, Son, & Roh, 2015). As a result, even in psychology, an area where women have outnumbered men for many years at the

BA, MA, and recently also at the PhD level, women are not equally represented at the highest job levels, and this pattern has not changed in the past 20 years (APA, 2017).

Thus, the overall summary of all the available evidence is that—despite the wide endorsement of individual merit ideology—women in academia have less return on academic investment and achievement than men do.

Implicit gender bias

These diverging outcomes are visible for all who care to see them. However, the preferred way of explaining them reflects the strong belief in individual merit ideology, leading people to assume that for whatever reason women are less committed to or less able to perform well in an academic career than men are. Thus, differential successes of men and women are mainly perceived as implicit indicators that something must be wrong with the performance, life choices, academic motivation, or career ambition of women ('fix the women'). While this may certainly be so in some cases, we suspect this is not the only reason, and is probably not the best explanation for the overall gender disparities observed ('fix the system'). Indeed, research shows that even those who intend to evaluate and treat men and women equally are not always able to do so. From childhood onwards, individuals are exposed to the same gender stereotypes and gender role divisions (Ellemers, 2018). As a result, men as well as women often display and suffer from implicit forms of gender bias, even if this happens unintentionally and is not always recognized as such.

The large body of research documenting such implicit biases can be structured into four distinct patterns (Williams & Dempsey, 2014). First, across a multitude of educational and work contexts it has been established that women generally need to offer more evidence of achievement to be evaluated as talented, competent, or deserving of employment or promotion ('prove it again'). As a result, even when they show the same performance and commitment to work, women tend to receive less work-related opportunities and rewards as a result of their efforts and achievement (Moss-Racusin, Dovidio, Brescoll, Graham, & Handelsman, 2012). Second, observed differences in career success or the persistence of gender pay gaps have been attributed to women's failure to show the behaviour that is required in many professional roles. Hence, it has been argued that women should adapt their demeanour to be more effective at work, for instance in negotiating about work conditions or in leadership roles. However, many studies have documented that the assertive behavioural styles that are invited and rewarded in men tend to be devalued and discouraged in women (Faniko, Ellemers, & Derks, 2016; Rudman, Moss-Racusin, Phelan, & Nauts, 2012). As a result, women have to walk a fine line to be effective in a work context without being dismissed as 'too aggressive' or 'too demanding' ('tightrope'). Third, even though men and women report similar levels of work-family conflict (Shockley, Shen, DeNunzio, Arvan, & Knudsen, 2017), working mothers are viewed differently than working fathers. Men who have children tend to be seen as more mature and responsible workers, and men who visibly take responsibility for their children are seen as good fathers. However, women who go back to work after having children are seen as less warm and committed mothers, and as less ambitious and reliable workers (Cuddy, Fiske, & Glick, 2004). Even women who have made arrangements to be available for work suffer from this implicit bias as they are offered less challenging assignments and less advancement opportunity when they become mothers ('maternal wall'). Fourth, while the desirability of having some diversity among employees is generally acknowledged (be it for socially responsible or for business reasons), many organizations are happy with a few token representatives as a show of good faith. In fact, often only a few 'women's slots' are made available in senior leadership positions or on boards of directors. By setting up women to compete with each other for the few opportunities provided for female representation, these organizations undermine the willingness of successful women to support or mentor more junior colleagues ('tug-of-war'; Duguid, 2011).

All these different forms and shapes in which implicit bias may materialize make it even more difficult to recognize or pinpoint the ways in which women fail to benefit from their individual merit. Together, however, they can set in motion a self-defeating cycle where women are under-represented and are not supported, feel undervalued and become less motivated, and eventually start to underperform and disengage from work (Derks, Van Laar, & Ellemers, 2007). The tendency for women to 'opt out' of demanding careers, for instance in academia, tends to be seen as a personal choice. Such accounts neglect the discouragement that is implicitly conveyed by systematically being provided limited career opportunities and lacking support from the organization—despite making great personal sacrifices and showing high performance and commitment to one's career (Ryan, Haslam, Hersby, Kulich, & Atkins, 2007).

Resistance to evidence of gender bias

Considering the subtle and—often—unintentional nature of gender bias, evidence of such bias has become increasingly important in identifying and mapping the occurrence and extent of gender inequality, as well as overcoming these inequalities. However, there seems to be reluctance in accepting evidence of ongoing differential opportunities and outcomes for men and women in academia. This appears to be fuelled by two trends: First, evidence of gender inequality seems mixed, with some studies showing gender disparities while other studies do not. Second, studies that reveal disparities are often met with methodological criticism and hence the existence of bias is considered controversial. Both trends contribute to the perseverance of individual merit ideology and shape perceptions of gender inequality.

Evidence of gender bias seems mixed

In contrast with the studies revealing *unequal* opportunities as outlined earlier, there are also studies being published arguing for *equal* opportunities for men and women in academia as well as studies arguing a *preferential* treatment of women (e.g. Ceci, Ginther, Kahn, & Williams, 2014; Williams & Ceci, 2015). To illustrate, in their study among (male and female) faculty of math-intensive and non-math-intensive fields, Williams and Ceci (2015) conclude a 2:1 hiring preference for the female applicant for tenure-track assistant professorships. They state that 'it is a propitious time for women launching careers in academic science' (p. 5360). However, it is not so easy to directly compare the results of studies showing bias versus studies not showing bias as they adopt different methodological approaches and hence speak to diverging situations. Comparing the study of Williams and Ceci (2015) revealing bias *favouring* female applicants for a research position among academic faculty with the study of Moss-Racusin et al. (2012) revealing gender bias *against* female applicants for a laboratory manager position among academic faculty, several important differences in the procedures can be observed that plausibly account for the different results and conclusions. In the case of Williams and Ceci (2015), the experiments consisted of three important conditions that left little room for implicit bias to affect the hiring decision. First, the (female) applicant was clearly highly qualified and detailed personal information was provided that was stereotype-disconfirming. Second, the applicant was already short-listed and the committee's positive evaluation was included. Third, the applicant was recommended by a person with high competence and high power: the committee chair. Under conditions such as these, in which the gender stereotype is clearly disconfirming, the chances of success for women tend to increase (e.g. Biernat & Fuegen, 2001). In comparison, in the experiments of Moss-Racusin et al. (2012), the applicant (male or female but with identical resumes) had ambiguous competence and faculty were asked to rate the applicant themselves. Faculty favoured the male student ('John') over the female student ('Jennifer') in terms of perceived competence, hiring intentions, mentoring, and salary (see also Steinpreis, Anders, & Ritzke, 1999). In more natural procedures like these, when evaluators are asked to form judgements about applicants—also in the case of unambiguous high competence—implicit bias affects applicant evaluation and hiring decision (see also Kaatz et al., 2014; Uhlmann & Cohenm, 2007). Thus, under highly controlled settings in which the provided information of the applicant is favourable and explicitly stereotype-disconfirming, women might enjoy preferential treatment. However, these controlled settings are unlikely to occur in natural application procedures, thereby leaving room for implicit biases to affect the hiring practices that disadvantage women in academia.

Taken together, evidence of gender bias might seem mixed, but this is actually not the case. Rather, different studies focus on different situations and produce different outcomes. Natural application procedures leave room for implicit bias to affect applicant evaluation and hiring decisions because these often require evaluators to judge the applicant(s) which in itself primes their sense of perceived objectivity. In addition, they also might include ambiguous information— or information that can be ambiguously interpreted—about the applicant(s). This is indeed reflected in studies that simulate such natural procedures (e.g. Moss-Racusin et al., 2012). In highly controlled experimental procedures, however, women tend to be favoured over men ('shifting standards'; Biernat & Fuegen, 2001; Williams & Ceci, 2015). These settings provide valuable information for interventions aimed at reducing implicit bias. However, when the methodological approaches are not closely scrutinized, it is easy to conclude that the evidence of gender bias is mixed. This, in turn, causes controversy about the existence of gender bias, and, together with upholding individual merit ideology, results in reluctance to acknowledge the necessity of implementing interventions aimed at solving gender inequality in academia.

Evidence of gender bias raises (methodological) debate

A second trend that fuels the resistance to evidence of gender bias is how people respond to evidence that refutes individual merit ideology. That is, studies showing empirical evidence of unequal opportunities or gender bias are often met with scepticism and are prone to public derogation (e.g. Leslie, Cimpian, Meyer, & Freeland, 2015; Moss-Racusin et al., 2012; van der Lee & Ellemers, 2015a). The study of Moss-Racusin et al. (2012), for example, revealing empirical evidence of gender bias in science, technology, engineering, and mathematics (STEM) fields, sparked controversy among the general public. Analyses of the online comments revealed that about 50% of the responses contained a negative comment. More specifically, men posted more negative responses than women, mostly by providing an essentialist justification of bias (e.g. 'I think one of the largest subconscious factors here is that women get pregnant'). Contrarily, women posted more positive responses than men, but this primarily pertained to acknowledgement of the existence of gender bias (e.g. 'I am a female scientist, and even I sometimes struggle with bias against women'; Moss-Racusin, Molenda, & Cramer, 2015).

Following this study, Handley and colleagues (2015) conducted an empirical study into the acceptance of evidence of gender bias against women in STEM (Handley, Brown, Moss-Racusin, & Smith, 2015). In a series of experiments, individuals from the general public as well as (STEM and non-STEM) university faculty read a journal abstract reporting gender bias in science. They then rated the overall quality of the research. Results showed that men, and especially male STEM faculty, evaluated gender bias research less favourably than women. This effect occurred regardless of the author's gender (which was varied across conditions), suggesting that these effects underlie a bias against the research rather than the researcher(s). Thus, men appear to be more sceptical of empirical research demonstrating gender bias and they tend to be more vocal about it than women.

In line with this, our own paper that revealed gender disparities in success rates of grant funding for early career researchers in The Netherlands (van der Lee & Ellemers, 2015a) sparked similar public controversy. To address this controversy, we set out to systematically analyze the online responses that were posted in the first 2 weeks after the paper was published online. The responses included comments directly emailed to us as well as those that appeared in (social) media. In accordance with the methodological approach of Moss-Racusin et al. (2015), the valence and length of the comment, as well as the gender of the commenter, were coded[1]. A total of 213 responses were analyzed, among which 38 email messages, 121 tweets, 8 dedicated blog posts, and 46 online comments. In addition, 23 news items appeared in national media outlets (e.g. newspapers).

Results revealed that 51.6% of the commenters were male, and 35.7% were female (for 12.7% of the commenters, the gender was unknown). Comments contained on average 81.53 words ($SD = 195.50$). As for the content of the comments, 65.4% included criticism (i.e. negative comment), whereas 39.5% included praise (i.e. positive comment). When examining the content of the comment by gender of the commenter, results revealed that men were less positive and more negative, and wrote on average longer comments than women ($\chi^2[1] = 49.50$, $p < 0.001$, Cramer's $V = 0.52$; $\chi^2[1] = 46.51$, $p < 0.001$, Cramer's $V = 0.50$; and $F[1, 184] = 6.58$, $p = 0.011$ respectively; see Figures 4.1 and 4.2). Thus, several independent analyses of naturally occurring online comments to research revealing evidence of gender bias, as well as an empirical study, show that men, especially male STEM faculty, respond with scepticism and derogation of the evidence that refutes individual merit ideology.

Statistical criticism

In addition to general scepticism of studies revealing gender disparities by the public, some of these studies are scrutinized by academic peers, particularly for their methodological and statistical procedures (e.g. Cimpian & Leslie, 2015). Such methodological debates might conceal ideological arguments (e.g. 'belief'

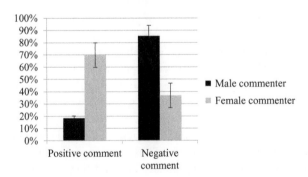

FIGURE 4.1 Valence of the comments (in percentages) by gender of the commenter.

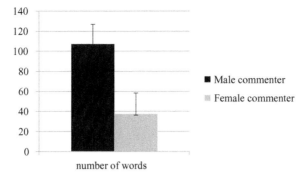

FIGURE 4.2   Length (i.e. number of words) of the comments by gender of the commenter.

in the existence of gender inequality in academia), for example, by raising 'spurious' problems of these studies in scientific jargon. Our recent study described earlier is one such example (van der Lee & Ellemers, 2015a). Many responses we received from peers following the publication of the paper claimed that the statistics were 'wrong' and recommended 'right' statistics. Interestingly, however, the recommendations were not at all consistent and opposing analytical strategies were proposed as the 'correct' way to analyze the data. Some critics argued against doing overall tests across scientific fields because this would not allow for the detection of different patterns within different disciplines (e.g. Albers, 2015). Other critics warned against the inclusion of multiple tests for different scientific fields and recommended to focus exclusively on the results of the overall tests (e.g. Volker & Steenbeek, 2015). In reality, the paper reported both: The main results held up regardless of the statistical test that was used, and the conclusion that there is evidence of gender bias was also based on other data, such as the gendered language in instructions to evaluators (see also van der Lee & Ellemers, 2015b, 2015c). Furthermore, other critiques included impossible demands, such as including the most recent round of funding decisions in the analyses, which were finalized months *after* the paper was submitted for publication.

Taken together, resistance to accept evidence of gender bias in academia is characterized by two trends: apparent mixed evidence and methodological debate. First, studies arguing for equal opportunities or even a preferential treatment of women tend to use highly controlled settings in which there is little room for implicit bias to disadvantage the career opportunities of women. Second, (field) studies that reveal empirical evidence of gender bias are publicly met with scepticism and derogation—in particular by academic peers for the methodological procedures they used. Of course, all research should be open to scientific debate with the aim of improving scientific knowledge as well as advancing knowledge utilization. Yet the discourse that often follows studies documenting gender bias such as those described here is often neither scientific nor constructive but appears to be ideological. This arouses controversy about the validity of the empirical evidence, hence negatively affecting perceptions of gender bias and willingness to support policy changes aimed at promoting equal opportunities. In this way, both trends sustain individual merit ideology.

Factors that contribute to resistance to evidence of gender bias

Incidental versus structural evidence of gender bias

Why would people be sceptical of empirical evidence revealing gender disparities in academia? In understanding the resistance to empirical evidence of gender inequality, we distinguish between incidental versus structural disadvantages (Van Zomeren, Postmes, & Spears, 2008). Incidental evidence of inequality is generally considered personal and anecdotal, as it revolves around situation-based disadvantages of a particular individual (e.g. 'my male co-worker, also a university lecturer, earns more than me'). Structural evidence of inequality, on the other hand, implies structural, systematic discrimination based on group membership (e.g. 'On average, the pay gap between male and female scientists of the same age in The Netherlands is EUR 390 in a full-time gross monthly salary'; De Goede et al., 2016). Structural disadvantage is, psychologically, more harmful for the individual than incidental disadvantage because it is more defining in terms of self-evaluation (i.e. over and above situation-specific and individual differences, women earn less than men). Consequently, structural disadvantage is harder to change due to lower identification with the disadvantaged group, decreased perceptions of unjust discrimination against the group, and diminished belief that change is possible, for example by means of protest (Van Zomeren et al., 2008). In other words, in order to solve the structural pay gap, women need to identify with the feminist cause (i.e. strive for gender equality), attribute their lower salary to unfair gender-based discrimination, and believe that protesting will result in a change of universities' rewarding system. In the example of incidental disadvantage, the individual woman might 'simply' negotiate a pay raise. Thus, structural evidence of gender inequality poses a greater threat to the status quo than incidental evidence, resulting in greater justification of the inequality and denial of structural discrimination (Van Zomeren et al., 2008).

This is especially true in the case of gender inequality because the factors that make protest (i.e. any type of individual or collective action behaviour aimed at achieving group-based improvements) likely affect gender more so than any other type of inequality (Radke, Hornsey, & Barlow, 2016). That is, first, women might not identify strongly with the feminist cause because the category 'women' is numerically so large that identification is less likely because women have interdependent and close contact with men (i.e. advantaged group) and because feminists are stigmatized. Second, women might have difficulty recognizing gender bias due to its subtle and benevolent nature, or they might even endorse such modern sexist beliefs themselves. In addition, gender roles prescribe women to control their emotions, in particular to inhibit their feelings of anger (i.e. anger in response to unjust treatment of their group, which is the primary emotion affecting the likelihood of protest). Thus, modern sexism, or implicit gender bias, is less likely to be perceived as discriminatory, less likely to elicit anger, and, consequently, less likely to prompt protest aimed at resolving structural gender inequality (Ellemers & Barreto, 2009). Third, because most protest for gender equality does not focus on legal change—in the West at least—but more on normative change, and because essentialist arguments are used to explain gender differences in behaviour, faith in effective change as the result of protest is relatively low among women. Taken together, the antecedents of collective action against group-based inequalities are particularly difficult for women, thereby making protest aimed at achieving gender equality less likely to occur when facing structural gender disadvantages as compared to other types of structural or incidental disadvantages.

The attribution of bias to an incidental instance versus structural disadvantage also affects how others judge the (coping) responses of the disadvantaged. That is, those who considered gender bias as incidental thought protest was inappropriate and devalued individuals (i.e. professional women) who claimed to be treated unfairly—even if this was clearly the case. Only when gender bias was presented as a structural problem did other women think it was appropriate to object against unfair treatment (Garcia, Schmitt, Branscombe, & Ellemers, 2010). For men, considering how their advantaged position might change due to a more gender equal society induced a cardiovascular threat response (Scheepers, Ellemers, & Sintemaartensdijk, 2009). Thus, whereas protesting against structural gender inequality might be considered appropriate by women, the evidence is threatening for men as it challenges their advantaged position and individual merit ideology.

Taken together, providing evidence of incidental instances of gender bias is generally accepted as discriminatory. And, although protesting over an incidental instance of gender discrimination might arouse backlash, it also—and importantly—creates support and improves the individual's sense of well-being (Garcia et al., 2010; Morello, 2015). Evidence of structural gender discrimination, however, is generally less accepted and arouses system justification tendencies such as denial of discrimination by derogation the empirical evidence because it poses a threat to individual merit ideology. Hence, perceptions of the existence of gender bias in academia remain controversial.

Towards a more inclusive academia

Diversity, and in particular gender diversity, among researchers has gained considerable attention in the last decade. Universities, research institutes, grant funding agencies, as well as individual researchers increasingly emphasize the importance of diversity, not only in terms of demographics (e.g. gender, race) but also in terms of ideological diversity (Chapters 9 and 10). In the case of gender, striving for equal gender representation seems the right thing to do ('moral case for diversity') and—arguably—also the smart thing to do ('business case for diversity'). Yet individual merit ideology is pervasive and perceptions of gender inequality remain controversial. One of the ways in which this manifest itself is resistance to evidence of gender inequality in academia. This is in particular the case for evidence of structural gender disadvantages (i.e. systematic discrimination based on group membership), more so than incidental instances (i.e. personal, situation-based disadvantage), because evidence of structural discrimination poses a greater threat to individual merit ideology. The resistance is characterized by two trends: First, evidence of gender bias appears to be mixed, with some studies showing unequal opportunities, whereas other studies show equal opportunities for men and women in academia. These different outcomes, however, can be explained by the methodological procedures used to examine evaluation processes such as hiring, promotion, and funding practices. Second, evidence of gender bias is prone to scepticism and derogation by both the public and academic peers, the latter often raising a—spurious—methodological debate about the statistical procedures revealing gender bias. In addition, there also appears to be a bias against research aimed to *examine* gender inequality, as gender bias research is less often funded than, for example, race bias research (Formanowicz, Cislak, & Saguy, 2017). These types of resistance shape perceptions of, and arouse controversy about, the existence of gender bias in today's academia. Taken together, perceptions of gender bias in academia are, on the one hand, fuelled by scepticism about whether gender inequality *exists* in academia in the first place (e.g. rejection and derogation of studies revealing unequal opportunities). On the other hand, there is scepticism about the extent to which current unequal gender representation is perceived as *problematic* and as requiring active policy interventions (e.g. the 'problem' will gradually disappear with the passing of time).

In addition, implicit gender bias is largely unintentional and subtle in nature, and arguably relatively small in different areas of academia (e.g. women have a disadvantage of about 4% compared to men in obtaining personal grant funding in The Netherlands; van der Lee & Ellemers, 2015a). This might be particularly detrimental to women's advancement in academia because it is less likely to be perceived as discrimination, thereby impairing the motivation to protest against gender inequality (Ellemers & Baretto, 2009; Radke, Hornsey, & Barlow, 2016). Effective gender diversity interventions should thus be aimed at controlling or overcoming implicit bias in evaluation and hiring procedures rather than focussing on the fairness of such procedures. That is, the mere presence of a diversity policy increases employees' belief in the fairness of the organization's procedures, which at the same time lowers their sensitivity towards discriminatory practices (Kaiser, Major, Jurcevic, Dover, Brady, & Shapiro, 2013). The implementation of diversity policies can thus, paradoxically, increase rather than decrease the occurrence of gender bias. The challenge for diversity chiefs and policymakers lays therefore primarily in designing policies and implementing interventions that tackle implicit bias (see also Carnes et al., 2012). These will only be effective, however, if there is consensus about the continuing existence of such biases. The implicit nature of gender bias thus only increases the importance of solid evidence of systematic inequality. Creating awareness about the different ways in which implicit bias might affect the evaluation process, as well about the pitfall of evaluators' tendency to believe in their personal objectivity, is a crucial first step. Key is, however, to design an intervention that is context-dependent so that it targets specific psychological processes relevant to the evaluation process at hand (Walton, 2014). There is, unfortunately, no 'silver bullet' or one-size-fits-all intervention that eliminates implicit biases and fosters equal opportunities. Yet reluctance in accepting evidence of gender bias hinders the perceived necessity of implementing these types of interventions and policy changes aimed at fostering equal opportunities for men and women and sustains individual merit ideology.

Note

1 Gender was only coded when indicated by the sender of the comment. Independent coders rated the anonymized comments orthogonally on valence (Positive: 1 = yes, 2 = no; Negative: 2 = yes, 2 = no), resulting in several comments rated as both positive and negative in terms of their content (e.g. 'I have recently read your paper in *PNAS* with interest. I wonder if you can send me the raw data as I am curious about the analyses of the differences between disciplines').

References

Albers, C.J. (2015). Dutch research funding, gender bias, and Simpson's paradox. *Proceedings of the National Academy of Sciences, 112*(50), E6828. doi:10.1073/pnas.1518936112.

American Psychological Association (2017). *Women in the American Psychological Association*. Washington, DC: APA.

Barreto, M., & Ellemers, N. (2015). Detecting and experiencing prejudice: New answers to old questions. *Advances in Experimental Social Psychology, 52*, 139–219. doi:10.1016/bs.aesp.2015.02.001.

Biernat, M., & Fuegen, K. (2001). Shifting standards and the evaluation of competence: Complexity in gender-based judgment and decision making. *Journal of Social Issues, 57*, 707–724. doi:10.1111/0022-4537.00237.

Carnes, M., Devine, P.G., Isaac, C., Manwell, L., Ford, C.E., Byars-Winston, A., … Sheridan, J. (2012). Promoting institutional change through bias literacy. *Journal of Diversity in Higher Education, 5*, 63–77. doi:10.1037/a0028128.

Ceci, S.J., Ginther, D.K., Kahn, S., & Williams, W.M. (2014). Women in academic science: A changing landscape. *Psychological Science in the Public Interest, 15*, 75–141. doi:10.1177/1529100614541236.

Cimpian, A., & Leslie, S.-J. (2015). Responses to comment on "Expectations of brilliance underlie gender distributions across academic disciplines". *Science, 349*, 391-c. doi:10.1126/science.aaa9892.

Cuddy, A.J.C., Fiske, S.T., & Glick, P. (2004). When professionals become mothers, warmth doesn't cut the ice. *Journal of Social Issues, 60*, 701–718. doi:10.1111/j.0022-4537.2004.00381.x.

De Goede, M., Van Veelen, R., & Derks, B. (2016). *Financiële beloning van mannen en vrouwen in de wetenschap [Financial rewards for men and women in academia]*. Research issued and published by the Dutch Network of Women Professors (LNVH).

Derks, B., Van Laar, C., & Ellemers, N. (2007). The beneficial effects of social identity protection on the performance motivation of members of devalued groups. *Social Issues and Policy Review, 1,* 217–256.

Duguid, M. (2011). Female tokens in high-prestige work groups: Catalysts or inhibitors of group diversification? *Organizational Behavior and Human Decision Processes, 116,* 104–115. doi:10.1016/j.obhdp.2011.05.009.

Ellemers, N. (1993). Sociale identiteit en sekse: Het dilemma van succesvolle vrouwen. *Tijdschrift voor Vrouwenstudies, 14,* 322–336.

Ellemers, N. (2012). The group self. *Science, 336,* 848–852. doi:10.1126/science.1220987.

Ellemers, N. (2017). *Morality and the regulation of social behavior: Groups as moral anchors.* Milton Park: Routledge/Taylor & Francis.

Ellemers, N. (2018). Gender stereotypes. *Annual Review of Psychology, 69,* 275–298. doi:10.1146/annurev-psych-122216-011719.

Ellemers, N., & Barreto, M. (2009). Collective action in modern times: How modern expressions of prejudice prevent collective action. *Journal of Social Issues, 65,* 749–768. doi:10.1111/j.1540-4560.2009.01621.x.

Ellemers, N., & Van Laar, C. (2010). Individual mobility: The opportunities and challenges members of devalued groups encounter when trying to avoid group-based discrimination. In: J.F. Dovidio, M. Hewstone, P. Glick, & V. Esses (Eds.). *Handbook of prejudice, stereotyping, and discrimination* (pp. 561–576). London: Sage.

European Commission (2016). *She Figures 2015.* Brussels: European Union.

Faniko, K., Ellemers, N., & Derks, B. (2016). Queen bees and alpha males: Are successful women more competitive than successful men? *European Journal of Social Psychology, 46,* 903–913. doi:10.1002/ejsp.2198.

Formanowicz, M., Cislak, A., & Saguy, T. (2017). *Bias against research on gender bias.* Paper presented at the 18th General Meeting of the European Association of Social Psychology, Granada, Spain.

Garcia, D., Schmitt, M.T., Branscombe, N.R., & Ellemers, N. (2010). Women's reactions to ingroup members who protest discriminatory treatment: The importance of beliefs about inequality and response appropriateness. *European Journal of Social Psychology, 40,* 733–745. doi:10.1002/ejsp.644.

Handley, I.M., Brown, E.R., Moss-Racusin, C.A., & Smith, J.L. (2015). Quality of evidence revealing subtle gender biases in science is in the eye of the beholder. *Proceedings of the National Academy of Sciences, 112*(43), 13201–13206. doi:10.1073/pnas.1211286109.

Joshi, A., Son, J., & Roh, H. (2015). When can women close the gap? A meta-analytic test of sex differences in performance and rewards. *Academy of Management Journal, 58,* 1516–1545. doi:10.5465/amj.2013.0721.

Jost, J.T., Banaji, M.R., & Nosek, B.A. (2004). A decade of system justification theory: Accumulated evidence of conscious and unconscious bolstering of the status quo. *Political Psychology, 25,* 881–919.

Kaatz, A., Gutierrez, B., & Carnes, M. (2014). Threats to objectivity in peer review: The case of gender. *Trends in Pharmacological Sciences, 35*(8), 371–373. doi:10.1016/j.tips.2014.06.005.

Kaiser, C.R., Major, B., Jurcevic, I., Dover, T.L., Brady, L.M., & Shapiro, J.R. (2013). Presumed fair: Ironic effects of organizational diversity structures. *Journal of Personality and Social Psychology, 104,* 504–519. doi:10.1037/a0030838.

Lerner, M.J. (1980). The belief in a just world. In: *Perspectives in social psychology* (pp. 9–30). Boston, MA: Springer. doi:10.1007/978-1-4899-0448-5_2.

Leslie, S-J., Cimpian, A., Meyer, M., & Freeland, E. (2015). Expectations of brilliance underlie gender distributions across academic disciplines. *Science, 347*(6219), 262–265. doi:10.1126/science.1261375.

Major, B., & Kaiser, C.R. (2017). Ideology and the maintenance of group inequality. *Group Processes & Intergroup Relations.* doi:1368430217712051.

Morello, L. (2015). Science and sexism: In the eye of the Twitterstorm. *Nature, 527*, 148–151. doi:10.1038/527148a.

Moss-Racusin, C.A., Dovidio, J.F., Brescoll, V.L., Graham, M.J., & Handelsman, J. (2012). Science faculty's subtle gender biases favour male students. *Proceedings of the National Academy of Sciences, 109*(41), 16474–16479. doi:10.1073/pnas.1211286109.

Moss-Racusin, C.A., Molenda, A.K., & Cramer, C.R. (2015). Can evidence impact attitudes? Public reactions to evidence of gender bias in STEM fields. *Psychology of Women Quarterly, 39*, 194–209. doi:10.1177/0361684314565777.

O'Connor, P., Montez Lopez, E., O'Hagan, C., Wolffram, A., Aye, M., …, Caglayan, H. (2017). Micro-political practices in higher education: A challenge to excellence as a rationalising myth? *Critical Studies in Higher Education, 41*, 1943–1957. doi:10.1080/17 508487.2017.1381629.

Radke, H.R.M., Hornsey, M.J., & Barlow, F.K. (2016). Barriers to women engaging in collective action to overcome sexism. *American Psychologist, 71*, 863–874. doi:10.1037/a0040345.

Rudman, L.A., Moss-Racusin, C.A., Phelan, J.E., & Nauts, S. (2012). Status incongruity and backlash effects: Defending the gender hierarchy motivates prejudice against female leaders. *Journal of Experimental Social Psychology, 48*, 165–179. doi:10.1016/j.jesp.2011.10.008.

Ryan, M, Haslam, S.A. Hersby, M.D. Kulich, C., & Atkins, C. (2007). Opting out or pushed off the edge? The glass cliff and the precariousness of women's leadership positions. *Social and Personality Psychology Compass, 1*, 266–279. doi:10.1111/j.1751–9004.2007.00007.x.

Sarsons, H. (2017). *Recognition for group work.* Working paper. Retrieved at February 15,2016viahttps://scholar.harvard.edu/sarsons/publications/note-gender-differences-recognition-group-work.

Scheepers, D., Ellemers, N., & Sintemaartensdijk, N. (2009). Suffering from the possibility of status loss: Physiological responses to social identity threat in high status groups. *European Journal of Social Psychology, 39*, 1075–1092. doi:10.1002/ejsp.609.

Sheltzer, J.M., & Smith, J.C. (2014). Elite male faculty in the life sciences employ fewer women. *Proceedings of the National Academy of Sciences, 111*(28), 10107–10112. doi:10.1073/pnas.1403334111.

Shen, H. (2013). Inequality quantified: Mind the gender gap. *Nature, 495*(7439), 22–24. doi:10.1038/495022a.

Shockley, K.M., Shen, W., DeNunzio, M. M., Arvan, M. L., & Knudsen, E. A. (2017). Disentangling the relationship between gender and work–family conflict: An integration of theoretical perspectives using meta-analytic methods. *Journal of Applied Psychology.* doi:10.1037/apl0000246.

Steinpreis, R.E., Anders, K.A., & Ritzke, D. (1999). The impact of gender on the review of the curricula vitae of job applicants and tenure candidates: A national empirical study. *Sex Roles, 41*, 509–528. doi:10.1023/A:1018839203698.

Stroebe, K., Barreto, M., & Ellemers, N. (2010). Experiencing discrimination: How members of disadvantaged groups can be helped to cope with discrimination. *Social Issues and Policy Review, 4*, 181–213. doi:10.1111/j.1751-2409.2010.01021.x.

Treviño, L.J., Gomez-Mejia, L.R., Balkin, D.B., & Mixon, F.G. (2015). Meritocracies or masculinities? The differential allocation of named professorships by gender in the academy. *Journal of Management*. doi:10.1177/0149206315599216.

UCAS (2016). *End of Cycle Report 2016*. Gloucestershire: UCAS Analysis and Research.

Uhlmann, E.L., & Cohen, G.L. (2007). "I think it, therefore it's true": Effects of self-perceived objectivity on hiring discrimination. *Organizational Behavior and Human Decision Processes, 104*, 207–223. doi:10.1016/j.obhdp.2007.07.001.

Van Arensbergen, P., Van der Weijden, I., & Van den Besselaar, P. (2012). Gender differences in scientific productivity: A persisting phenomenon? *Scientometrics, 93*, 857–868. doi:10.1007/s11192-012-0712-y.

van der Lee, R., & Ellemers, N. (2015a). Gender contributes to personal research funding success in the Netherlands. *Proceedings of the National Academy of Sciences, 112*(40), 12349–12353. doi:10.1073/pnas.1510159112.

van der Lee, R., & Ellemers, N. (2015b). Reply to Albers: Acceptance of empirical evidence for gender disparities in Dutch research funding. *Proceedings of the National Academy of Sciences, 112*(50), E6830. doi:10.1073/pnas.1521336112.

van der Lee, R., & Ellemers, N. (2015c). Reply to Volker and Steenbeek: Multiple indicators point toward gender disparities in grant funding success in The Netherlands. *Proceedings of the National Academy of Sciences, 112*(51), E7038. doi:10.1073/pnas.1521331112.

van Zomeren, M., Postmes, T., & Spears, R. (2008). Toward an integrative social identity model of collective action: A quantitative research synthesis of three socio-psychological perspectives. *Psychological Bulletin, 134*, 504–535. doi:10.1037/0033-2909.134.4.505.

volker, B., & Steenbeek, W. (2015). No evidence that gender contributes to personal research funding success in The Netherlands: A reaction to van der Lee and Ellemers. *Proceedings of the National Academy of Sciences, 112*(50), E7036. doi:10.1073/pnas.1519046112.

Wagner, N., Rieger, M., & Voorvelt, K.J. (2016). *Gender, ethnicity and teaching evaluations: Evidence from mixed teaching teams* (No. 617). ISS Working Paper Series/General Series (Vol. 617, pp. 1–32). International Institute of Social Studies of Erasmus University (ISS).

Walton, G.M. (2014). The new science of wise psychological interventions. *Current Directions in Psychological Science, 23*, 73–82. doi:10.1177/0963721413512856.

Williams, W.M., & Ceci, S.J. (2015). National hiring experiments reveal 2:1 preference for women on STEM tenure track. *Proceedings of the National Academy of Sciences, 112*(17), 5360–5365. doi:10.1073/pnas.1418878112.

Williams, J.C., & Dempsey, R. (2014). *What works for women at work: Four patterns working women need to know*. New York and London: New York University Press.

THEME 3

Threat

5

POPULISM AS POLITICAL MENTALITY UNDERLYING CONSPIRACY THEORIES

Jan-Willem van Prooijen

In the current political climate, citizens frequently are confronted with fake news and alternative facts. Such alternative portrayals of reality often take the form of conspiracy theories, which have been particularly salient during the 2016 US presidential election. Donald Trump propagated a range of conspiracy theories such as that climate-change is a hoax perpetrated by the Chinese, that Obama was not born in the United States (and hence should never have been president), that the pharmaceutical industry suppresses evidence of a link between vaccines and autism, and that Hillary Clinton was part of a major conspiracy to cover up illegal activities. It is quite plausible to assume that Trump got elected not despite but *because* of these conspiracy theories, particularly in light of findings that large portions of normal, nonpathological citizens endorse such theories (Oliver & Wood, 2014; Sunstein & Vermeule, 2009). Other impactful political developments were also clearly associated with conspiracy theories. For instance, belief in conspiracy theories was a major predictor of a "Leave" vote in the UK Brexit referendum: Polling shortly before the referendum revealed that 64% of supporters of the populist UK Independence Party (UKIP) expected the referendum to be rigged. Moreover, over one-third of "Leave" voters believed in a conspiracy between MI5 and the UK government to prevent the Brexit.[1]

These examples are consistent with the idea that conspiracy theories are associated with populist political movements. Indeed, empirical findings reveal that radical political ideologies predict a tendency to believe conspiracy theories. For instance, political extremists at both the left and right of the ideological spectrum are more likely to believe conspiracy theories than political moderates (van Prooijen, Krouwel, & Pollet, 2015; see also Imhoff, 2015). Likewise, political extremists at both the left and right are less trustful of societal institutions than moderates, a finding that was observed following an analysis of Eurobarometer survey data in five out of six investigated countries (Inglehart, 1987).

Complementary findings from various scientific disciplines further support a link between radical political ideologies and conspiracy theories. For instance, historians have observed that the radical regimes that our world has seen in the past century (e.g., communism, fascism) are characterized by excessive conspiracy theorizing (Pipes, 1997). Moreover, content analyses of the writings and speeches of over 50 ideologically radical—and sometimes even violent—fringe groups in society (e.g., neo-Nazis, anti-globalization extremists, religious fundamentalist groups) reveal that such extremist documentation typically contains excessive conspiracy theorizing (Bartlett & Miller, 2010). One may wonder, however, what these insights imply exactly for the relationship between populism and conspiracy theories. Not all populist currents are ideologically extreme, and moreover, little is known about the underlying psychological processes that may account for a possible relationship between populism and conspiracy theories.

Conspiracy theories are commonly defined as beliefs that a group of actors colludes in secret to attain goals that are widely seen as malevolent (Bale, 2007; Zonis & Joseph, 1994). Although many conceptually different conspiracy theories exist—ranging from theoretically possible or even plausible (e.g., it can be rational to suspect corruption among certain power holders) to completely outlandish (e.g., conspiracy theories that the world is ruled by alien lizards disguised as human)—accumulating research suggests that different conspiracy theories emerge through similar psychological processes. For instance, an excellent predictor of belief in one conspiracy theory is belief in a different conspiracy theory (Abalakina-Paap, Stephan, Craig, & Gregory, 1999; Lewandowski, Oberauer, & Gignac, 2013; Swami et al., 2011; van Prooijen & Acker, 2015). Even beliefs in mutually incompatible conspiracy theories are positively correlated (e.g., the belief that Princess Diana faked her own death vs. the belief that she was murdered; Wood, Douglas, & Sutton, 2012). People hence differ in the extent to which they have a conspiratorial mindset—that is, a general propensity to explain impactful geopolitical events through conspiracy theories—which is shaped by a range of personal, situational, and ideological factors (Goertzel, 1994).

Irrational conspiracy theories can be harmful as they are associated with a range of detrimental psychological and societal outcomes, including negative emotions, destructive health behaviors (e.g., vaccine refusal, decreased contraceptive use), decreased civic virtue, climate-change skepticism, and aggression (Grebe & Nattrass, 2012; Jolley & Douglas, 2014; Swami et al., 2011; Thorburn & Bogart, 2005; van Prooijen, Krouwel, & Pollet, 2015). Also, in a political context, certain conspiracy theories can be dangerous, as underscored by the 2016 incident in which a Trump supporter opened fire in a pizza restaurant, assuming it to be a Democrats-run center for pedophiles (the "pizza-gate" conspiracy theory). It is therefore important to establish the psychological and political variables that predict citizens' susceptibility to conspiracy theories.

This chapter seeks to increase understanding of the psychological and political roots of conspiracy theories by examining how belief in such theories is related with populism. Are citizens who support populist movements more likely than others to be susceptible to conspiracy theories, and if so, why exactly? For this purpose, in the following, I will first illuminate what populism is by defining the term and identifying its underlying psychological dimensions. Then, based on the research literature, I will assess how each of these dimensions predicts belief in conspiracy theories. At the end, I integrate these insights, and conclude that populism is a key political mentality underlying conspiracy theories.

What is populism?

While populism is a popular and highly prevalent term in news reports and public discourse, social scientists have not yet reached consensus about its definition or underlying psychological dimensions (e.g., Judis, 2016; Mudde & Kaltwasser, 2017; Müller, 2016; Oliver & Rahn, 2016). What different conceptualizations of populism share, however, is that populism is a political mentality that construes society as a dichotomous struggle between "the people" versus "the establishment." As such, populism is not a novel political phenomenon but has had an impact on society throughout the past few centuries (e.g., the French Revolution was inspired by strong populist sentiments). Of importance, this definition implies that populism is not exclusive to the political right or left. As noted by Müller (2016), populism is not an ideology but a way of thinking about politics, and can in principle occur everywhere at the political spectrum. In practice, however, populism is most common at the edges of the political spectrum (i.e., the left and right extremes; see Mudde & Kaltwasser, 2017).

Popular media frequently portray "populism" within the same breath as "right-wing," and, indeed, at present populism predominantly occurs among right-wing political movements in, for instance, the United States (e.g., Trump, the Tea Party) and Northern Europe (e.g., UKIP in the UK, Alternative für Deutschland in Germany, Front National in France, Partij voor de Vrijheid (PVV) in the Netherlands). It would be a mistake, however, to assume that populism is a right-wing political phenomenon only. In various Southern European countries, strong left-wing populist movements exist (e.g., Syriza in Greece, Podemos in Spain). Furthermore, in various Latin-American countries populism is mostly a left-wing political phenomenon. A prime example of a left-wing populist leader is Hugo Chavez, who was president of Venezuela from 1999 to 2013, and was succeeded by the left-wing populist leader Nicholas Maduro. Examples of other Latin-American countries that currently have strong left-wing populist movements are Ecuador, Bolivia, and Brazil. Furthermore, some political leaders are clearly populist yet not clearly left- or right-wing, such as Duterte in the Philippines.

Furthermore, the political signature of populist movements is culturally flexible and therefore subject to change. For instance, in various Eastern European countries—that have been under communist rule for decades—populist movements have recently emerged at the political right (e.g., Poland, Hungary). Moreover, in the United States and Northern Europe, left-wing populist movements appear to be gaining momentum: In the United States, the relatively extreme segment of Bernie Sanders supporters expressed an unwillingness to vote for Hillary Clinton, who in their view represented the political establishment ("Bernie or Bust"). Likewise, in the 2017 French presidential election, Jean-Luc Mélenchon of the populist left-wing party "La France Insoumise" acquired over 19% of the votes in the first round; in the second round, he indicated not only that did he not support Le Pen but also that he refused to support Macron. In sum, populism is widespread and culturally subject to change, and although left- and right-wing populist movements have obvious ideological differences (some of which will be illuminated later), populism occurs at both the left and right ends of the political spectrum.

What are the underlying psychological dimensions that characterize populism? In this chapter, I propose three related but distinct factors that together provide a parsimonious model to predict whether citizens will support populist movements. The first two factors are drawn from Müller (2016) and are referred to as anti-elitism and anti-pluralism. Furthermore, based on an integration of empirical political psychological findings (Hogg, Meehan, & Farquharson, 2010; McGregor, Prentice, & Nash, 2013; van Prooijen, Krouwel, Boiten, & Eendebak, 2015) with macro-political insights (Midlarsky, 2011), I propose a third factor, which I tentatively label threatened nationalism. In the following, I will define and illuminate these three dimensions.

Anti-elitism means that populist leaders and citizens have a deep-rooted distrust of the ruling political and societal elites. Left- and right-wing populists may differ in what specific societal elites they distrust most, depending on ideological differences. For instance, left-wing populists are likely to distrust "capitalist" elites, such as CEOs and bankers (e.g., the "Occupy Wall Street" movement). Right-wing populists are likely to distrust mainstream media (which often are perceived as left-wing), scientists, and labor union leaders (for related arguments, see Brandt, Reyna, Chambers, Crawford, & Wetherell, 2014; Chambers, Schlenker, & Collison, 2013; Wetherell, Brandt, & Reyna, 2013). Left- and right-wing populist movements share an aversion against mainstream politicians: For instance, across Europe, left- and right-wing populist parties are skeptic of the European Union (EU). Intriguingly, such anti-elitism persists even when populist leaders seize power and effectively become part of the establishment themselves: A case in point is Trump's aversion to certain media that he believes to produce "fake news" (e.g., CNN) (see also Müller, 2016).

Anti-pluralism means that populists tend to believe that they—and they alone—represent the true voice of "the people." For instance, after the first results of the Brexit referendum came in—predicting a majority for "Leave"—UKIP leader Nigel Farage gave a speech in which he literally proclaimed the following:

> This, if the predictions now are right, this will be a victory for real people,
> a victory for ordinary people, a victory for decent people. We have fought
> against the multinationals, we have fought against the big merchant banks,

we have fought against big politics, we have fought against lies, corruption and deceit. And today honesty, decency and belief in nation, I think now is going to win.

Put differently, according to Farage, the 48% of UK citizens that voted "Remain" were not real, ordinary, or decent people but instead represented the voice of the corrupt elites (Müller, 2016). Relatedly, Marine Le Pen tends to present herself as "La voix du peuple" ("the voice of the people"). Finally, Dutch PVV leader, Geert Wilders, often proclaims to be the spokesperson of "Henk and Ingrid," which are typical Dutch names, to model "the people," that is, the large group of ordinary citizens that—according to Wilders—have been forgotten or exploited by the "corrupt elites." A direct implication of such anti-pluralism, however, is that populists are particularly likely to perceive their own beliefs are morally superior and are hence intolerant of different views. After all, if only they speak on behalf of "the people," dissenting voices necessarily represent the "corrupt elites." Empirical findings are consistent with the notion that populists at both the left and right are less tolerant of different views than politically moderate citizens (van Prooijen & Krouwel, 2017; see also Crawford & Pilanski, 2014).

Finally, *threatened nationalism* means that although populists are strongly nationalistic and believe in the intrinsic superiority of their own country, they also believe that this national glory is under threat by external forces. This insight is consistent with the political-historical analysis of Midlarsky (2011), who studied the rise of politically extremist regimes across the world in the 20th century. He found evidence for a societal condition termed "Ephemeral Gains" as main precursor of increased populist and extremist sentiments. Specifically, populist and extremist political movements are most likely to rise to power in societies that first experience a short-lived period of collective gains (e.g., economic prosperity, territorial expansion) that is followed by a period of critical losses. Under those circumstances, citizens are susceptible to populist leaders who promise to reinstall their country's previous glory through a set of straightforward policies. Ephemeral gain theory resonates well with typical populist one-liners (e.g., Trump's "Make America great again"; Farage's "We want our country back"). More importantly, it is consistent with empirical studies within the domain of political psychology that, for instance, found a relationship between political extremism and feelings of uncertainty or fear (e.g., McGregor, Prentice, & Nash, 2013; van Prooijen, Krouwel, Boiten, & Eendebak, 2015), combined with findings that uncertainty increases both group cohesion (Hogg, 2007; Schmid & Muldoon, 2015) and group members' preference for rigid and radical leaders (Hogg et al., 2010).

Such threatened nationalism may take different forms for left- versus right-wing populist movements. For instance, Judis (2016) speculated that differential threats may explain differences in the ideological signature of populist movements across the EU. Specifically, due to their wealthy economies, Northern European countries (as well as the United States) are relatively attractive for immigrants, stimulating right-wing populist movements that focus on anti-immigration policies. Southern European countries, in contrast, face more economic hardship and are therefore relatively sensitive to financial and economic threats (e.g., EU austerity measures), stimulating left-wing populist movements that promise financial security for people who are poor, unemployed, and less educated. Put differently, social-cultural threat may particularly stimulate right-wing populism and economic threat may particularly stimulate left-wing populism, a prediction that awaits further testing. What left- and right-wing populist movements share, however, is the perception of an external threat that causes the downfall of their nation's previous glory.

In sum, populism is a complex and multifaceted phenomenon, and only recently researchers started to recognize populism as a political mentality that is conceptually distinct from ideology (e.g., traditional liberal-conservative distinctions). In the following, I will utilize this three-dimensional structure (i.e., anti-elitism, anti-pluralism, threatened nationalism) to examine the relationship between populism and conspiracy theories.

Populism and conspiracy theories

Empirical research has established a relationship between radical ideological beliefs and conspiracy theories (Imhoff, 2015; Inglehart, 1987; van Prooijen, Krouwel, & Pollet, 2015), and hence conspiracy theories are more likely to flourish among populist instead of moderate political movements. Furthermore, in their dichotomous perception of the world, populists often perceive "the establishment" as a direct enemy of "the people," setting the stage for allegations of corruption and conspiracy theories (Müller, 2016). It is yet unclear, however, what specific aspects of populism stimulate conspiracy theories. In order to reach a more fine-grained understanding of the relationship between populism and conspiracy theories, in the following I review empirical findings that connect the dimensions of populism with belief in conspiracy theories.

Anti-elitism

Particularly, the dimension of anti-elitism has straightforward implications for conspiracy theories: If one deeply distrusts societal and political elites, it is a small step to also assume those elites to pursue malevolent goals by forming conspiracies. To clarify, distrust and conspiracy theories are conceptually distinct, as one can easily distrust an authority or institution without perceiving a conspiracy. Distrust refers to an abstract, uncomfortable feeling that undermines perceivers' willingness to accept vulnerability in their relationship with another person or group; a conspiracy theory, however, is a concrete and specific allegation of immoral, and often criminal conduct (van Prooijen & De Vries, 2016). Nevertheless, it stands to reason that perceivers are more likely to accuse distrusted rather than trusted authorities of conspiracy formation. Consistently, distrust and conspiracy beliefs are moderately but significantly correlated, indicating distinct yet related constructs (Abalakina-Paap et al., 1999; Goertzel, 1994).

If anti-elitism is associated with belief in conspiracy theories, two key predictions follow. The first prediction is that people who generally are uncomfortable with powerful groups in society are more likely to believe conspiracy theories. In line with this prediction, feelings of alienation from politics predict conspiracy beliefs (Goertzel, 1994). Furthermore, a study by Imhoff and Bruder (2014) specifically investigated the relationship between negative stereotypes of high- versus low-power groups and conspiracy mentality, that is, a general propensity to perceive conspiracies in the world. Their results revealed that negative stereotypes of powerful groups (e.g., Americans, Capitalists, Jews) but not of powerless groups (e.g., Roma, Muslims) predicted conspiracy mentality. These findings generalized to stereotypes of discrete societal groups that are powerful (e.g., politicians, managers) versus powerless (e.g., drug addicts, homeless people).

Two conclusions emerged from the study by Imhoff and Bruder (2014). First, conspiracy mentality is conceptually different from the ideological variables, right-wing authoritarianism (RWA) and social dominance orientation (SDO), which were statistically associated particularly with negative stereotypes of power*less* groups. Second, and more important for the present purposes, these findings suggest that people who have negative stereotypes about power holders—and hence would score high on the anti-elitism dimension—are more likely than others to perceive a world full of conspiracies.

The second, and closely related prediction is that conspiracy theories are prevalent particularly among citizens who feel powerless in society. This prediction was first raised by Hofstadter (1966), who theorized that conspiracy theories occur mostly among citizens who feel powerless or voiceless. Perceivers hence need to classify themselves as part of the powerless "people" to endorse conspiracy theories that implicate the ruling "establishment." Empirical findings reveal that people are more likely to believe conspiracy theories to the extent that they feel more powerless in society (Abalakina-Paap et al., 1999). Furthermore, conspiracy theories occur more frequently among relatively powerless societal groups (e.g., ethnic minority groups; Crocker, Luhtanen, Broadnax, & Blaine, 1999; Goertzel, 1994; Thorburn & Bogart, 2005) as well as among the lower educated segment of society, a finding that is partially mediated by feelings of powerlessness (van Prooijen, 2017).

A common explanation for this relationship is that the subjective state of powerlessness is closely associated with negative emotions such as anxiety, feelings of being out of control, and uncertainty. These aversive emotions instigate a desire to make sense of one's social environment, prompting conspiracy theories to explain complex societal events that are difficult to understand otherwise (Hofstadter, 1966; see also Bale, 2007). Experimental findings support a causal effect of these aversive emotional experiences on belief in conspiracy theories. For instance, threatening people's feeling that they can control their environment increases belief in conspiracy theories (Sullivan, Landau, & Rothschild, 2010; Van Harreveld, Rutjens, Schneider, Nohlen, & Keskinis, 2014; van Prooijen & Acker, 2015; Whitson & Galinsky, 2008). Furthermore, aversive societal events that are highly consequential (e.g., a politician is assassinated), and are hence likely to elicit such negative emotions, elicit stronger conspiracy theories than aversive societal events that are not particularly consequential (e.g., the assassination attempt fails; McCauley & Jacques, 1979; see also van Prooijen & Van Dijk, 2014). The effects of these aversive emotions on conspiracy theories occur only in the context of power holders that one considers to be immoral (van Prooijen & Jostmann, 2013).

In sum, the populist dimension of anti-elitism has clear implications for conspiracy theories. Both negative stereotypes of power holders and the experience of powerlessness increase the likelihood of endorsing conspiracy theories. In a dichotomous struggle between the powerless "people" and the powerful "establishment," perceivers attribute many harmful events in society to the intentional actions of powerful and malevolent conspiracies.

Anti-pluralism

The dimension of anti-pluralism often reflects itself in an inability to reach compromises and intolerance of competing beliefs (Müller, 2016). Consistently, radical political views predict increased attitudinal certainty (Brandt, Evans, & Crawford, 2015; Toner, Leary, Asher, & Jongman-Sereno, 2013; van Prooijen, Krouwel, & Emmer, 2018), a decreased ability to compromise (Tetlock, Armor, & Peterson, 1994), and a tendency to reject, and consider as inferior, any ideological belief that differs from one's own (i.e., dogmatic intolerance; van Prooijen & Krouwel, 2017). It is likely that such anti-pluralism is associated with conspiracy theories: Anti-pluralism implies a worldview in which citizens who disagree with populist rhetoric are part of the establishment, suggesting that such dissenting citizens either conspire with, or are string puppets of, the establishment. Although no research has yet directly tested for a relationship between anti-pluralism and conspiracy theories, empirical findings support two predictions that indirectly follow from the idea that the anti-pluralism dimension of populism is related with conspiracy theories.

The first prediction that can be inferred from the anti-pluralism dimension is that the more strongly citizens believe that their own political preferences represent the simple and only solution to the complex problems that society faces, the more strongly they endorse conspiracy theories. Research reveals that such belief in simple political solutions mediates the relationship between radical political beliefs and conspiracy theories (van Prooijen, Krouwel, & Pollet, 2015). It is plausible that this finding is at least partly related with the insight that conspiracy theories emerge from feelings of uncertainty and fear: After all, simple solutions offer clarity, which may mitigate these aversive emotions. But above and beyond that, a rigid belief in simple solutions is also related with people's analytic thinking capacities. Decreased analytic thinking predicts belief in conspiracy theories (Swami, Voracek, Stieger, Tran, & Furnham, 2014), and belief in simple solutions mediates the link between analytic thinking and conspiracy beliefs (van Prooijen, 2017). These findings suggest that conspiracy theories emerge from an inability or unwillingness to consciously reflect on multiple points of view.

The second prediction that follows from the anti-pluralism dimension is that the more strongly people believe conspiracy theories, the more likely they are to respond with hostility when their beliefs are threatened. This prediction is consistent with Hofstadter's (1966) notion that conspiracy theories occur mostly among people who have an "angry mind," as reflected in increased hostility and suspiciousness toward others. Various complementary research findings support this prediction. Belief in conspiracy theories is empirically related with increased hostility (Abalakina-Paap et al., 1999) as well as with disagreeableness, a personality trait frequently associated with conflict and aggression (Swami et al., 2011). Furthermore, belief in conspiracy theories is correlated with narcissism—an individual difference variable characterized by an inflated self-view, which often determines a tendency to respond with hostility and aggression when one's beliefs are challenged (Cichocka, Marchlewska, & Golec de Zavala, 2016). Finally, a strong predictor of belief in conspiracy theories is interpersonal paranoia, that is, a general tendency to be suspicious of possibly hostile intentions of others in one's direct social environment (Darwin, Neave, & Holmes, 2011). Taken together, these findings suggest that an increased susceptibility to conspiracy beliefs is associated with relatively conflict-prone interpersonal relationships.

Behavioral data is currently lacking in empirical psychological research on conspiracy theories. Yet evidence from different disciplines suggests a link between conspiracy theories and aggression. Historians have noted that most—if not all—wars that have been fought in recent history showed excessive conspiracy theorizing about the enemy group at both sides of the conflict (Pipes, 1997). Furthermore, in their content analysis of radical fringe groups in society, Bartlett and Miller (2010) examined possible differences between violent versus nonviolent groups. While they did not find evidence for a direct link between conspiracy theories and violence—in the sense that both violent and nonviolent fringe groups strongly endorsed conspiracy theories—they did find evidence for a role of conspiracy theories as "radicalization multiplier." Specifically, conspiracy theories accelerate the processes through which ideological groups turn radical, and through which radical groups turn violent.

In sum, the more strongly people believe that their own ideology represents the simple and only solution to the problems that society faces, the more likely they are to endorse conspiracy theories. Furthermore, ideological disagreements are particularly likely to lead to conflict, hostility, and aggression in encounters with people who strongly believe conspiracy theories. Although at present somewhat circumstantial, the available evidence is consistent with the notion that the anti-pluralism dimension of populism predicts belief in conspiracy theories.

Threatened nationalism

The dimension of threatened nationalism implies that the glory of one's own nation is under threat by external forces. Due to such threatened nationalism, populist movements at the political right typically have strong anti-immigration sentiments. Furthermore, threatened nationalism leads populist movements at both sides of the ideological spectrum to reject international trade treaties, oppose financial cutbacks and economic austerity measures, embrace protectionism, and be skeptical of powerful multination political alliances (e.g., the EU, NATO). At a psychological level, it stands to reason that such threatened nationalism predicts belief in conspiracy theories for two complementary reasons. First, the belief that one's nation is under threat is a likely source of uncertainty and fear, which stimulates conspiracy beliefs (e.g., van Prooijen & Acker, 2015; Whitson & Galinsky, 2008). But in addition to that, conspiracy theories by definition involve intergroup dynamics where "they" (i.e., the powerful conspiracy) collude in secret to harm "us" (e.g., fellow citizens, fellow employees). As such, it might be reasoned that feelings of uncertainty and fear increase conspiracy beliefs only in situations where one can realistically blame a suspect out-group for the problems experienced by a valued in-group.

Building on these insights, it can be predicted that conspiracy theories flourish when people associate feelings of uncertainty and fear with a valuable but vulnerable in-group. Multiple studies support this prediction. In a series of experiments, participants read a newspaper article about the political situation in an African country. Half of the participants were asked to take the perspective of the citizens of that country while reading the article, and to imagine that they themselves were born in that country. The purpose of such perspective taking was to increase the extent to which participants would align themselves with the target group in the article. In the control condition, participants were asked to read the article as objectively as possible. Then, the article described how a political opposition leader, who was likely to win the upcoming elections in this African country, was involved in a car crash. Half of the participants read that the opposition leader died (high threat) and half of the participants read that the opposition leader miraculously survived the car crash (low threat). Results revealed stronger belief in conspiracy theories—suggesting that the car crash was not an accident but an assassination attempt by the government—in the high as opposed to low threat condition. This effect emerged only among participants who took the perspective of the citizens of the African country, however, and not among citizens who read the article in a detached fashion. These findings suggest that threatening societal circumstances only increase conspiracy theories among perceivers who feel close to the affected citizens (van Prooijen & Van Dijk, 2014).

Additional findings further support the idea that threatening events increase conspiracy theories only among people who experience strong interpersonal connections with the people who are harmed by the events. In a series of studies, van Prooijen (2016) found that feelings of self-uncertainty predicted belief in conspiracy theories but only among participants who were primed with feelings of inclusion, not among participants who were primed with feelings of exclusion. Furthermore, conspiracy theories are driven mostly by feelings of in-group superiority (i.e., collective narcissism), and not by regular in-group identification (Cichocka, Marchlewska, Golec de Zavala, & Olechowski, 2016). This latter finding is consistent with the notion of threatened nationalism, which assumes one's own country to be superior as compared to other countries.

Finally, Mashuri and Zaduqisti (2013, 2015) found support for these intergroup dynamics in the context of Indonesian citizens' conspiracy theories about the causes of terrorist attacks in their country. Their results revealed that identification with the Muslim community predicted a tendency to believe conspiracy theories suggesting that the Western world was behind these terrorist attacks. These effects only emerged, however, among citizens who considered the West to be threatening to their Islamic identity. In the context of distressing societal circumstances (i.e., frequent terrorist strikes), the specific combination of perceiving a threatening out-group (i.e., the West), along with strong affective connections to the in-group that one considers to be under threat (i.e., the Muslim community in Indonesia), stimulates belief in conspiracy theories.

The findings reviewed here together support the idea that the threatened nationalism dimension of populism is associated with belief in conspiracy theories. While high levels of regular in-group identification do not shape belief in conspiracy theories per se, conspiracy theories emerge from vulnerable forms of in-group identification (i.e., collective narcissism), or from situations where high identifiers are confronted with distressing events that cause feelings of fear and uncertainty. Conspiracy theories flourish particularly among citizens who believe that external forces damage the greatness of their country.

Discussion and conclusion

In this chapter, I sought to examine the relationship between populism and belief in conspiracy theories. The research literature supports such a link not only through findings that radical political ideologies in general predict belief in conspiracy theories (van Prooijen, Krouwel, & Pollet, 2015) but also through findings that more specifically address the underlying dimensions of populism. Conspiracy theories are related to (a) an aversion toward power holders and feelings of powerlessness (i.e., anti-elitism); (b) a tendency to perceive simple solutions to complex problems and a tendency to respond with hostility if one's beliefs are challenged (i.e., anti-pluralism); and (c) a tendency to believe in the superiority of one's nation and the perception that a valued but vulnerable in-group is under threat by external forces (i.e., threatened nationalism).

One might speculate about the causality of these effects: Does populism increase belief in conspiracy theories, or do conspiracy theories increase populist sentiments? Some of the findings reviewed here were experimental, indicating causal effects of populism dimensions on conspiracy theories (e.g., Mashuri & Zaduqisti, 2015; Swami et al., 2014; van Prooijen & Acker, 2015; van Prooijen & Van Dijk, 2014; Whitson & Galinsky, 2008). At the same time, these findings do not exclude the additional possibility that conspiracy beliefs also increase populist sentiments. Conspiracy theories may be a source of uncertainty and fear, and such negative emotions are associated with radical political beliefs (van Prooijen, Krouwel, Boiten, & Eendebak, 2015). Moreover, empirical research suggests that the relationship between populist voting and discontent with the political elites is bidirectional: Anti-elitism stimulates populist voting, but the rhetoric of populist leaders also stimulates anti-elitism among the public (Rooduijn, van der Brug, & De Lange, 2016). Finally, recall that conspiracy theories may serve as radicalization multiplier, hence causally contributing to the process of radicalization (Bartlett & Miller, 2010). Integrating these arguments, it is plausible that the relationship between populism and conspiracy theories is bidirectional and self-reinforcing. Consistent with this view, it has been argued that conspiracy theories may be an unavoidable and intrinsic aspect of populism (Müller, 2016).

Throughout the chapter, I have used the terms "populism" and "extremism" somewhat interchangeably. To some extent, this reflects conceptual pragmatism that can be justified by the notion that most present-day populist movements are situated at the far-left or far-right end of the political spectrum (Mudde & Kaltwasser, 2017). It should be noted, however, that extremism and populism do not always converge. In fact, some popular political leaders are populist yet not politically extremist. A well-known example in recent history is Silvio Berlusconi, who had all the characteristics of a populist leader, yet was commonly conceived of as ideologically center-right but not far-right. An interesting question for future research, therefore, is whether populism or extremism more parsimoniously explains the relationship between political attitudes and conspiracy theories.

Furthermore, it is important to recognize that many differences between populist movements exist. One should be particularly careful not to overgeneralize contemporary populist movements with the ideologies of some of the most infamous extremist regimes of the 20th century. For instance, following the inauguration of Donald Trump in January 2017, Pope Francis warned against global populism by drawing a direct comparison with the rise of Adolf Hitler in the 1930s. Such a comparison may be tempting but is historically ill-informed. Although Hitler certainly would qualify as populist, there are many important ideological differences between the Nazis and present-day populist leaders like Trump, Farage, Le Pen, or Wilders. For instance, contemporary populist movements tend to be protectionist (i.e., they wish to better protect their country's existing borders); the Nazis, however, from the very beginning were expansionist in their ideologies (i.e., they wanted to *expand* Germany's borders). Naturally, Nazi expansionism made war inevitable, which is not a given for present-day populist protectionism (Judis, 2016).

These qualifications notwithstanding, the arguments of this chapter suggest that the recent electoral successes of populist movements are reason for concern. Our world is facing real challenges, including climate-change, epidemics, poverty, inequality, terrorism, and war. Such challenges require rational, science-based political solutions, and constructive collaborations between national governments. Populist movements, however, approach such challenges with irrational and far-fetched conspiracy theories, leading to impoverished decision-making and a deterioration of the international relationships that are needed to effectively address these challenges. Specifically, populist movements have—more so than mainstream political movements—an alternative perception of reality that is poorly grounded in reason or science. This may manifest itself in dismissing real solutions to global problems, as underscored by the anti-vaccine movement's rejection of decades of immunologic research and the decreasing number of citizens who have their children vaccinated. But besides rejecting real solutions, alternative perceptions of reality may also lead one to deny the existence of real problems that threaten our existence (e.g., denial of anthropogenic climate-change). Conspiracy theories typically are part of such alternative facts, and society may therefore benefit from interventions that promote rationality among the public.

Note

1 www.independent.co.uk/news/uk/politics/eu-referendum-poll-brexit-live-leave-voters-mi5-conspiracy-government-a7092806.html.

References

Abalakina-Paap, M., Stephan, W., Craig, T., & Gregory, W. L. (1999). Beliefs in conspiracies. *Political Psychology, 20,* 637–647.

Bale, J. M. (2007). Political paranoia v. political realism: On distinguishing between bogus conspiracy theories and genuine conspiratorial politics. *Patterns of Prejudice, 41,* 45–60.

Bartlett, J., & Miller, C. (2010). *The power of unreason: Conspiracy theories, extremism and counter-terrorism.* London: Demos.

Brandt, M. J., Evans, A. M., & Crawford, J. T. (2015). The unthinking or confident extremist? Political extremists are more likely than moderates to reject experimenter-generated anchors. *Psychological Science, 26,* 189–202.

Brandt, M. J., Reyna, C., Chambers, J. R., Crawford, J. T., & Wetherell, G. (2014). The ideological-conflict hypothesis: Intolerance among both liberals and conservatives. *Current Directions in Psychological Science, 23,* 27–34.

Chambers, J. R., Schlenker, B. R., & Collisson, B. (2013). Ideology and prejudice: The role of value conflicts. *Psychological Science, 24,* 140–149.

Cichocka, A., Marchlewska, M., & Golec de Zavala, A. (2016). Does self-love or self-hate predict conspiracy beliefs? Narcissism, self-esteem, and the endorsement of conspiracy theories. *Social Psychological and Personality Science, 7,* 157–166.

Cichocka, A., Marchlewska, M., Golec de Zavala, A., & Olechowski, M. (2016). "They will not control us": In-group positivity and belief in intergroup conspiracies. *British Journal of Psychology, 107,* 556–576.

Crawford, J. T., & Pilanski, J. M. (2014). Political intolerance, right and left. *Political Psychology, 35,* 841–851.

Crocker, J., Luhtanen, R., Broadnax, S., & Blaine, B. E. (1999). Belief in U.S. government conspiracies against blacks among black and white college students: Powerlessness or system blame? *Personality and Social Psychology Bulletin, 25*, 941–953.

Darwin, H., Neave, N., & Holmes, J. (2011). Belief in conspiracy theories: The role of paranormal belief, paranoid ideation and schizotypy. *Personality and Individual Differences, 50*, 1289–1293.

Goertzel, T. (1994). Belief in conspiracy theories. *Political Psychology, 15*, 733–744.

Grebe, E., & Nattrass, N. (2012). AIDS conspiracy beliefs and unsafe sex in Cape Town. *AIDS Behavior, 16*, 761–773.

Hofstadter, R. (Ed.). (1966). The paranoid style in American politics. In *The paranoid style in American politics and other essays* (pp. 3–40). New York, NY: Knopf.

Hogg, M. A. (2007). Uncertainty–identity theory. *Advances in Experimental Social Psychology, 39*, 69–126.

Hogg, M. A., Meehan, C., & Farquharson, J. (2010). The solace of radicalism: Self-uncertainty and group identification in the face of threat. *Journal of Experimental Social Psychology, 46*, 1061–1066.

Imhoff, R. (2015). Beyond (right-wing) authoritarianism: Conspiracy mentality as an incremental predictor of prejudice. In M. Bilewicz, A. Cichocka, & W. Soral (Eds.), *The psychology of conspiracy* (pp. 122–142). Oxon, UK: Routledge.

Imhoff, R., & Bruder, M. (2014). Speaking (un-)truth to power: Conspiracy mentality as a generalized political attitude. *European Journal of Personality, 28*, 25–43.

Inglehart, R. (1987). Extremist political position and perceptions of conspiracy: Even paranoids have real enemies. In C. F. Graumann, & S. Moscovici (Eds.), *Changing conceptions of conspiracy* (pp. 231–244). New York, NY: Springer-Verlag.

Jolley, D., & Douglas, K. (2014). The social consequences of conspiracism: Exposure to conspiracy theories decreases intentions to engage in politics and to reduce one's carbon footprints. *British Journal of Psychology, 105*, 35–56.

Judis, J. B. (2016). *The populist explosion: How the great recession transformed American and European politics.* New York, NY: Columbia Global Reports.

Lewandowski, S., Oberauer, K., & Gignac, G. (2013). NASA faked the moon landing—Therefore (climate) science is a hoax: An anatomy of the motivated rejection of science. *Psychological Science, 24*, 622–633.

Mashuri, A., & Zaduqisti, E. (2013). The role of social identification, intergroup threat, and out-group derogation in explaining belief in conspiracy theory about terrorism in Indonesia. *International Journal of Research Studies in Psychology, 3*, 35–50.

Mashuri, A., & Zaduqisti, E. (2015). The effect of intergroup threat and social identity salience on the belief in conspiracy theories over terrorism in Indonesia: Collective angst as a mediator. *International Journal of Psychological Research, 8*, 24–35.

McCauley, C., & Jacques, S. (1979). The popularity of conspiracy theories of presidential assassination: A Bayesian analysis. *Journal of Personality and Social Psychology, 37*, 637–644.

McGregor, I., Prentice, M., & Nash, K. (2013). Anxious uncertainty and reactive approach motivation (RAM) for religious, idealistic, and lifestyle extremes. *Journal of Social Issues, 69*, 537–563.

Midlarsky, M. L. (2011). *Origins of political extremism.* Cambridge, UK: Cambridge University Press.

Mudde, C., & Kaltwasser, C. R. (2017). *Populism: A very short introduction.* New York, NY: Oxford University Press.

Müller, J.-W. (2016). *What is populism?* Philadelphia, PA: University of Pennsylvania Press.

Oliver, J. E., & Rahn, W. M. (2016). Rise of the *Trumpenvolk*: Populism in the 2016 election. *Annals of the American Academy of Political and Social Science, 667*, 189–206.

Oliver, J. E., & Wood, T. (2014). Medical conspiracy theories and health behaviors in the United States. *JAMA Internal Medicine, 174*, 817–818.

Pipes, D. (1997). *Conspiracy: How the paranoid style flourishes and where it comes from*. New York, NY: Simon & Schuster.

Rooduijn, M., van der Brug, W., & De Lange, S. L. (2016). Expressing or fuelling discontent? The relationship between populist voting and political discontent. *Electoral Studies, 43*, 32–40.

Schmid, K., & Muldoon, O. T. (2015). Perceived threat, social identification, and psychological well-being: The effects of political conflict exposure. *Political Psychology, 36*, 75–92.

Sullivan, D., Landau, M. J., & Rothschild, Z. K. (2010). An existential function of enemyship: Evidence that people attribute influence to personal and political enemies to compensate for threats to control. *Journal of Personality and Social Psychology, 98*, 434–449.

Sunstein, C. R., & Vermeule, A. (2009). Conspiracy theories: Causes and cures. *The Journal of Political Philosophy, 17*, 202–227.

Swami, V., Coles, R., Stieger, S., Pietschnig, J., Furnham, A., Rehim, S., & Voracek, M. (2011). Conspiracist ideation in Britain and Austria: Evidence of a monological belief system and associations between individual psychological differences and real-world and fictitious conspiracy theories. *British Journal of Psychology, 102*, 443–463.

Swami, V., Voracek, M., Stieger, S., Tran, U. S., & Furnham, A. (2014). Analytic thinking reduces belief in conspiracy theories. *Cognition, 133*, 572–585.

Tetlock, P. E., Armor, D., & Peterson, R. S. (1994). The slavery debate in antebellum America: Cognitive style, value conflict, and the limits of compromise. *Journal of Personality and Social Psychology, 66*, 115–126.

Thorburn, S., & Bogart, L. M. (2005). Conspiracy beliefs about birth control: Barriers to pregnancy prevention among African Americans of reproductive age. *Health Education & Behavior, 32*, 474–487.

Toner, K., Leary, M., Asher, M. W., & Jongman-Sereno, K. P. (2013). Feeling superior is a bipartisan issue: Extremity (not direction) of political views predicts perceived belief superiority. *Psychological Science, 24*, 2454–2462.

Van Harreveld, F., Rutjens, B. T., Schneider, I. K., Nohlen, H. U., & Keskinis, K (2014). In doubt and disorderly: Ambivalence promotes compensatory perceptions of order. *Journal of Experimental Psychology: General, 143*, 1666–1676.

van Prooijen, J.-W. (2016). Sometimes inclusion breeds suspicion: Self-uncertainty and belongingness predict belief in conspiracy theories. *European Journal of Social Psychology, 46*, 267–279.

van Prooijen, J.-W. (2017). Why education predicts decreased belief in conspiracy theories. *Applied Cognitive Psychology, 31*, 50–58.

van Prooijen, J.-W., & Acker, M. (2015). The influence of control on belief in conspiracy theories: Conceptual and applied extensions. *Applied Cognitive Psychology, 29*, 753–761.

van Prooijen, J.-W., & De Vries, R. E. (2016). Organizational conspiracy beliefs: Implications for leadership styles and employee outcomes. *Journal of Business and Psychology, 31*, 479–491.

van Prooijen, J.-W., & Jostmann, N. B. (2013). Belief in conspiracy theories: The influence of uncertainty and perceived morality. *European Journal of Social Psychology, 43*, 109–115.

van Prooijen, J.-W., & Krouwel, A. P. M. (2017). Extreme political beliefs predict dogmatic intolerance. *Social Psychological and Personality Science, 8,* 292–300.

van Prooijen, J.-W., Krouwel, A. P. M., Boiten, M., & Eendebak, L. (2015). Fear among the extremes: How political ideology predicts negative emotions and outgroup derogation. *Personality and Social Psychology Bulletin, 41,* 485–497.

van Prooijen, J.-W., Krouwel, A. P. M., & Emmer, J. (2018). Ideological responses to the EU refugee crisis: The left, the right, and the extremes. *Social Psychological and Personality Science, 9,* 143–150.

van Prooijen, J.-W., Krouwel, A. P. M., & Pollet, T. (2015). Political extremism predicts belief in conspiracy theories. *Social Psychological and Personality Science, 6,* 570–578.

van Prooijen, J.-W., & Van Dijk, E. (2014). When consequence size predicts belief in conspiracy theories: The moderating role of perspective taking. *Journal of Experimental Social Psychology, 55,* 63–73.

Wetherell, G. A., Brandt, M. J., & Reyna, C. (2013). Discrimination across the ideological divide: The role of value violations and abstract values in discrimination by liberals and conservatives. *Social Psychological and Personality Science, 4,* 658–667.

Whitson, J. A., & Galinsky, A. D. (2008). Lacking control increases illusory pattern perception. *Science, 322,* 115–117.

Wood, M. J., Douglas, K. M., & Sutton, R. M. (2012). Dead and alive: Beliefs in contradictory conspiracy theories. *Social Psychological and Personality Science, 3,* 767–773.

Zonis, M., & Joseph, C. M. (1994). Conspiracy thinking in the middle east. *Political Psychology, 15,* 443–459.

6

THE ROLE OF CULTURAL BELIEFS AND EXISTENTIAL MOTIVATION IN SUFFERING PERCEPTIONS

Daniel Sullivan, Roman Palitsky, and Isaac F. Young

Across the social sciences, scholars have argued that people have a deep-seated need to explain their suffering and that of their loved ones. This need is often understood as stemming from practical epistemic motivations: understanding the causes of suffering ensures that one can avoid future calamity. At the same time, however, it is clear that people's practical need to explain suffering does not always lead them to embrace rationally "objective" beliefs about reality. Indeed, when confronted with extreme suffering, an individual's primary motivation is not necessarily to understand exactly why the suffering occurred in a mechanistic sense but rather to assign it a particular *meaning*. Several writers (e.g. Berger & Luckmann, 1966; Janoff-Bulman, 1992; Nietzsche, 1967) contend that, for symbolically self-aware humans, the primary affront posed by severe suffering is the threat or experience of subsequent trauma – a "second wound" (Caruth, 2016, p. 4), the breakdown in a basic sense of culturally buffered ontological security (Herman, 1997). Although painful experiences may pressure individuals toward more accurate accounts of reality, it is often the case that suffering binds us even more closely to motivated, culturally constructed worldviews that are variable and potentially "detached" from reality.

This is so because the meaningful interpretation of suffering is a primary function of culture: culture solves the problem of theodicy (i.e. of potentially meaningless suffering) and thus contains the potential for nihilism (Sullivan, 2013). It does so by providing individuals with interpretations that make sense of suffering in light of their local worldview. However, there is a great deal of variation in the belief systems that perform this function (Shweder, Much, Mahapatra, & Park, 1997). Cultures filter what forms of suffering register as threats and provide normative interpretations of and responses to these forms (Gillin & Nicholson, 1951). In fact, the relationship between the individual's experience of suffering and the surrounding culture could be considered a cycle of mutual constitution: cultural patterns orient individuals toward interpretations of and responses to suffering that attach them even more deeply to those patterns (a "threat-culture cycle"; Sullivan, 2016).

One primary implication of this perspective is that it is possible to predict variations in suffering construal in light of cultural and social structural variables. In this chapter, we focus on two prominent forms of culturally afforded suffering construal – *repressive* construals of suffering as indicating individual deviance and the need for social order, and *redemptive* construals of suffering as necessary for personal growth and individuation. We will also discuss how variation in cultural dimensions – individualism-collectivism and the worldviews of humanism and normativism – systematically predict tendencies to rely on these construals.

Cultural-existential psychology

Our framework integrates experimental existential and cultural psychology. Experimental existential psychology was inaugurated three decades ago with the creation of terror management theory (Greenberg, Pyszczynski, & Solomon, 1986), which proposes that people are motivated to maintain the symbolic resources of self-esteem and a meaningful *cultural worldview* to protect themselves from the awareness of inevitable death. Hundreds of studies carried out in dozens of countries have shown that reminding people of their mortality prompts compensatory investment in cultural beliefs or markers of self-worth, even to the point of aggression against others who endorse opposing ideologies (Pyszczynski, Solomon, & Greenberg, 2015). These studies demonstrate that humans often rely on *symbolic* resources to maintain equanimity in the face of symbolic threats to life's meaning. Although experimental existential psychology has alerted social psychologists to people's "irrational" need for bulwarks of cultural meaning, researchers in this area tend to conceive of this as a universal functional process, largely ignoring the great diversity that exists in the *content* of cultural repertoires for solving existential dilemmas such as death awareness.

The cultural-existential framework aims to overcome this limitation by enriching experimental existential research with insights from cultural psychology. Cultural psychologists have conducted hundreds of studies over the past 25 years documenting extensive psychological variability between cultures. Famously, research has demonstrated that in some cultures people are more individualistic – they think of themselves in terms of personal identities and prioritize personal goals – while in others they are more collectivistic – they think of themselves in terms of relational attachments and prioritize the well-being of others (Triandis, 1995). In its effort to catalog such diversity, cultural psychology "de-naturalizes" conventional psychology. Certainly, there are undeniable aspects of human biology that contribute to the universal potentialities of our experience, but the field of human symbolism makes the manifestation of these potentialities extremely malleable.

One of the guiding dictums of cultural psychology is the notion of mutual constitution (Markus & Kitayama, 2010): culture and mind "make each other up" in reciprocal processes. Thus, the products and environments that constitute the "public sphere" – such as media texts, works of art, or elements of urban design – are infused with the intentions of individuals. In individualistic (collectivistic) cultures, news stories make more dispositional (situational) attributions; artworks emphasize individual actors (surrounding landscapes); and street corners tend to have more clearly defined and streamlined (ambiguous and cluttered) features (Morling & Lamoreaux, 2008). This intentionality in cultural environments in turn feeds back into the intentionalities of subjects. For instance, settings where individuals have higher rates of residential mobility become filled with bureaucratic and standardized spaces, which then attract more residentially mobile individuals (Oishi, Miao, Koo, Kisling, & Ratliff, 2012).

Most social psychological meta-theorizing posits the "person" and the "situation" interact in the moment to determine behavior. Experimental existential and cultural psychology shift theoretical focus to the fluid motivational *bloodlines* running between the individual and the environment (Schrag, 1961; Shweder, 1995). In some sense, the primary difference between experimental existential and cultural psychology lies in the fact that the former focuses on how individual motivations give rise to culture, while the latter focuses on how different cultures give rise to certain kinds of individuals. By bringing together these two research fields, cultural-existential psychology provides a comprehensive understanding that emphasizes the interlocking functionality of culture and suffering construal.

This new framework yields three "guiding principles" (Sullivan, 2016). The first is that humans are unique animals by virtue of their capacity for symbolic consciousness, a notion rooted in philosophical anthropology (Langer, 1988). Phenomena like the experience of suffering have to be understood in the human context as being heavily symbolically and linguistically mediated (Daniel, 1994). This brings us to the second principle, namely that cultural systems provide "threat orientations" – they predispose us to experience certain kinds of suffering as especially problematic while also simultaneously providing characteristic means of interpreting and defending against this suffering. Finally, the third principle of cultural-existential psychology is that multiple, interdisciplinary methods, ranging from history to (quasi-)experiments to ethnography, are required to fully understand culturally afforded styles of suffering construal. Accordingly, we will draw on various sources of evidence throughout this chapter, including a qualitative study of suffering narratives.

Cultural variation in suffering construal

When considering suffering construals, it is important to parse out *causal* and *teleological* components. People want to know what factor(s) caused an instance of suffering to occur and what its ultimate purpose is (Taylor, 1983). It is important to distinguish between these two (generally interrelated) aspects of a suffering construal because often the same causal explanation for an instance of suffering might be accompanied by different teleological aspects in different cultural contexts.

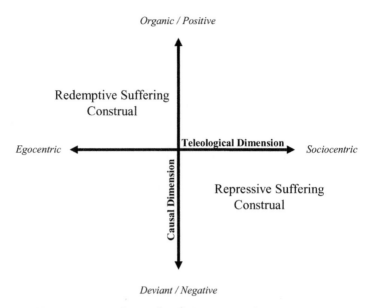

FIGURE 6.1 Two prominent forms of suffering construal.

A survey of the classic theoretical literature suggested that two interpretive dimensions could be combined to reveal two "ideal types" of suffering construal that have been especially prominent across cultures (Durkheim, 1893/1997; Sullivan, 2013). As seen in Figure 6.1, the first, causal dimension is whether suffering is construed as resulting from *deviant* behavior and is therefore *negative*; or whether suffering is construed as *organic* (i.e. natural, endemic) to existence and is therefore neutral or even *positive*. The second, teleological dimension is whether suffering's purpose is interpreted in a *sociocentric* or *egocentric* manner.

Two common culturally afforded interpretations arise from particular combinations of these dimensions, namely *repressive suffering construals* and *redemptive suffering construals*. A repressive suffering construal is the combination of a causal account of suffering as deviance (thus possessing a negative valence) and a teleological account of suffering as having a sociocentric function. Suffering is seen as the result of some form of deviant, immoral, or antisocial behavior, and as having the ultimate result of strengthening social bonds or the moral order by preventing such behavior from occurring in the future. For example, if I were to interpret an acquaintance's illness as caused by their decision to lie to one of their neighbors, and if I were to recommend that this acquaintance makes confession to their neighbor and avoids lying in the future, I would be construing this acquaintance's suffering repressively.

A redemptive suffering construal is the combination of a causal account of suffering as being organic to existence and unavoidable (and hence more neutrally valenced or even positively reframed), and a teleological account of suffering as having an egocentric function. Suffering is interpreted as spontaneously caused by processes of individuation and growth, and as having the result of shaping our identities and strengthening us in necessary ways. For example, if I were to interpret an acquaintance's illness as brought on by exposure to natural elements, and if I were prompted by their survival to develop a new conception of this acquaintance as more resilient than I previously believed, I would be construing this acquaintance's suffering redemptively.

Although the psychological processes governing suffering construals are motivated and reactive to threats, they are typically experienced as natural and even inevitable in light of *a priori* worldview assumptions. As such, they constitute effective resolutions to theodicy because they are founded on epistemic and ontological propositions about the nature of things (Berger, 1990). Therefore, repressive and redemptive suffering construals not only imply a set of interpretations and responses to events but also ways in which culture affords certain perceptions of the world in which these events occur.

Although these two forms of suffering interpretation have been fairly common across settings and epochs, they should be afforded by different cultural belief systems in ways that reflect and reinforce the intentionalities built into those systems. We now turn to a systematic review of mounting evidence that repressive suffering construals are especially afforded by collectivist (as opposed to individualist) attitudes, beliefs, and forms of social organization, whereas redemptive suffering construals are especially afforded by humanist (as opposed to normativist) belief systems.

Repressive suffering construals and collectivist culture

Individualism and collectivism have been associated with a wide variety of attitudinal, behavioral, and cognitive tendencies (e.g. Cross, Hardin, & Gercek-Swing, 2011). In an ideal-typical collectivist society, the individual is more or less interchangeable while continuation of group norms and values takes precedence. As a result, the individual is not permitted to stray significantly from shared expectations. Supporting this claim, studies have shown that collectivists' valuing of shared norms and conformity reduces their tolerance and lenience for deviant individuals (Bond & Smith, 1996; Brauer & Chaurand, 2010). This reflects collectivists' (vs. individualists') stronger endorsement of *social morality*: the belief that morals are determined by the community rather than by self-interested individuals (Shweder et al., 1997).

Where cultural differences in suffering construal are concerned, the collectivist orientation toward social morality should lend itself to repressive construals that portray suffering as the consequence of deviance from shared norms. On a teleological level, repressive construals portray suffering as ultimately preserving the social order. In collectivist cultures, if a person believes suffering to be a punishment for antisocial behavior, then they are likely to also believe that suffering has the ultimate effect of preventing people from breaking moral norms, and of reintegrating deviants into society through atonement rituals (Braithwaite, 1989).

In the first systematic correlational and experimental investigations of this link, we and our colleagues constructed survey items to capture this form of construal at a general level (Sullivan, Landau, Kay, & Rothschild, 2012). Some items pertained to the causal (e.g. "By and large, the people who suffer most severely in life are the people who break society's rules") while others to the teleological aspect (e.g. "By suffering, the sufferer is often paying back a debt owed to society or other people"). An initial correlational study of US participants (Sullivan et al., 2012; Study 1) supported the mediational model that dispositional collectivism predicts greater endorsement of repressive construals via higher social morality (endorsing the notion that morality is a social, rather than personal, construct). Converging experimental evidence from North American samples (Sullivan et al., 2012; Studies 2–4) showed that primed collectivist orientation increased repressive suffering construals. This effect was consistent whether collectivist orientation was primed consciously or nonconsciously, and whether the target suffering was abstract (i.e. "suffering in general"), or a specific type of relatively low-impact (teenage angst) or high-impact suffering (the experience of AIDS).

While these initial investigations established the internal, causal validity of the link between collectivism and repressive construal, subsequent cross-cultural work has demonstrated its external validity. A focused examination of religious subcultures in the United States found that members of more collectivistic religions endorsed repressive construals to a greater extent than members of more individualistic religions (Sullivan, Stewart, Landau, Liu, Yang, & Diefendorf, 2016). A comparison of three cultural groups in Costa Rica – college students exposed to global culture, typical urban community members, and residents of the culturally insulated and ethnically diverse region of Cahuita – showed an increasing gradation of endorsement of repressive construals that mirrored increasing levels of self-reported collectivism (McGarrh, Descamps, & Sullivan, 2017). In China, a country historically high in collectivism, we (Sullivan et al., 2016) have found that citizens show higher (compared to US average) levels of teleological, but not causal, repressive construal of the suffering that arises from mental and physical illness. In other words, Chinese and North American participants are equally likely to make moralistic attributions for suffering, but the former are more likely to see suffering as ultimately having a prosocial function.

Recent investigations have adopted a more socioecological stance (Oishi, 2014) toward the relationship between collectivism and repressive construal. These studies show that people living under social structural conditions that typically afford greater collectivism are more likely to interpret suffering repressively. For example, in a representative US sample, people living in rural (vs. urban) areas were more likely to agree that a variety of maladies might be partly caused by the sufferer's "bad character" (Yang, Liu, Sullivan, & Pan, 2016; Study 1). And in China, even health care providers working in a lower socioeconomic environment were more likely to interpret patients' illnesses repressively compared to those working in a higher socioeconomic environment

(Yang et al., 2016; Study 2). Interestingly, both these associations were statistically mediated by the size of participants' families – an ecologically valid indicator of collectivism.

Cultural belief systems such as collectivism shape perceptions of suffering, and in turn these perceptions directly influence the reality of people's experience of suffering and the societal use of suffering as a form of social control. For instance, Breitborde, López, Aguilera, and Kopelowicz (2013) observed that among Mexican-American patients with schizophrenia, the Emotional Over-Involvement (EOI) of relatives – typically a predictor of relapse (Hooley, 2007) – instead predicted *reduced* relapse at moderate levels. This surprising outcome is understandable in light of the likely suffering construals of Mexican-American families, which have higher tendencies toward collectivism (Falicov, 2016). When suffering can have a socially integrative function, the sufferer may be in a better position to benefit from social connection. If suffering serves to affirm social bonds, the sufferer's engagement with these bonds may serve a salutary function that could be lacking or reversed in individualist contexts. Beyond impacting the experience of suffering, perceptions of the meaning of suffering also have an impact on policy attitudes. A study of US parents (Sullivan et al., 2012; Study 5) found that when collectivist self-construal was primed, participants were more likely to construe the suffering of children repressively, and this in turn predicted greater endorsement of plans to institute corporal punishment in one's own school district. Policies that involve the direct use of suffering as a social control mechanism are controversial, but different attitudes toward such policies can be sensible in light of varying belief systems. If suffering is interpreted as having an ultimately prosocial function and educating children to avoid deviant acts, parents may be more willing to inflict suffering on their children.

Redemptive suffering construals and the humanistic worldview

While repressive construals involve perceiving suffering as the negative consequence of deviance and as functioning to uphold the social order, redemptively construed suffering is considered an organic and ultimately positive part of life that unleashes the individual's potential for growth. Redemptive suffering construals are almost ubiquitous in contemporary individualist cultures, and they take many forms in academic, therapeutic, media, and popular discourses. An assumption underlying redemptive construals is that the experience of extreme suffering necessitates a change in one's understanding of the world and the self. Growth occurs when one allows either one's worldview or one's self-concept to change positively as the autobiographical meaning of the suffering is formulated (e.g. Triplett, Tedeschi, Cann, Calhoun, & Reeve, 2012). Crucial for such positive growth – according to the standard narrative – is the sense that new knowledge, enhanced creativity, or both are gained through suffering (e.g. learning through survival that one is stronger than one thought), concluding in a state where one's life is actually *improved* compared to the pre-suffering state. The sufferer may not believe that the suffering was a necessary event in their life story, but ideally they will be convinced that they are better off in some ultimate sense as a consequence.

Just as repressive construals mesh functionally within a collectivist cultural context, redemptive construals represent a clearly functional perspective on suffering in an individualist setting. But this does not imply that all residents in an individualist country such as the United States will be equally predisposed to redemptive construals. US residents obviously differ on a variety of dimensions – political, religious, etc. – that can sometimes appear to be insurmountable cultural divides (as many chapters in the present volume attest). Many of these differences are related to variation in personal worldviews (e.g. beliefs about human nature, epistemology, society, and the nature and value of affective experience), the two most common of which were identified by Tomkins' (1965) polarity theory.

Tomkins (1965) outlined in particular the contrast between *normativist* and *humanist* worldviews (Nilsson, 2014; Sullivan, 2016). As these were recently summarily described:

> Normativism … is associated with an implicit metaphysics of essentialism and determinism, an absolutist epistemology, and moral intuitions, values, and aspirations pertaining to conformity with norms and the pursuit of excellence … [Humanism] is associated with an anthropocentric metaphysics, a subjectivist epistemology, and moral intuitions, values, and aspirations pertaining to intrinsic preferences and the pursuit of human well-being.
>
> *(Nilsson & Strupp-Levitsky, 2016, p. 86)*

In other words, even if they mutually endorse some of the underlying tenets of modern individualism, when faced with a critical trade-off, normativists tend to prioritize an "objective" world outside the self (be it material reality, a supernatural belief system, or a community), whereas humanists prioritize the "subjective" inner world of the self. Normativists tend to take a Hobbesian view of individual selves and believe they can be sacrificed, if necessary, for the greater good; humanists, adopting a perspective in the mold of Rousseau, believe the needs of society should be sacrificed, if necessary, to preserve the individual.

We assert that scores on measures of these personal worldviews are important in identifying those individuals within the broader US culture who are most likely to endorse redemptive suffering construals. Given that such construals have the ultimate effect of inoculating the individual's value from the threat of suffering, it stands to reason that humanists – who prioritize the sacred individual above all else – will be predisposed towards them. Furthermore, because humanists are more likely than normativists to believe that intense emotional experiences can have some value for the self, they may be comparatively likely to find redemptive aspects in the strong affective elements of suffering.

Although redemptive construals are prominent in the media, lay, and psychological discourses of individualist cultures such as the United States, there remain many alternate attitudes toward suffering. Importantly, not all forms of suffering are valorized, and many sufferers continue to face high levels of stigmatization in individualist cultures (Cole, 2007). US culture is permeated by the biomedical model of suffering dominant among healthcare providers and experts, which construes suffering not as an inevitable phenomenon to be accepted or embraced but, rather, tends to reduce it to an aberrance with clearly identifiable causes that can and should be eradicated whenever possible (Geniusas, 2013; Singer, Valentín, Baer, & Jia, 1992).

Normativists, in contrast with humanists, value the orderly functioning of society and believe that laws and institutions are required to defend that order. They also tend to view emotion as an irrational side of human nature and believe that emotions need to be controlled, rather than given free reign, for individuals to function in society. Therefore, it stands to reason that normativists will be especially predisposed to endorse more conventional biomedical perspectives on human suffering – to treat all its forms as varieties of illness that should be managed and mitigated if possible through drugs, therapy, or other controlled procedures.

In a recent series of investigations, we (Palitsky, Sullivan, Dong, & Young, 2018) have examined how relative endorsement of humanism and normativism relates to differential construals of the suffering caused by mental illness, specifically depression. In an initial study with a US student population, we first administered the short form of Nilsson's (2014) humanism/normativism scale. We then administered a scale designed to assess different interpretations of the suffering caused by depression. Our redemptive suffering construal measure consisted of seven items such as "Having depression can be an opportunity for personal growth and development," whereas our biomedical suffering construal measure consisted of three items such as "People with depression who are opposed to taking medication would be doing harm to themselves in the same manner as a diabetic who won't take insulin."

The pattern of correlations for our measures accorded with our theoretical analysis. Specifically, redemptive construals of depression were positively ($r = 0.20$, $p < 0.05$) correlated with dispositional humanism, but uncorrelated ($r = 0.03$) with dispositional normativism. When it came to biomedical construals, these were negatively ($r = -0.20$, $p < 0.05$) associated with humanism, but positively ($r = 0.31$, $p < 0.05$) associated with normativism. We subsequently replicated this pattern of associations in a pooled sample including three other independent samples (total N across studies = 375).

In a follow-up study, we sought to better establish causality by creating an experimental prime of humanist and normativist worldview endorsement. We randomly assigned US internet users to read and answer questions about a newspaper editorial from a reputable source. We fabricated the two articles that participants read and manipulated whether the author endorsed and extolled the virtues of humanism or normativism. Given that many US citizens harbor core values that resonate with both of these worldviews (e.g. Katz & Hass, 1988), we reasoned that, despite the realities of strong dispositional variation in worldview endorsement, it would be possible to temporarily increase agreement with either one of them. Indeed, when we administered the humanism/normativism scale (Nilsson, 2014) to participants after the prime, the results indicated that the articles successfully influenced participants' self-reported levels of humanism/normativism.

More importantly, when participants were asked to answer the same measures of different construals of depression-related suffering used in our correlational study, we found that worldview prime also had a significant impact. As shown in Figure 6.2, those participants primed with a humanist worldview showed elevated endorsement of redemptive and decreased endorsement of biomedical construals of depression. By contrast, the normativism prime had no impact on construals of depression. Summarizing across these preliminary investigations, there is encouraging relational and experimental evidence that, within a broadly individualist culture, internalization of a humanist worldview is associated with a greater tendency to interpret suffering in a redemptive manner.

Because the belief systems of humanism and normativism afford different perceptions of suffering, they can undergird fierce debates about how the social reality of illness should be constructed and managed. These debates can manifest in areas such as the benefits and disadvantages of chemical versus talk therapies; the wisdom and pitfalls of universal insurance; and the best social approaches for managing suffering. For example, the rise of biomedical construals that treat illnesses as problems to be avoided has led to an increased focus in the medical,

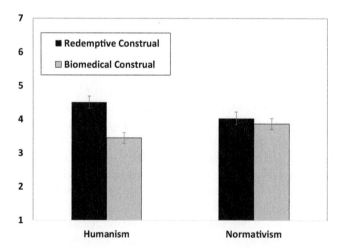

FIGURE 6.2 Redemptive and biomedical construals of depression as a function of primed humanism and normativism.

Source: Palitsky, Sullivan, Dong, and Young (2018).

insurance, and policy realms on controlling risk factors and lifestyle choices that might be considered "pre-diseases" (e.g. an unhealthy diet that might cause diabetes; Dumit, 2012). As another example, consider oft-contentious debates for and against vaccination. This discourse revolves around moral propositions (the well-being of children, adherence to a scientific worldview and progress) and mobilizes individuals' construals of suffering. If a redemptive construal of suffering positions illness as the outcome of natural developmental factors – and ultimately in service of individuating ends – then the attempt to control it by means of normative influences (e.g. the medical establishment) may be regarded with suspicion. Conversely, biomedical construals suggest not only that illness should be regulated by expert institutions but also that individual departures from such attempts at regulation are immoral, as they enable the further spread of disease processes. Some evidence suggests the importance of humanism and normativism for these debates. Nan and Madden (2014) examined how vaccination attitudes are influenced by whether people possess more hierarchical beliefs (operationalized as prioritizing social norms over individual needs, related to normativism) or more egalitarian beliefs (operationalized as prioritizing individual opportunity over the status quo, related to humanism). They found that framing vaccination in terms of loss (greater suffering that would occur if the vaccine were not mandated) led those with hierarchical views to increase favorability for vaccination, whereas those with egalitarian views decreased their support. If suffering has a purpose and is a private matter, as redemptive narratives would suggest, loss-framed arguments for vaccination may not be as effective. However, if suffering is deemed the result of a dysfunction as consistent with biomedical views, arguments that emphasize loss may have more traction.

To conclude our discussion, we will fulfill the principles of the cultural-existential perspective by considering suffering interpretations at a deeper level. Namely, we will briefly consider a qualitative investigation of US residents' spontaneous efforts at construing their own suffering in either a redemptive or biomedical fashion.

A qualitative investigation of stress-related suffering narratives

A critical component of cultural-existential psychology is understanding how individuals' phenomenological experiences of suffering and coping are permeated by certain widespread cultural patterns and archetypes. To provide a thorough account of the role of culture in suffering construal, it is important to examine how people spontaneously invoke culturally afforded interpretations to make sense of their suffering experience. Qualitative investigations of people's idiographic suffering narratives can offer directions for future research and clarify the role of threat interpretation in perpetuating individual allegiance to particular cultural ideals.

To this end, we (Palitsky & Sullivan, 2017) asked a sample of undergraduate students to write about the suffering they experienced during an especially stressful life episode and prompted them to consider particular meanings that suffering might have in their life. To examine qualitative differences in the ways participants draw upon different culturally prominent suffering construals, we randomly assigned participants to respond to different prompts pointing toward either redemptive or biomedical construals. Participants were asked to write one or two paragraphs about "a recent time in your life when you experienced a great deal of stress." In the *redemptive suffering construal* condition, participants responded to the following prompts:

- Please briefly state how this stressful situation helped you grow as a human being.
- Please briefly state how others might have seen the value of the stressful situation you went through.
- In what ways do you think you might have been "ripe" or ready, to experience that kind of stressful situation at that time?
- Now that you've gone through this situation, are there any ways in which you've gained insights about yourself because of the stress you went through?

In the *biomedical suffering construal* condition, participants instead wrote short responses to these prompts:

- Please identify at least one thing that can remove this kind of stress from your life in the future.
- If someone else were looking at your situation, how might they diagnose the cause of the stress?
- What was different, or abnormal, about your life at that time, which led to the stress?
- Now that you've gone through this situation, are there any steps you've taken to prevent this kind of stress in the future?

Finally, participants assigned to a *control* condition answered a series of neutral questions that were not intended to elicit interpretive reflection on the suffering (e.g. to recall their favorite book at the time of the stressful situation).

Additionally, before and after answering the condition-specific prompts, participants were asked to rate the level of stress they experienced during this previous episode on a 1–10 scale. Initial average stress ratings across conditions were in the 7- to 8-point range. A multivariate analysis revealed (at $p < 0.05$) that participants who construed their suffering in *either* a redemptive or biomedical fashion showed decreased stress ratings after answering the prompts. Participants in these conditions showed a stress reduction of about one scale point after writing their narratives, but this amelioration effect was not observed among control participants who answered neutral, trivial questions about the stressful period. Thus, within the broadly individualist US upper-middle class culture of our participants, construing the problem of stress either redemptively or biomedically has a meaning-conferring function that reduces the raw anxiety associated with stress.

More important for our perspective, however, were the particular phenomenological interpretations participants produced in response to our prompts. To address this issue, we subjected 25 redemptive suffering (68% of the total narratives produced in this condition) and 21 biomedical suffering (75%) narratives to a global qualitative analysis. The most common types of stressful events recalled across both conditions were general academic stress and interpersonal conflicts (e.g. with family members, peers, or romantic partners). Events ranged in severity and uniqueness from the stress of finals week to coping with a sibling's suicide attempt.

We separately examined the redemptive and biomedical narrative datasets with the *a priori* aim of identifying passages that typified either frequent themes or themes we expected on the basis of prior theory and research. Ultimately, we identified three primary and contrasting themes frequently represented in the responses to the different prompts that were given according to suffering construal condition. These themes, and representative examples of statements from particular narratives, are presented in Table 6.1.

We observed three themes among the responses. First, redemptive (vs. biomedical) interpretations were characterized by *Global* (vs. *Local*) lessons. Redemptively prompted participants evoked lessons about life, the world, and themselves ("being through this emotional turmoil made me a lot stronger mentally"), whereas biomedically prompted individuals focused on specific, local strategies ("Created a financial plan" or needed to plan "out the month ahead on what obligations I have"). Second, redemptive prompts yielded an emphasis on *Transformation*, whereas biomedical prompts elicited greater focus on *Adaptation*. Transformation themes capitalized on notions of growth and approach ("I've learned that I can use the stress as motivation and energy to meet a goal"; "It is really okay to have stress once and awhile"), whereas adaptation involved recognizing and amending faults in the self ("I saw others around me growing up, changing, and advancing in the real world with job/experience while I had remained stagnant and unchanged"). Finally, further extending themes of approach and avoidance, we observed that redemptive prompts led participants to describe *Fostering independence*, whereas biomedical prompts yielded accounts of *Reduced dependence*. Fostering independence was characterized by increased self-awareness, independent growth, and a narrative of moving toward one's values ("It forced me to be more aware of my character and … who I actually was"; "It inspired me to get back into writing"). Reduced dependence tended to emphasize the harm that social dependence can bring and the mitigation of that harm ("Try not to invest so much emotionally next time").

Reflecting on the themes that emerged from our participants' spontaneous redemptive and biomedical suffering narratives, clear links to the humanist and normativist worldviews can be observed. These links provide insight into how the threat-culture cycle operates. Our quantitative studies suggest that people who dispositionally endorse humanist versus normativist worldviews are more likely to have phenomenological suffering experiences informed by redemptive

TABLE 6.1 Major themes and associated examples from a qualitative analysis of redemptive and biomedical suffering narratives

	Redemptive suffering narratives			Biomedical suffering narratives		
Themes	Global lessons	Suffering to transform	Fostering (creative) independence	Local lessons	Suffering to adapt	Reducing (emotional) dependence
Examples	"I've learned that I am a stronger person than I think I am"	"I think people would put a lot of value on the stress that I went through because as a result I am a way better person and have changed immensely"	"I became more aware of what I needed to work on and certain goals I had for myself. It forced me to be more aware of my character and acted as reminder of who I actually was"	"Planning out the month ahead on what obligations I have"	"I knew that I could not take that time for myself and life would move on whether I was ready or not"	"People around me caused me to become irrationally stressed, as I took on the emotional burden of family members … [I need to be] able to separate my emotions from my focus on a particular task"

versus biomedical themes and language, respectively. In turn, our qualitative study offers suggestive evidence that these phenomenological experiences, if repeated, might attach people more deeply to the respective worldviews that encourage them. For instance, the themes of the redemptive narratives tended to be approach-oriented and to encourage emotional self-expression, whereas the themes of the biomedical narratives were more avoidance-oriented and encouraged emotional suppression. This is consistent with prior research (Nilsson, 2014; Nilsson & Strupp-Levitsky, 2016) showing that one of the fundamental dimensions on which humanistic and normativistic individuals differ is their (positive vs. negative) attitude toward emotion, and that endorsement of humanism is associated with more approach-oriented intrinsic aspirations, whereas endorsement of normativism is associated with avoidance-oriented conservation values.

Summary

Culture confers the sense that one lives in an orderly, navigable world and secures a meaningful place for the person living in it. Suffering threatens this sense of order when it is not ascribed a cause and a purpose consistent with the epistemic, teleological, and moral assumptions of one's broader worldview. For this reason, humans are motivated to construe suffering in a way that reaffirms their cultural frame of reference, a process that helps constitute the reference frame itself. From this standpoint, cultural-existential psychology furthers an understanding of the ways in which culture shapes different styles of suffering construal.

We identified a set of cultural attributes that appear to shape assumptions about suffering, its purpose, and meaning, and which in turn are reinforced by distinctive construals of suffering. In repressive construals, consistent with collectivism, suffering serves to reaffirm the social order and return deviant individuals to established norms. Redemptive construals, consistent with individualism and humanism, see suffering as affirming the unique development of the individual and their inherent worth. Biomedical construals, which correspond with individualistic normativism, localize suffering within a process of disease or dysfunction and enjoin its eschewal by eliminating these processes and minimizing risk.

These differences mean that, when ideological divisions hinge on perceptions of suffering, it is unlikely that conflicting parties draw on a common pool of facts and, more importantly, values. On the contrary, responses to suffering draw on cardinal assumptions about the nature of the self and the purpose of suffering which, in turn, reaffirm distinct (e.g. individualist vs. collectivist) social priorities and worldview assumptions. We observe that making features of humanist and normativist worldviews salient influences people's perception of the causes and purpose (if any) of depression. We also point to qualitative data showing that, when redemptive suffering construals are prompted, people respond with approach-oriented growth narratives, and that when biomedical construals are elicited, people respond with avoidance-oriented narratives of adaptation.

Importantly, these data contribute to more than a set of predictions about attitudes and behavior. They suggest that if suffering threatens foundational elements of one's worldview, then interpretations of suffering are most effective when they reinforce the cornerstones of these foundations. In turn, each response to suffering entails its own set of vulnerabilities and may lead to further ideological conflict. These differences shape how individuals steer their own lives, traversing present and potential encounters with the suffering of others, and the exigencies they themselves will undoubtedly face.

References

Berger, P. L. (1990). *The sacred canopy: Elements of a sociological theory of religion*. New York, NY: Anchor Books.

Berger, P. L., & Luckmann, T. (1966). *The social construction of reality*. New York, NY: Anchor.

Bond, R., & Smith, P. B. (1996). Culture and conformity: A meta-analysis of studies using Asch's (1952b, 1956) line judgment task. *Psychological Bulletin, 119*, 111–137.

Braithwaite, J. (1989). *Crime, shame and reintegration*. New York, NY: Cambridge UP.

Brauer, M., & Chaurand, N. (2010). Descriptive norms, prescriptive norms, and social control: An intercultural comparison of people's reactions to uncivil behaviors. *European Journal of Social Psychology, 40*, 490–499.

Breitborde, N. J. K., López, S. R., Aguilera, A., & Kopelowicz, A. (2013). Perceptions of efficacy, expressed emotion, and the course of schizophrenia: The case of emotional overinvolvement. *The Journal of Nervous and Mental Disease, 201*(10), 833–840.

Caruth, C. (2016). *Unclaimed experience: Trauma, narrative, and history* (20th Anniversary Ed.). Baltimore, MA: Johns Hopkins UP.

Cole, A. M. (2007). *The cult of true victimhood*. Stanford, CA: Stanford UP.

Cross, S. E., Hardin, E. E., & Gercek-Swing, B. (2011). The *what, how, why*, and *where* of self-construal. *Personality and Social Psychology Review, 15*, 142–179.

Daniel, E. V. (1994). The individual in terror. In T. J. Csordas (Ed.), *Embodiment and experience: The existential ground of culture and self* (pp. 229–247). Cambridge: Cambridge University Press.

Dumit, J. (2012). *Drugs for life: How pharmaceutical companies define our health*. Durham, NC: Duke University Press.

Durkheim, E. (1997). *The division of labor in society* (Original work published 1893). Trans. W. D. Halls. New York, NY: Free Press.

Falicov, C. J. (2016). *Latino families in therapy* (2nd Ed.). New York: Guilford Press.

Geniusas, S. (2013). On Nietzsche's genealogy and Husserl's genetic phenomenology. In C. Daigle & É. Boublil (Eds.), *Nietzsche and phenomenology: Power, life, subjectivity* (pp. 44–60). Bloomington: Indiana University Press.

Gillin, J., & Nicholson, G. (1951). The security functions of cultural systems. *Social Forces, 30*, 179–184.

Greenberg, J., Pyszczynski, T., & Solomon, S. (1986). The causes and consequences of a need for self-esteem: A terror management theory. In R. F. Baumeister (Ed.), *Public self and private self* (pp. 189–212). New York, NY: Springer.

Herman, J. (1997). *Trauma and recovery*. New York, NY: Basic Books.

Hooley, J. M. (2007). Expressed emotion and relapse of psychopathology. *Annual Review of Clinical Psychology, 3*(1), 329–352.

Janoff-Bulman, R. (1992). *Shattered assumptions: Towards a new psychology of trauma.* New York, NY: Free Press.

Katz, I., & Hass, R. G. (1988). Racial ambivalence and American value conflict: Correlational and priming studies of dual cognitive structures. *Journal of Personality and Social Psychology, 55,* 893–905.

Langer, S. K. (1988). *Mind: An essay on human feeling* (Abridged Ed.). Baltimore, MA: Johns Hopkins UP.

Markus, H. R., & Kitayama, S. (2010). Cultures and selves: A cycle of mutual constitution. *Perspectives on Psychological Science, 5,* 420–430.

McGarrh, D., Descamps, O., & Sullivan, D. (2017). *Cultural worldviews and attitudes toward alcoholism: A comparison of Costa Rica and the United States.* Dallas, TX: Southern Methodist University. Unpublished manuscript.

Morling, B., & Lamoreaux, M. (2008). Measuring culture outside the head: A meta-analysis of individualism–collectivism in cultural products. *Personality and Social Psychology Review, 12,* 199–221.

Nan, X., & Madden, K. (2014). The role of cultural worldviews and message framing in shaping public opinions toward the human papillomavirus vaccination mandate. *Human Communication Research, 40*(1), 30–53.

Nietzsche, F. (1967). *On the genealogy of morals/Ecce Homo.* Trans. W. Kaufmann. New York, NY: Vintage.

Nilsson, A. (2014). Humanistic and normativistic worldviews: Distinct and hierarchically structured. *Personality and Individual Differences, 64,* 135–140.

Nilsson, A., & Strupp-Levitsky, M. (2016). Humanistic and normativistic metaphysics, epistemology, and conative orientation: Two fundamental systems of meaning. *Personality and Individual Differences, 100,* 85–94.

Oishi, S. (2014). Socioecological psychology. *Annual Reviews of Psychology, 65,* 581–609.

Oishi, S., Miao, F. F., Koo, M., Kisling, J., & Ratliff, K. A. (2012). Residential mobility breeds familiarity-seeking. *Journal of Personality and Social Psychology, 102,* 149–162.

Palitsky, R., & Sullivan, D. (2017). *A qualitative investigation of redemptive and biomedical narratives of stress-related suffering.* Tucson: University of Arizona. Unpublished data.

Palitsky, R., Sullivan, D., Dong, S., & Young, I.F. (2018). *Worldviews and the construal of suffering from depression.* Tucson: University of Arizona. Manuscript submitted for publication.

Pyszczynski, T., Solomon, S., & Greenberg, J. (2015). Thirty years of terror management theory: From genesis to revelation. *Advances in Experimental Social Psychology, 52,* 1–70.

Schrag, C. (1961). *Existence and freedom: Towards an ontology of human finitude.* Evanston, IL: Northwestern University Press.

Shweder, R. A. (1995). Cultural psychology: What is it? In N. R. Goldberger & J. B. Veroff (Eds.), *The culture and psychology reader* (pp. 744–766). New York, NY: New York University Press.

Shweder, R. A., Much, N. C., Mahapatra, M., & Park, L. (1997). The "Big Three" of morality (autonomy, community, divinity) and the "Big Three" explanations of suffering. In A. Brandt & P. Rozin (Eds.), *Morality and health* (pp. 119–169). New York, NY: Routledge.

Singer, M., Valentín, F., Baer, H., & Jia, Z. (1992). Why does Juan García have a drinking problem? The perspective of critical medical anthropology. *Medical Anthropology, 14,* 77–108.

Sullivan, D. (2013). From guilt-oriented to uncertainty-oriented culture: Nietzsche and Weber on the history of theodicy. *Journal of Theoretical and Philosophical Psychology, 33,* 107–124.

Sullivan, D. (2016). *Cultural-existential psychology: The role of culture in suffering and threat.* Cambridge: Cambridge University Press.

Sullivan, D., Landau, M. J., Kay, A. C., & Rothschild, Z. K. (2012). Collectivism and the meaning of suffering. *Journal of Personality and Social Psychology, 103,* 1023–1039.

Sullivan, D., Stewart, S. A., Landau, M. J., Liu, S., Yang, Q., & Diefendorf, J. (2016). Exploring repressive suffering construal as a function of collectivism and social morality. *Journal of Cross-Cultural Psychology, 47,* 903–917.

Taylor, S. E. (1983). Adjustment to threatening events: A theory of cognitive adaptation. *American Psychologist, 38,* 1161–1171.

Tomkins, S. S. (1965). Affect and the psychology of knowledge. In S. S. Tomkins & C. E. Izard (Eds.), *Affect, cognition, and personality* (pp. 72–97). New York, NY: Springer.

Triandis, H. C. (1995). *Individualism and collectivism.* Boulder, CO: Westview Press.

Triplett, K. N., Tedeschi, R. G., Cann, A., Calhoun, L. G., & Reeve, C. L. (2012). Posttraumatic growth, meaning in life, and life satisfaction in response to trauma. *Psychological Trauma, 4,* 400–410.

Yang, Q., Liu, S., Sullivan, D., & Pan, S. (2016). Interpreting suffering from illness: The role of collectivism and repressive suffering construal. *Social Science and Medicine, 160,* 67–74.

THEME 4

Scientists interpreting science

7
DIRECT AND INDIRECT INFLUENCES OF POLITICAL IDEOLOGY ON PERCEPTIONS OF SCIENTIFIC FINDINGS

Sean T. Stevens, Lee Jussim, Stephanie M. Anglin, and Nathan Honeycutt

Science places a primary value on findings and empirical evidence obtained via the scientific method. Yet, scientists are also urged to maintain skepticism when presented with scientific findings (Merton, 1942/1973; Popper, 1959). Recent controversies over the reliability and validity of findings in the social sciences (Gelman, 2016; Simonsohn, Nelson, & Simmons, 2013) raise concerns over how accurate and robust such conclusions are, and if they accurately reflect social reality. A variety of reasons have been offered as to why the veracity of social scientific findings has become suspect (e.g. Haidt, 2011; Jussim, 2012; Simmons, Nelson, & Simonsohn, 2011). Of these, we contend that political beliefs (Jussim, Crawford, Anglin, & Stevens, 2015; Jussim, Crawford, Anglin, Stevens, & Duarte, 2016a; Jussim, Crawford, Stevens, & Anglin, 2016b; Jussim, Crawford, Anglin, Stevens, & Duarte, 2016c) and the level of ideological homogeneity of certain disciplines (Honeycutt & Freberg, 2017; Inbar & Lammers, 2012) pose significant threats. This chapter proposes a model of how political beliefs can influence social scientists' perceptions of empirical evidence, their interpretation of empirical findings, and thus, in part, their beliefs about social reality.

In our proposed model, confirmation bias takes two forms. *Theoretical confirmation bias* occurs when researchers are more accepting and less critical of scientific evidence that comports well with their theoretical inclinations, when non-politicized research topics are under investigation. *Political confirmation bias*, on the other hand, occurs when researchers are more accepting and less critical of scientific evidence that comports well with their *political beliefs*. Both forms can influence a researcher's beliefs about social reality via a direct route and an indirect route. In the direct route, researchers are more accepting and less critical of evidence that comports well with their preexisting beliefs – theoretical and/or political. In the indirect route, theoretical confirmation bias occurs when the theory endorsed by a researcher influences the research design and

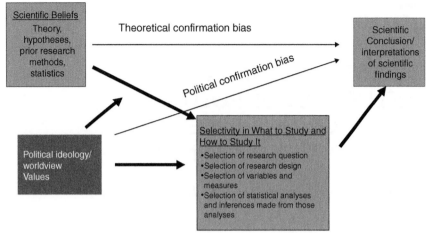

Thin arrows represent the direct route. Thick arrows represent the indirect route

FIGURE 7.1   Direct and indirect influences on perceptions of scientific facts.

the conclusions drawn so that they are consistent with this orientation. Political confirmation bias occurs when researchers' political beliefs influence the research design and the conclusions drawn so that they are consistent with the researcher's political beliefs about social reality.

In this chapter, we briefly review evidence for the ideological homogeneity of the social sciences. Then, we present our proposed model. We briefly describe the direct route before turning our attention to the indirect route, which we suspect may have more influence than the direct route. Our proposed model (Figure 7.1) suggests that political confirmation bias occurs when researchers' ideological beliefs influence what topics they select to study, how they study them, and what conclusions they draw from the results. Because the conclusions produced by a field that investigates politicized topics may be influenced by the ideological beliefs of its practitioners (Jussim, 2012; Tetlock, 1994), this indirect influence of politics on science may exceed that of the direct route. We conclude with recommendations for limiting the impact of political beliefs on the interpretation of scientific evidence.

Ideological homogeneity of the social sciences

At the very least, academics within the United States and the United Kingdom is composed of growing majorities of left-leaning faculty (Cardiff & Klein, 2005; Carl, 2017; Rothman, Lichter, & Nevitte, 2005), majorities that are particularly pronounced within the social sciences (Gross & Simmons, 2007; Honeycutt & Freberg, 2017; Inbar & Lammers, 2012). It is common for social science faculty to cover political material in the classroom and in their research. Thus, ideological beliefs may play a greater role than they would in other academic areas

(Klein & Stern, 2009). Without colleagues who, because of their different political beliefs, raise different questions, frame hypotheses differently, and generally see the world in a different way, the domination of the social sciences by individuals of one ideological orientation may create blind spots. These blind spots may increase the risk that certain questions are not asked or investigated, data are misinterpreted or are interpreted with bias, or conclusions are generated that are convenient, exaggerated, distorted, or advance a political agenda (Duarte et al., 2015; Tetlock, 1994).

Direct route

A host of cognitive mechanisms have been identified that lead people to process evidence in ways that support their desired conclusions (MacCoun, 1998). Many theorists argue that such processes are "hot," motivated biases (MacCoun, 1998; Taber & Lodge, 2006). However, they can also be driven by "cold" cognitive strategies (Koehler, 1993). These strategies can be logical, as it may be rational to give more weight to evidence confirming prior beliefs while scrutinizing or dismissing evidence inconsistent with prior experience.

Even so, process models often depict motivated reasoning as affective. When information supports prior beliefs, people experience positive affect; they process information heuristically and quickly assimilate it into their existing views (Munro & Ditto, 1997). When information challenges prior beliefs, negative arousal induces more effortful processing aimed at disconfirming the evidence (Munro & Ditto, 1997; Taber & Lodge, 2006). Consistent with these models, people analyze belief-inconsistent evidence longer and generate more counterarguments than in response to belief-consistent evidence (Munro & Ditto, 1997; Taber & Lodge, 2006; but see Kahan, Peters, Dawson, & Slovic, 2017).

When belief preservation motives distort reasoning and judgment, people believe their reasoning is objective because they quickly rationalize their automatic response (Haidt, 2001). If motivated reasoning is unintentional, this poses an obstacle to the generation of valid scientific knowledge (Hamilton, 2011). Recent evidence suggests that people may possess some awareness of their bias, and although laypeople attribute polarizing research findings to the researchers' ideological beliefs (Anglin, 2016), they perceive researchers to be less biased than themselves (Anglin, 2016). However, accumulating evidence suggests that those with greater knowledge, education, and expertise (e.g. researchers) may be more prone to belief-driven processing (Anglin & Jussim, 2017; Hamilton, 2011).

Indirect route

Controversies over replication (Gelman, 2016), effect sizes (Ioannidis, 2008), p-hacking (Simonsohn et al., 2013), and null hypothesis testing (Cohen, 1994) have led a number of scientists to question the reliability and validity of findings across many disciplines. Critics of this view emphasize confidence in the scientific method, and, for many disciplines, inferential statistics (Fiske, 2016). It appears that one unstated implication of this criticism is that scientific reformers have lost confidence in the scientific method. Yet, in our view, this is not the case. The problem is not with the scientific method, it is with human error in employing it. We strongly suspect that the problem is behavioral and *largely unintentional* – people may assign greater weight to desirable information (e.g. Tappin, van der Leer, & McKay, 2017). We thus contend that one manifestation of this problem is the indirect route of political confirmation bias in our proposed model.

Debates as to whether hypothesis testing and the use of inferential statistics are impacted by beliefs and value judgments are not new (see Meehl, 1990; Rudner, 1953). Rudner (1953) was one of the first to argue that the decision-making process involved in hypothesis testing was value based:

> For the scientist to close his eyes to the fact that the scientific method *intrinsically* requires the making of value decisions, for him to push out of his consciousness the fact that he does make them, can in no way bring him closer to the ideal of objectivity. To refuse to pay attention to the value decisions which *must* be made, to make them intuitively, unconsciously, haphazardly, is to leave an essential aspect of scientific method scientifically out of control.
>
> *(p. 6)*

We agree with this position and contend it is flawed to assume that the scientific method ensures that a researcher's beliefs and values cannot influence how findings are interpreted. We propose that political beliefs and values can indirectly influence the research process by impacting any of the following, alone or in combination: the selection of the research question; the research design; what variables are measured and how they are measured; and the statistical analyses performed and the inferences made from them. This section describes each of these elements of the research process through examples from social psychological literature.

Research question

One way that a researcher's political beliefs can indirectly influence conclusions is by influencing which questions they ask and how they ask them. The horrific events of World War II sparked greater interest in explaining the psychological roots of fascism and authoritarianism (see Adorno, Frenkel-Brunswik, Levinson, & Sanford, 1950). Adorno et al. (1950) defined authoritarianism as a personality syndrome characterized by ethnocentrism, aggression, submissiveness to recognized authority figures, and political conservatism. They also developed the F-Scale to identify those predisposed to an authoritarian personality. Although this work was criticized (e.g. Rokeach, 1960; Shils, 1954) and the F-Scale was demonstrated to be psychometrically flawed (Altemeyer, 1996), study on authoritarianism remains a burgeoning area of research.

Shils (1954), one of the earliest and most prominent critics, suggested that the work of Adorno et al. (1950) was politicized because its conceptualization of political ideology was insufficient, and that the F-Scale was confounded with right-wing politics (see also Feldman, 2003). He objected to the idea of a unidimensional approach that placed fascism and authoritarianism on the extreme right, and supporters of a democratic system of government on the left. Shils (1954) argued that there was an authoritarian of the left and that Adorno et al. (1950) did not find one because it placed its focus on fascism, and Nazism in particular, and ignored communism, particularly in the Soviet Union under Stalin (see also Greenberg & Jonas, 2003; Rokeach, 1960).

The myth of left-wing authoritarianism

Stone (1980), on the other hand, has concluded that left-wing authoritarianism (LWA) is a myth (Stone, 1980; Stone & Smith, 1993) and contends that belief in LWA persists because of a *centrist bias* in social science (Stone, 1980). Stone (1980) noted that evidence demonstrating that fascists and communists have similar underlying personality dynamics is scant (Altemeyer, 1996; Rokeach, 1960). Brown (1965) reached a similar conclusion 25 years earlier: "It has not been demonstrated that fascists and communists resemble one another in authoritarianism or any other dimension of ideology" (p. 542).

Myth or reality?

Brown (1965) and Stone (1980) support their claims with empirical findings. Yet, we suspect there are at least two possible reasons for the dearth of evidence of LWA. First, it is possible that people on the left are not prone to authoritarianism (Altemeyer, 1996; Stone, 1980). Second, it is possible that the Adorno group's goal of understanding Nazism and anti-Semitism – and not communism and other left-wing ideologies – may have, over time, combined with an increasingly leftward ideological tilt of the field (Duarte et al., 2015) to create obstacles to measuring LWA.

What are the key elements of "authoritarianism" that *could* manifest on the left? We speculate that they include intolerance of political differences, willingness to suppress others' human rights if they are perceived as political rivals, and a willingness to engage in violent protest. Consistent with this, Crawford and Pilanski (2014) reported that political liberalism and conservatism both predicted intolerance of rival political targets based on the perceived threat from these targets. More recently, across three studies, van Prooijen and Krouwel (2017) found evidence that dogmatic intolerance was predicted by extreme political beliefs, on the left and the right. Importantly, they also found evidence that dogmatic intolerance may result in an increased willingness to curtail the free speech of political opponents and increased support for violence against political opponents.

An error of omission?

In short, the methods typically used to study right-wing authoritarianism may not identify LWA. It remains possible that LWA is more than a myth, but, if so, a different approach may be needed to capture it. Thus, demonstrating that communists do not possess the same underlying personality dynamics as fascists may be a red herring and we suspect the scholarship on authoritarianism may suffer from an *error of omission*.

Indeed, Stone (1980, p. 7) has also opined that "had the F Scale not correlated with conservatism, something would have been wrong with the conceptualization." Thus, from its inception, the psychological measurement of authoritarianism could only have been a right-wing phenomenon. Furthermore, despite Adorno et al. (1950) and Altemeyer (1996) explicitly stating that conservatism and authoritarianism were distinct constructs, much of the literature has come to treat them as synonymous (e.g. Jost, Glaser, Kruglanski, & Sulloway, 2003; Wilson, 1973). Again, there are two possibilities here: (1) The consensus that LWA is a myth is true, as stated or (2) Social psychologists have trouble recognizing and measuring authoritarianism of the left.

Research design and the selection of variables and measures

The power of the situation

Social psychologists have long emphasized the "power of the situation" – the conclusion that situations are better predictors of behavior than personality (Funder, 2006). In other words, behavior is not a result of personality, except to the extent that those characteristics result from one's environment – society, socialization, the media, etc. Although this debate has been largely resolved in favor of an interactionist perspective, a narrative about "the power of the situation" persists in much of the social psychological literature (Funder, 2006). There are reasons to suspect that this persistence reflects, in part, political beliefs and values (Funder, 2006).

Funder (2006) contends that the situationist outlook begins "with a basic belief in equality" (pp. 32–33) and is thus consistent with egalitarian political beliefs. How might this reflect an effect of political beliefs and values? The person-centered approach, in contrast, is more consistent with beliefs emphasizing personal responsibility, a belief more consistent with conservatism (Haidt, 2012; Pinker, 2002). In other words, the persistence of the power of the situation narrative, in the face of disconfirming evidence, may reflect, in part, a subtle distorting effect of social psychology's ideological imbalance (Honeycutt & Freberg, 2017; Inbar & Lammers, 2012).

Demographic gaps

Where do demographic gaps come from? One of the go-to explanation in the social sciences is discrimination (Moss-Racusin, Dovidio, Brescoll, Graham, & Handelsman, 2012; Williams & Smith, 2015). We consider this explanation as "selective" because it is primarily applied when the group is one the left per-ceives as oppressed and protected in some way. In contrast, concerns about the lack of political diversity in academia are expressed far less frequently, and often dismissed (Gilbert, 2011; Jost, 2011). Academics offer a variety of alternatives to "discrimination" when explaining the ideological imbalance in many disciplines (see, e.g. the commentaries on Haidt, 2011). But, these alternative explanations are absent when considering demographic gaps, such as the gender gap in Sci-ence, Technology, Engineering and Mathematics (STEM).

Simpson's paradox I

Obtaining empirical evidence that bears on alternative explanations is a variable selection problem because they will be overlooked if they are not tested. Some demographic gaps result from Simpson's paradox (Simpson, 1951): A pattern that describes a population may not describe any subset of that population. For ex-ample, there can be a gender gap in college admissions because men or women differentially apply to programs with different acceptance rates. In one famous case, Berkeley successfully defended itself against charges of discrimination in graduate admissions (Bickel, Hammel, & O'Connell, 1975; see also Jussim et al., 2016a) by showing that even though admission rates were considerably higher for men (44%) than women (35%), there was no systematic discrimination against women *within departments*. Rather women disproportionately applied to programs that had more stringent admissions standards. What was the "variable selection problem"? Not *examining* admission rates within *departments.*

Simpson's paradox II

van der Lee and Ellemers (2015a) found that, in The Netherlands, men had higher funding rates than women, and concluded that (p. 12349) "Results showed evidence of gender bias in application evaluations and success rates..." These results demonstrated a gap, but they did not show a gender bias. Consistent with Simpson's Paradox, Albers (2015) showed that women tended to apply for funding in disciplines where it was more difficult to obtain (for a response, see van der Lee & Ellemers, 2015b).

Ignoring changes over time I

Budden et al. (2008) found that a higher proportion of articles by women were accepted after Behavioral Ecology adopted double-blind review. Their interpre-tation was that if submitters' names were known to reviewers, gender biases could occur. Because there were more female authors after adoption of double-blind review, researchers believed gender bias had contributed to the gender gap. These findings made enough of a splash that it was cited in an editorial by Nature (2008) calling for double-blind review to combat unjustified gender bias.

Webb, O'Hara, and Freckleton (2008) did not dispute the data; however, they showed that the proportion of female authors *also* increased in many other ecology journals that *did not* adopt double-blind review. Put differently, *something* was increasing the proportion of female authors, but blinding reviewers to authors' gender was irrelevant. What was the "variable selection problem" here? It was failure to include other journals that did not adopt double-blind review for comparison.

All but ignoring changes over time II

Brown and Goh (2016) found evidence of a gender gap in social-personality psychology in publications and prestigious awards, a finding primarily interpreted as evidence of gender bias. One of us was a reviewer of this paper, and pointed out that the gaps they studied were decreasing over time. Indeed, the calculation of an approximate correlation between time and percent of women publishing equaled .64, a correlation that was included in the paper.

This is important because it raises the possibility that all or some of the current publication gaps are because, historically, the most senior and successful social psychologists were mostly men, and that as the percentage of women entering the field has increased, women are publishing more. What is the variable selection problem identified here? Not considering the differing distributions of men and women in the field *over time.* Even though this analysis was reported, the original interpretation prevailed. Yet, time is only one possible relevant omitted variable. It is also possible that women publish less and receive fewer awards for all sorts of other unexamined reasons that were not considered (e.g. fewer papers are submitted for publication or the journals submitted to have higher rejection rates).

Analyses and interpretation

Sound and fury signifying almost nothing

Lewandowsky, Oberauer, and Gignac (2013) published a paper that suggested conspiratorial thinking contributes to the rejection of science. They assessed 1,145 people's belief in various conspiracies and acceptance of scientific conclusions. Latent variable modeling found that "conspiracist ideation" negatively predicted acceptance of climate science. The "endorsement of free markets" also predicted the rejection of other established findings, such as that HIV causes AIDS and that smoking causes lung cancer. These claims were supported by standard statistical analyses, so, what was the problem?

Lewandowski et al. (2013) drew an explicit link between belief in the moon-landing hoax and belief in a climate science hoax. Yet, a closer inspection of the data reveals that a total of *10* participants endorsed the moon-landing hoax. Furthermore, of the 134 participants who believed climate science was a hoax, *three* endorsed the moon-landing hoax. Although the statistical analyses revealed significant correlations, only a fraction of 1% of the sample believed the moon-landing was a hoax and also reported that climate change was a hoax.

Endorsement of free markets also predicted the rejection of other established scientific findings (Lewandowski et al., 2013). Yet, only *16* participants rejected the fact that HIV causes AIDS, and only *11* participants rejected the fact that smoking causes lung cancer. There were 176 free market endorsers in the sample. *Nine* of them rejected the HIV-AIDS link, and *seven* of them rejected the smoking-lung cancer link. Thus, 95% and 96% of free market endorsers agreed with those findings. It thus seems hasty to draw a causal connection between believing in hoaxes and conspiracy theories, and a rejection of legitimate scientific findings.

More importantly, even if more people had actually endorsed the hoaxes, any causal claim would still be unfounded. Covariance in levels of positive *agreement* with scientific facts drove the linear associations, which resulted from covariance in levels of agreement among reasonable positions (e.g. disbelieving the moon-landing hoax and disbelieving that climate science is a hoax). No analyses directly compared those who believed the moon-landing hoax with those who did not. Thus, the conclusions drawn (Lewandowski et al., 2013) conflated the sign of the correlational results with participants' actual placement on the items.

Implicit Association Test scores predict egalitarianism

The problem of conflating correlations with levels of a construct is not an isolated incident. For instance, McConnell and Leibold (2001) reported that the Implicit Association Test (IAT) predicted anti-Black discrimination because the IAT was correlated with discrimination. Blanton et al. (2009) critique of these findings simply displayed a scatterplot of the data, which showed little evidence of anti-Black discrimination. Most participants treated the African-American target more positively than the White target, and most of the remainder treated targets nearly equally. The significant correlation occurred because higher IAT scores were indicative of *egalitarian behavior*, whereas lower IAT scores corresponded to anti-White behavior.

The not so impressive power of self-fulfilling prophecies

Finally, social psychologists have long emphasized the power of expectations to create social reality through self-fulfilling prophecies. Although many experimental studies and many naturalistic studies provide statistically significant evidence of self-fulfilling prophecies, this evidence does not demonstrate the *pervasive* power of expectancies to fuel self-fulfilling prophecies (Jussim, 2012). Indeed, Jussim (2012) demonstrated that (1) many of the studies serving as sources for these claims have been subject to replication failures; (2) the effect size for self-fulfilling prophecies runs about $r = .20$ to $.30$ in most experimental studies involving human (as opposed to animal) behavior and lower for studies

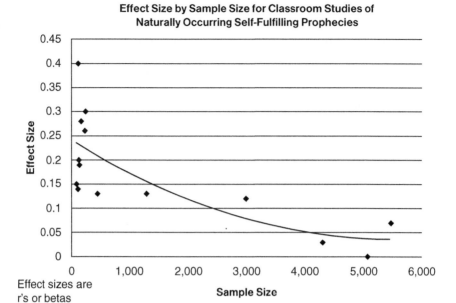

Effect Size by Sample Size for Classroom Studies of Naturally Occurring Self-Fulfilling Prophecies

FIGURE 7.2 Data from Table 13.1 in Jussim (2012).

conducted in field settings; and (3) in most naturalistic studies of real people making real judgments (e.g. teachers in elementary schools), accuracy was two to three times larger than self-fulfilling prophecies. Finally, Figure 7.2 shows that as sample sizes increase, self-fulfilling prophecy effects decrease, a pattern consistent with publication biases producing a literature overstating the typical effect size.

Nonetheless, it is worth considering how "powerful" an $r = .20$ effect is. As per a binomial effect size display, it means that self-fulfilling effects of real-world teacher expectations substantially change the achievement of about 10% of all students. This would mean changing the achievement of two students in a class of 20, which, of course, means the achievement of 18 students was not changed. Some have claimed that even small effects can be important because they can accumulate (Greenwald, Banaji, & Nosek, 2015). However, such an argument is plausibly interpretable as consistent with the main argument of this chapter because Greenwald et al. (2015) provided no evidence that the small effects actually did accumulate. As Oswald, Mitchell, Blanton, Jaccard and Tetlock (2013, p. 568) put it, "cumulative effect modeling is more complex than invoking a compound interest formula." Can this controversy be resolved by evidence rather than argument? Indeed, it can. To date, evidence shows that self-fulfilling prophecies dissipate rather than accumulate (Jussim, 2012). Thus, there is scant evidence that expectancies fuel self-fulfilling prophecies which then create social reality.

Recommendations

Social scientists often subject politically unpalatable findings to far more skeptical scrutiny than politically palatable findings (for reviews, see Jussim & Crawford, 2018; Jussim, 2012; Pinker, 2002). But the strongest and most valid scientific claims, especially about controversial issues, will withstand even withering criticisms. Therefore, we embrace and are calling for a renewal of Mertonian skepticism and Popperian falsificationism.

Embrace Mertonian skepticism

Merton (1942/1973) argued that organized skepticism is one of the core norms of science. He used the term "skepticism" in its modern colloquial sense: To be dubious, critical, and even suspicious of any claim until the evidence in support of that claim was overwhelmingly clear and compelling. "Organized" meant not restricting skepticism to the personal beliefs of individual scientists (although such skepticism was certainly a component), but that it was built into the fabric of science. Therefore, one of the core norms of science is to subject claims to intense, highly critical scrutiny before accepting them as valid.

Although subsequent work has suggested that Merton presented more of an ideal than a norm (Mulkay, 1976), our view is that it is an ideal worth invigorating. Specifically, scientific claims *should* be subject to intense skepticism and scrutiny so that unjustified claims are sifted out from justified claims. Extraordinary claims should require extraordinary evidence.

We suspect that the research areas we reviewed above were not subjected to the intense scrutiny deemed necessary by Mertonian Skepticism because the conclusions about social reality generally supported an egalitarian perspective, and thus potentially advanced a politically desirable narrative. Perhaps this is why claims of powerful stereotype effects in person perception and powerful and pervasive self-fulfilling prophecies have not held up (see Jussim, 2012; Kunda & Thagard, 1996). It may also help explain why a high-powered replication failed to find any evidence of a stereotype threat effect, and why reviews and meta-analyses have concluded that the validity of the stereotype threat phenomenon is in doubt (Flore & Wicherts, 2015; Stoet & Geary, 2012).

Neo-Popperian falsification

"Neo-Popperian falsificationism" refers to a modern adaptation of Popper's notion of falsification (Popper, 1959). There are limits to pure falsificationism. Predictions can fail for many reasons that do not invalidate the underlying theory (e.g. the methods were poor) and it is almost impossible to conclusively falsify *any* theory in psychology (Meehl, 1990). Thus, few psychological theories or claims can be falsified in an absolute sense – it is essentially impossible to justify a conclusion that some phenomenon is nonexistent everywhere, among everyone and all conditions, for all time.

Nonetheless, neo-Popperian falsification strongly encourages researchers to conduct Mertonian tests of important hypotheses. Even if some claim cannot be "ultimately" falsified, specifically stated predictions that were informed by existing scholarship and tested in particular studies can be disconfirmed (see e.g., Brandt, 2017). When specifically stated predictions are repeatedly disconfirmed, especially by other high-quality studies (e.g. highly powered, with pre-registered predictions), one can conclude that the claim is either generally false or requires modification. Even the suggestion that rare and arcane circumstances exist under which the claim holds true would warrant being held in abeyance until such evidence was produced.

Increasing Mertonian skepticism and neo-Popperian falsification by promoting diversity of political beliefs

Research on minority influence (Crano, 2012) shows that there are two beneficial scientific outcomes when a minority attempts to change the majority's view: (1) The minority is wrong, but by mounting a strong challenge, it leads the majority to provide even stronger and clearer evidence that it was correct all along or (2) The minority is right, and eventually produces such a mountain of evidence that it wins over and corrects the majority's initially incorrect view.

Given the benefits of skeptical scrutiny for scientific validity, an influx of political diversity into fields that investigate topics that can become politicized may spur an embrace of Mertonian skepticism and could possibly improve the quality of research. For instance, increasing political diversity should improve social psychology because those in the ideological minority (e.g. conservative, libertarian, anarchist) will probably be far more skeptical of claims that advance the dominant perspectives in the field. Those in the ideological minority may not always be correct, but that skepticism will force others to either produce strong data or retreat from their strong claims.

For instance, Clark McCauley is one of the few social psychologists who has publicly acknowledged that he is politically conservative (Haidt, 2011). He was also the first to demonstrate that the conclusion that "stereotypes are inaccurate" was erroneous, first by providing one of the earliest and clearest empirical demonstrations that people held a slew of stereotypes about differences between Black and other Americans who corresponded well to census data (McCauley & Stitt, 1978), and then with a review highlighting a slew of logical and empirical failures on the part of perspectives declaring stereotypes to be inaccurate (McCauley, Stitt, & Segal, 1980). In other words, it is likely that McCauley's political orientation led him to be less blindly accepting of unjustified claims of "stereotype inaccuracy" and, ultimately, to a major corrective in social psychology (for other proactive steps to increase political diversity, see Duarte et al., 2015).

More importantly, skepticism and a more robust falsificationism can be directly incorporated into researchers' personal practices. We strongly suspect that if researchers proactively attempted to falsify rather than confirm some hypothesis, it would lead to different research questions and, possibly, a different methodology. For instance, one recommendation that can be implemented by the individual researcher is to apply a turnabout test (see Tetlock, 1994) when assessing the veracity of an empirical claim that is consistent with their political beliefs.

For other examples, see Crawford (2018) for a review of evidence identifying conditions under which liberals show a greater propensity for bias and double standards than do conservatives, and Brandt (2017) who specified clear falsifiable predictions and then assessed the accuracy of those predictions. Such a disconfirmation-seeking process can be greatly facilitated by designing studies to explicitly compare the validity of plausible alternative hypotheses. If they are true alternatives, then at least one, and possibly several hypotheses will ultimately be disconfirmed, unless they can be integrated into some sort of unified perspective, which, in a different way, will also advance scientific knowledge.

Conclusion

Concern over the potential for political bias to impact and distort scientific findings is not new (Shils, 1954; Tetlock, 1994), and, considering the growing ideological homogeneity of the social sciences (Honeycutt & Friberg, 2017), it appears that previous attempts have fallen on deaf ears. Yet, we are optimistic that this time such concerns are not falling by the wayside. The aforementioned concerns over p-hacking, replication, and null hypothesis testing have spurred a growing scientific reform movement (see, Jussim, Krosnick, Vazire, Stevens, & Anglin, 2015). Less than 10 years ago, concerns over the ideological homogeneity of the social sciences, specifically social psychology (Haidt, 2011), were frequently dismissed (Gilbert, 2011; Jost, 2011). This is no longer the case (Duarte et al., 2015 and the responses) although disagreement over the causes remains. Those disagreements, however, represent fertile ground for new, and in our view, important research.

We return to Rudner's (1953, p. 6) observation, made almost 70 years ago and emphasize that researchers need to pay attention to how their own beliefs impact value judgments made throughout the research process. There is nothing wrong with making these value judgments. However, when a field becomes dominated by ideologically homogeneity, blind spots can develop and the field risks shining a narrow spotlight on the phenomena of interest. In other words, shining the light exclusively in one spot will not provide a full understanding, and one never knows what they will find in the dark until they shine the light there and look.

References

Adorno, T. F., Frenkel-Brunswik, E., Levinson, D. J., & Sanford, R. N. (1950). *The Authoritarian Personality*. New York, NY: Harper & Row.

Albers, C. J. (2015). Dutch research funding, gender bias, and Simpson's paradox. *Proceedings of the National Academy of Sciences, 112*, E6828–E6829.

Altemeyer, R. A. (1996). *The authoritarian specter.* Cambridge, MA: Harvard University Press.

Anglin, S. M. (2016). The psychology of science: Motivated processing of scientific evidence, awareness, and consequences. Unpublished doctoral dissertation.

Anglin, S. M., & Jussim, L. (2017). Science and politics: Do people support the conduct and dissemination of politicized research? *Journal of Social and Political Psychology, 5*, 142–172.

Bickel, P. J., Hammel, E. A., & O'Connell, J. W. (1975). Sex bias in graduate admissions: Data from Berkeley. *Science, 187*, 396–404.

Blanton, H., Jaccard, J., Klick, J., Mellers, B., Mitchell, G., & Tetlock, P. E. (2009). Strong claims and weak evidence: Reassessing the predictive validity of the IAT. *Journal of Applied Psychology, 94*, 567–582. doi:10.1037/a0014665.

Brandt, M. J. (2017). Predicting ideological prejudice. *Psychological Science, 28(6)*, 713–722.

Brown, R. (1965). *Social psychology.* New York, NY: Free Press.

Brown, A. J., & Goh, J. X. (2016). Some evidence for a gender gap in personality and social psychology. *Social Psychological and Personality Science, 7*, 1–7.

Budden, A. E., Tregenza, T., Aarssen, L. W., Koricheva, J., Leimu, R., & Lortie, C. J. (2008). Double-blind review favours increased representation of female authors. *Trends in Ecology and Evolution, 23*, 4–6.

Cardiff, C. F., & Klein, D. B. (2005). Faculty partisan affiliations in all disciplines: A voter registration study. *Critical Review, 17(3/4)*, 237–255.

Carl, N. (2017). Lackademia: Why do academics lean left? *The Adam Smith Institute.*

Cohen, J. (1994). The earth is round (*p* <.05). *American Psychologist, 49*, 997–1003.

Crano, W.D. (2012). *The rules of influence: Winning when you're in the minority.* New York, NY: St. Martin's Press.

Crawford, J. T. (2018). The politics of the psychology of prejudice. In: J. T. Crawford, & L. Jussim (Eds.), *The politics of social psychology* (pp. 99–115). New York, NY: Routledge.

Crawford, J. T., & Pilanski, J. M. (2014). Political intolerance, right *and* left. *Political Psychology, 35*, 841–851.

Duarte, J. L., Crawford, J. T., Stern, C., Haidt, J., Jussim, L., & Tetlock, P. E. (2015). Political diversity will improve social psychological science. *Behavioral and Brain Sciences, 38*. doi:10.1017/S0140525X14000430.

Feldman, S. (2003). Enforcing social conformity: A theory of authoritarianism. *Political Psychology, 24*, 41–74.

Fiske, S. (2016). Mob rule or wisdom of crowds? Presidential guest column for *Association for Psychological Science: Observer.* Retrieved on 1/20/17 from: www.drop box.com/s/9zubbn9fyi1xjcu/Fiske%20presidential%20guest%20colum_APS%20 Observer_copy-edited.pdf.

Flore, P. C., & Wicherts, J. M. (2015). Does stereotype threat influence performance of girls in stereotyped domains? A meta-analysis. *Journal of School Psychology, 53(1)*, 25–44.

Funder, D. C. (2006). Towards a resolution of the personality triad: Persons, situations, and behaviors. *Journal of Research in Personality, 40*, 21–34.

Gelman, A. (2016). What has happened down here is the winds have changed. Retrieved on 7/19/17 from: http://andrewgelman.com/2016/09/21/what-has-happened-down-here-is-the-winds-have-changed/.

Gilbert, D. T. (2011). Comment on Haidt's "bright post-partisan future of social psychology." *The Edge.* Retrieved on 1/20/17 from: www.edge.org/conversation/jonathan_ haidt-the-bright-future-of-post-partisan social-psychology.

Greenberg, J., & Jonas, E. (2003). Psychological motives and political orientation – The left, the right, and the rigid: Comment on Jost et al. (2003). *Psychological Bulletin, 129*, 376–382.

Greenwald, A. G., Banaji, M. R., & Nosek, B. A. (2015). Statistically small effects of the implicit association test can have societally large effects. *Journal of Personality and Social Psychology, 108*, 553–561.

Gross, N., & Simmons, S. (2007). The social and political views of American professors. *Working Paper presented at a Harvard University Symposium on Professors and Their Politics.*

Haidt, J. (2001). The emotional dog and its rational tail: A social intuitionist approach to moral judgment. *Psychological Review, 108*, 814–834.

Haidt, J. (2011). *The bright future of post-partisan social psychology.* Retrieved from www.edge.org/3rd_culture/haidt11/haidt11_index.html.

Haidt, J. (2012). *The righteous mind: Why good people are divided by politics and religion.* New York, NY: Vintage.

Hamilton, L. C. (2011). Education, politics and opinions about climate change evidence for interaction effects. *Climatic Change, 104*, 231–242.

Honeycutt, N., & Freberg, L. (2017). The liberal and conservative experience across academic disciplines: An extension of Inbar and Lammers. *Social Psychological and Personality Science, 8*(2), 115–123. doi:10.1177/1948550616667617.

Inbar, Y., & Lammers, J. (2012). Political diversity in social and personality psychology. *Perspectives on Psychological Science, 7*(5), 496–503.

Ioannidis, J. P. A. (2008). Why most discovered true associations are inflated. *Epidemiology, 19*, 640–648.

Jost, J. T. (2011). Comment on Haidt's "bright post-partisan future of social psychology". *The Edge.* Retrieved on 1/20/17 from www.edge.org/conversation/jonathan_haidt-the-bright-future-of-post-partisan social-psychology.

Jost, J. T., Glaser, J., Kruglanski, A. W., & Sulloway, F. J. (2003). Political conservatism as motivated social cognition. *Psychological Bulletin, 129*, 339–375.

Jussim, L. (2012). *Social perception and social reality. Why accuracy dominates bias and self-fulfilling prophecy.* New York, NY: Oxford University Publishing.

Jussim, L., & Crawford, J. T. (2018). Possible solutions for a less politicized social psychological science. In: J. T. Crawford, & L. Jussim (Eds.), *The politics of social psychology* (pp. 265–282). New York, NY: Routledge.

Jussim, L., Crawford, J. T., Anglin, S. M., & Stevens, S. T. (2015). Ideological bias in social psychological research. In: J. Forgas, W. Crano, & K. Fiedler (Eds.), *Social psychology and politics* (pp. 91–109). Taylor & Francis.

Jussim, L., Crawford, J. T., Anglin, S. M., Stevens, S. M., & Duarte, J. L. (2016a). Interpretations and methods: Towards a more effectively self-correcting social psychology. *Journal of Experimental Social Psychology, 66*, 116–133.

Jussim, L., Crawford, J. T., Stevens, S. T. & Anglin, S. M. (2016b). The politics of social psychological science: Distortions in the social psychology of intergroup relations. In: P. Valdesolo, & J. Graham (Eds.), *Social psychology of political polarization* (pp. 165–196). New York, NY: Routledge.

Jussim, L., Crawford, J. T., Stevens, S. T., Anglin, S. M. & Duarte, J. L. (2016c). Can high moral purposes undermine scientific integrity? In: J. Forgas, L. Jussim & P. van Lange (Eds.), *The social psychology of morality* (pp. 173–195). New York, NY: Taylor and Francis.

Jussim L., Krosnick, J. A., Vazire, S., Stevens, S. T., & Anglin, S. M. (2015). Toward robust scientific research methods in the United States. An overview invited by John Holdren, Director of the White House Office of Science and Technology policy.

Kahan, D. M., Peters, E., Dawson, E. C., & Slovic, P. (2017). Motivated numeracy and enlightened self-government. *Behavioral Public Policy, 1*, 54–86.

Klein, D. B., & Stern, C. (2009). By the numbers: The ideological profile of professors. In: R. Maranto, R. E. Redding, & F. M. Hess (Eds.), *The politically correct university: Problems, scope, and reforms.* Washington, DC: AEI Press.

Koehler, J. J. (1993). The influence of prior beliefs on scientific judgments of evidence quality. *Organizational Behavior and Human Decision Processes, 56,* 28–55.

Kunda, Z., & Thagard (1996). Forming impressions from stereotypes, traits, and behaviors: A parallel-constraint-satisfaction theory. *Psychological Review, 103(2),* 284–308.

Lewandowsky, S., Oberauer, K., & Gignac, G. E. (2013). NASA faked the moon landing – therefore, (climate) science is a hoax: An anatomy of the motivated rejection of science. *Psychological Science, 24,* 622–633.

MacCoun, R. J. (1998). Biases in the interpretation and use of research results. *Annual Review of Psychology, 49,* 259–287.

McCauley, C., & Stitt, C. L. (1978). An individual and quantitative measure of stereotypes. *Journal of Personality and Social Psychology, 36,* 929–940.

McCauley, C., Stitt, C. L., & Segal, M. (1980). Stereotyping: From prejudice to prediction. *Psychological Bulletin, 87(1),* 195–208.

McConnell, A. R., & Liebold, J. M. (2001). Relations among the implicit association test, discriminatory behavior, and explicit measures of racial attitudes. *Journal of Experimental Social Psychology, 37,* 435–442.

Meehl, P. E. (1990). Appraising and amending theories: The strategy of Lakatosian defense and the two principles that warrant it. *Psychological Inquiry, 1(2),* 108–141.

Merton, R. K. (1942/1973). The normative structure of science. In N. W. Storer (Ed.), *The sociology of science* (pp. 267–278). Chicago, IL: University of Chicago Press.

Moss-Racusin, C. A., Dovidio, J. F., Brescoll, V. L., Graham, M. J., & Handelsman, J. (2012). Science faculty's subtle gender biases favor male students. *Proceedings of the National Academy of Sciences, 109,* 16474–16479.

Mulkay, M. J. (1976). Norms and ideology in science. *Social Science Information, 15(4–5),* 637–656.

Munro, G. D., & Ditto, P. H. (1997). Biased assimilation, attitude polarization, and affect in reactions to stereotype-relevant scientific information. *Personality and Social Psychology Bulletin, 23,* 636–653.

Nature (2008). Working double-blind. Editorial. Retrieved on 12/3/17 from www.nature.com/articles/451605b.

Oswald, F. L., Mitchell, G., Blanton, H., Jaccard, J., & Tetlock, P. E. (2013). Predicting ethnic and racial discrimination: A meta-analysis of IAT criterion studies. *Journal of Personality and Social Psychology, 105,* 171–192.

Pinker, S. (2002). *The blank slate: The modern denial of human nature.* New York, NY: Viking.

Popper, K. R. (1959). *The logic of scientific discovery.* London: Hutchinson.

Rokeach, M. (1960). *The open and closed mind.* New York, NY: Basic Books.

Rothman, S., Lichter, S. R., & Nevitte, N. (2005). Politics and professional advancement among college faculty. *The Forum, 3(1).* doi:10.2202/1540-8884.1067.

Rudner, R. (1953). The scientist qua scientist makes value judgments. *Philosophy of Science, 20(1),* 1–6.

Shils, E. A. (1954). Authoritarianism: "Right" and "left." In: R. Christie, & M. Jahoda (Eds.), *Studies in the scope and method of "the authoritarian personality"* (pp. 24–49). Glencoe, IL: Free Press.

Simmons, J. P., Nelson, L. D., & Simonsohn, U. (2011). False-positive psychology: Undisclosed flexibility in data collection and analysis allows presenting anything as significant. *Psychological Science, 22(11),* 1359–1366.

Simonsohn, U., Nelson, L. D., & Simmons, J. (2013). *P*-curve: A key to the file drawer. *Journal of Experimental Psychology: General.* doi:10.1037/a0033242.

Simpson, E. H. (1951). The interpretation of interaction in contingency tables. *Journal of the Royal Statistical Society, Series B, 13,* 238–214.

Stoet, G., & Geary, D. C. (2012). Can stereotype threat explain the gender gap in mathematics performance and achievement? *Review of General Psychology, 16,* 93–102.

Stone, W. F. (1980). The myth of left-wing authoritarianism. *Political Psychology, 2,* 3–19.

Stone, W. F., & Smith, L. D. (1993). Authoritarianism: Left and right. In: W. F. Stone, G. Lederer, & R. Christie (Eds.), *Strengths and weaknesses: The authoritarian personality today.* New York, NY: Springer-Verlag.

Taber, C. S., & Lodge, M. (2006). Motivated skepticism in the evaluation of political beliefs. *American Journal of Political Science, 50,* 755–769.

Tappin, B. M., van der Leer, L., & McKay, R. T. (2017). The heart trumps the head: Desirability bias in political belief revision. *Journal of Experimental Psychology: General, 146,* 1143–1149.

Tetlock, P. E. (1994) Political psychology or politicized psychology: Is the road to scientific hell paved with good moral intentions? *Political Psychology, 15,* 509–529.

van der Lee, R., & Ellemers, N. (2015a). Gender contributes to personal research funding success in The Netherlands. *Proceedings of the National Academy of Sciences, 112,* 12349–12353.

van der Lee, R., & Ellemers, N. (2015b). Reply to Albers: Acceptance of empirical evidence for gender disparities in Dutch research funding. *Proceedings of the National Academy of Sciences of the United States of America, 112*(50), E6830.

van Prooijen, J.-W., & Krouwel, A. P. M. (2017). Extreme political beliefs predict dogmatic intolerance. *Social Psychological and Personality Science, 8,* 292–300.

Webb, T. J., O'Hara, B., & Feckleton, R. P. (2008). Does double-blind review benefit female authors? *Trends in Ecology and Evolution, 7,* 351–352.

Williams, J. C. & Smith, J. L. (2015). The myth that academic science isn't biased towards women. *The Chronicle of Higher Education.* Retrieved from: www.chronicle.com/article/The-Myth-That-Academic-Science/231413.

Wilson, G. D. (1973). *The psychology of conservatism.* London: Academic Press.

8

STRATEGIES FOR PROMOTING STRONG INFERENCES IN POLITICAL PSYCHOLOGY RESEARCH

Anthony N. Washburn and Linda J. Skitka

Professor X grew up in the rural countryside and had a long-standing belief that country living was healthier than living in an urban setting. She decided that this might be a decent area of inquiry, and so developed a theory explaining why rural upbringings are especially wholesome compared to urban upbringings and set out to conduct research to confirm her hypothesis. Professor X examined differences in crime exposure, safety, violence, etc., between rural and urban settings to test her theory. All her findings collected over a very long career in fact revealed evidence that there are many positives to growing up in rural as compared to urban settings. Should the question of where to raise wholesome children therefore be considered settled science?

There are at least two reasons why the answer to this question is "no." First, Professor X relied on positive test strategies, that is, she only tested the benefits, but not the possible harms or costs of rural as compared to urban living. Second, Professor X focused on hypothesis confirmation to the neglect of falsification. For example, she only considered contexts where rural upbringing would perform better than urban upbringing (e.g. exposure to crime) without considering contexts where urban upbringing might perform better than rural upbringing (e.g. exposure to greater diversity)—that is, contexts that would be more likely to falsify her theory.

The same problems emerge when one tests hypotheses about ideological differences using a constrained set of stimuli and with a goal to confirm rather than provide a strong test of a hypothesis. Someone might have the hypothesis, for example, that conservatives are more prejudiced than liberals, and tests this hypothesis by examining whether there are ideological differences in racial animus, only to confirm her hypothesis. Does this mean a tendency toward prejudice is hard-baked into conservative thinking? Without testing the same hypothesis using a wider variety of possible targets of prejudice with the explicit goal of possible hypothesis *dis*confirmation, we cannot be certain. Strong inferences require testing hypotheses not only in the contexts most favorable for hypothesis confirmation but also in the contexts most favorable for hypothesis disconfirmation (Platt, 1964).

The goals of this chapter are to first describe two common pitfalls of social psychological approaches to the study of ideological differences, specifically, a pre-occupation with explaining conservatives to the neglect of liberals and an over-reliance on positive test strategies. As guards against these potential pitfalls, we recommend that researchers shift their orientation toward negative test strategies, something that can be facilitated using a "grid" approach to hypothesis generation. The grid approach to hypothesis generation forces researchers to consider a set of competing explanations for liberal and conservative thoughts, feelings, and behavior that vary in possible normative spin, which helps protect against possible researcher bias. Before turning to the specifics of the grid approach and providing examples of it in action, we first review these common pitfalls in this area of research that the grid approach is designed to address.

A one-sided coin

Social and political psychology has tended to focus on a single side of the "ideological coin," without fully appreciating that a more complete description of the coin would emerge if both sides were considered in concert. In other words, social and political psychology has been in the business of "explaining" conservatism for years (e.g. Jost, Glaser, Kruglanski, & Sulloway, 2003), starting with a focus on the authoritarian personality (e.g. Adorno, Frenkel-Brunswick, Levinson, & Sanford, 1950; Frenkel-Brunswick, 1949) something that eventually morphed into a focus on explaining right-leaning political beliefs more generally (e.g. Altemeyer, 1981). The dominant problem to be explained seemed to be that conservatives were "different" or non-normative, an orientation that remained relatively unchallenged until recently (e.g. Brandt, Reyna, Chambers, Crawford, & Wetherell, 2014; Conway et al., 2015; Frimer, Skitka, & Motyl, 2017; Morgan, Mullen, & Skitka, 2010).

One reason for the focus on explaining conservatism to the relative neglect of liberalism may be that the field is liberally biased (e.g. Duarte et al., 2015). Consistent with this idea, the ratio of liberal to conservative professors in psychology has been conservatively estimated to be about 11:1 (Rothman & Lichter, 2008). The ideological imbalance of researchers in psychology, particularly in social psychology, has the potential to undermine the integrity of psychological research by allowing liberal values to become embedded into theories and methods (Duarte et al., 2015). Social psychologists may concentrate on research topics or tests that confirm liberal narratives and avoid topics that contradict or challenge their biases. Due to lack of ideological diversity, liberal values and positions manifest as the norm, and conservative values and positions become the deviation that needs to be explained. Outside of a massive influx of conservative graduate students or faculty into the field, social psychologists who study ideological differences need to become aware of these biases to rule out their influence in the scientific process (see Mullen, Bauman, & Skitka, 2003; Tetlock, 1994; Washburn, Morgan, & Skitka, 2015 for other discussions of these issues).

An over-reliance on positive test strategies to test ideological differences

Compounding the issues of one-sided thinking and ideological homogeneity in social psychology is the tendency for researchers to rely on positive test strategies when testing for ideological differences. Positive test strategies occur when researchers test hypotheses by examining situations in which the hypothesized effect should occur if true or by examining instances in which differences are known to have occurred to see whether the hypothesized conditions prevail (e.g. Klayman & Ha, 1987). In other words, researchers often design studies with the goal of confirming a given hypothesis, rather than with the goal of testing its falsifiability. Compounding this problem is the natural human bias to believe evidence that is consistent with one's hypotheses is more likely to represent "truth" (specifically, confirmation bias, Kunda, 1990). Therefore, positive test strategies are focused on hypothesis confirmation, rather than hypothesis testing, and researchers are likely to be biased toward accepting conclusions congenial with their own preconceptions.

A related issue is a bias toward discovering differences rather than similarities. Similar to how people think of themselves as more extraverted when asked specifically about extraversion (as compared to introversion; e.g. Sanitioso, Kunda, & Fong, 1990), researchers who specifically (and exclusively) ask about how liberals and conservatives are different will be more likely to find evidence supporting differences without ever giving proper vetting to the idea of ideological similarity. Because ideological differences are often hypothesized, claims of ideological similarity have often relied on interpreting null results, a practice discouraged in the world of null hypothesis significance testing (e.g. Cohen, 1994). Alternatively, researchers could take a strong inferences approach to test ideological differences where one designs crucial experiments that test mutually incompatible hypotheses under conditions that allow for hypothesis elimination rather than hypothesis confirmation (e.g. McGuire, 2004; Platt, 1964); in other words, they could use both positive and negative test strategies.

The grid approach to hypothesis testing

One approach to developing competing, rather than confirmatory, hypotheses is to take a grid approach to hypothesis construction. The grid approach to hypothesis testing uses both positive and negative testing strategies to develop competing hypotheses for ideological differences and similarities that can be tested in one research program. The grid approach also borrows heavily from perspectivism, or the idea that all hypotheses can be both true and false depending on one's perspective and taking into account potential moderators (see McGuire, 2004 for a review). We detail each aspect of the grid approach in turn.

Using negative test strategies

One way to avoid the potential pitfalls of positive testing strategies in political psychology is to consider ideological differences in terms of moderators, or conditions when one might expect to find evidence of ideological similarities versus differences for one psychological construct or another. A negative testing strategy is when one hypothesizes the exact opposite of one's preferred hypothesis, and tests this alternative hypothesis under conditions that should be maximally amenable to confirming it. For example, common hypotheses in political psychology are that conservatives are more prejudiced and intolerant (e.g. Sibley & Duckitt, 2008) and are more obedient to and respectful of authorities than liberals (e.g. Altemeyer, 2004; Graham, Haidt, & Nosek, 2009; Pratto, Sidanius, Stallworth, & Malle, 1994). Although these predictions were based on sound theoretical rationales, the results of these studies were nonetheless products of positive test strategies because the conditions for testing differences in intolerance and prejudice were especially conducive to finding that conservatives were higher on these traits than liberals.

More recent research on ideological differences in prejudice, intolerance, and authority obedience, however, have generated competing hypotheses and designed studies to allow for the possibility of arriving at the exact opposite conclusion (e.g. liberals are more intolerant; Brandt et al., 2014; Frimer, Gaucher, & Schaefer, 2014). This research found that conservatives are more prejudiced against groups that pose perceived threats to cherished conservative values (e.g. racial or sexual minorities). But liberals express similar levels of prejudice and discrimination against groups that violate *their* cherished values (e.g. pro-life advocates and Tea Party supporters; Brandt et al., 2014). Additionally, both liberals and conservatives have positive views about obeying authorities, once one takes into account whether the authority is generally perceived as a more liberal or conservative one (Frimer et al., 2014). Both groups are positive about obeying authorities that they see as representing their respective values. The moderator of ideological effects on intolerance and obedience is the type of group one is being intolerant of or obedient toward. Of course, the type of group is undoubtedly not the sole moderator of the relationship between ideology and these psychological outcomes, but manipulating the target group allows for researchers to explicitly *test* competing hypotheses rather than *confirm* one set of hypotheses or one direction of hypotheses.

Using perspectivism to develop competing hypotheses

Perspectivism argues that one can generate possible conditions where a given hypothesis should be true and should be false. For example, exposure to television

	More Flattering	Less Flattering
Explaining Conservatives	Conservatives are dispassionately applying what we know about learning theory: We shouldn't reward misbehavior [shouldn't involve anger]	Conservatives are punishing people for being irresponsible [should involve anger]
Explaining Liberals	Liberals' sympathy toward people who need help trumps attributions of responsibility in driving helping decisions [should require cognitive effort]	Liberals are mindlessly helping everyone instead of making the tragic choices needed for a well-ordered society to function well [effect should disappear if we make them think carefully about responsibility]

FIGURE 8.1 Example grid approach explaining ideological differences in willingness to help people personally responsible for their plight (see also Skitka & Tetlock, 1993). Highlighted cells indicated supported hypotheses.

violence may increase or decrease violent behavior for different theoretical reasons (e.g. McGuire, 2004). Exposure to television violence may legitimize violent behavior by portraying it as acceptable, thus leading to increase violent behavior (e.g. Berkowitz, Corwin, & Heironimus, 1963). Alternatively, television violence exposure may reduce violent behavior because watching television violence provides a cathartic release for aggressive individuals (e.g. Feshbach & Singer, 1971). A perspectivist orientation requires designing studies that allow one to test competing hypotheses for any given phenomena. The grid approach builds on the strong inference goal of testing competing hypotheses by recommending that researchers also test flattering and unflattering explanations for any given phenomena (cf. Tetlock & Mitchel, 1993). In short, researchers are recommended to generate hypotheses using a 2 × 2 grid (Figure 8.1).

Constructing the grid

The grid approach to hypothesis construction starts with posing an initial research question about ideology. For example, the initial question might focus on conservatives, such as "Why are *conservatives* less willing than liberals to want to help the poor or personally responsible?" Then, using a hypothesis-generation strategy of accounting for the contrary of a hypothesis (McGuire, 1997), the goal is to reverse the focus of the initial research statement to explain liberals, rather than conservatives. This simply involves replacing liberals for conservatives as the subject of the research question, such as "Why are *liberals* more willing than conservatives to want to help the poor and personally responsible?" Specifically, laying out research questions that implicate both sides of the political spectrum allows one to develop more balanced theoretical explanations and hypothesis tests. This strategy ensures that researchers think equally hard about the psychology of both conservatives *and* liberals.

The grid approach to hypothesis construction intentionally guides the researcher to also develop more and less flattering explanations for politicized research questions as a protection against bias. In other words, researchers should come up with at least two possible hypotheses when posing questions about why liberals and conservatives might differ—an explanation that is normatively more flattering and unflattering for each group (see Figure 8.1 for an example). When one interacts the dual-sided research question with more and less flattering explanations, a 2 × 2 grid emerges that forces the researcher to test equally plausible hypotheses for why liberals' or conservatives' behavior is consistent with a normatively more or less flattering explanation.

The grid in action

The grid approach might be most easily understood if we provide a concrete example of it in use, as we have hinted in our example questions above—that is, by generating theoretically plausible competing explanations for why there are ideological differences in willingness to help people personally responsible for their plight, even when there are sufficient resources to help everyone (Skitka & Tetlock, 1992), that also vary in normative valence. Skitka and Tetlock (1993) provides a useful example.

Explaining conservatives' unwillingness to help the personally responsible

The goal of the grid approach, again, is to generate equally plausible theoretical explanations for conservatives' unwillingness to help that vary in normative implication. Toward this end, Skitka and Tetlock (1993) posited that one reason why conservatives are less willing than liberals to help the poor or personally responsible is that they want to punish people who failed to take sufficient care of themselves. The punitiveness hypothesis suggests that conservatives respond angrily to claimants seeking public assistance for problems for which they are personally responsible because conservatives are more motivated than liberals to punish violators of traditional values and norms of hard work and self-reliance. If this rather unflattering characterization of conservative motivation is true, anger and hostility should mediate the relationship between ideology and willingness to help those personally responsible for their plight.

A more flattering explanation for the same behavior, however, might be that conservatives are not acting in a blind rage, but instead might be dispassionately applying principles of learning theory (e.g. McClelland, 1987). Instead of responding with anger to claims of need by those responsible for their plight, conservatives might dispassionately withhold assistance because a properly functioning society depends on enforcing certain social norms and avoiding a

slippery slope, and because of a need to model to others that there are consequences for misbehavior (e.g. Jencks, 1992; Murray, 1984). If the deterrence hypothesis is true, anger should not mediate the relationship between ideology and
willingness to help. Moreover, ideological differences in willingness to help the
responsible should disappear if the personally responsible show credible evidence
of reform.

Explaining liberals' willingness to help the personally responsible

The next step in the grid approach is to develop explanations for liberals' behavior, rather than focusing exclusively on explanations for conservatives' behavior
in this context. In other words, how can we explain why liberals tend to help
those personally responsible for their quandary? One possible explanation might
be that liberals want to avoid making difficult decisions or tradeoffs or to think
too carefully about why people need help. From a cognitive effort perspective,
making equal allocations to claimants regardless of why they need help is much
simpler than carefully scrutinizing each claim, and developing a mental algo-
rithm of what counts as deserving versus undeserving need (e.g. Kahneman,
2003; Langer, 1978; Stanovich & West, 2000). If the mindlessness hypothesis is
true, liberals should be more likely to fail to notice a mistaken "extra" person
on a "who to help" checklist than will conservatives, and liberals should allocate
resources more like conservatives when they are forced to think carefully about
why people need help.

A more flattering interpretation of liberals' willingness to help might be that
liberals are effortfully down-regulating negative reactions to those personally
responsible to their plight. In other words, liberals and conservatives might be
equally likely to feel initial distaste toward those who refuse to help themselves.
Liberals' commitment to humanitarianism and egalitarianism, however, may
create a sense of dissonance that will lead them to check a more automatic tendency to make person-centered attributions for behavior and to feel anger or
distaste, and to generate some sympathy instead. If this motivated correction hypothesis is true, liberals should only be more likely than conservatives to help the
personally responsible when they have sufficient cognitive resources to engage in
downregulation of anger and disgust, and the upregulation of sympathy instead.

Testing the grid

After fleshing out comparatively flattering and unflattering hypotheses for observed ideological differences in willingness to help the personally responsible,
the next step is to develop a set of studies that test each of these competing hypotheses (something that is unlikely to be possible in a single study). Skitka and
Tetlock (1993) found that negative affect did mediate the relationship between
conservatism and willingness to help those personally responsible for their plight.
However, conservatives were just as willing to help reformed claimants as they

were willing to help those who were not responsible for their plight. In other words, conservatives were not merely seeking to punish free-riders, but were carefully considering the potential future repercussions of providing assistance to those who might not use the money wisely. They also found that liberals were not mindlessly egalitarian but instead considered the tradeoffs between spending resources wisely and helping those in need. When the suffering or need outweighed the goal of the resource allocation, liberals were more likely to provide assistance than not. In short, Skitka and Tetlock (1993) found stronger support for the motivated correction explanation for liberals' willingness to help (and no support for the mindlessness hypothesis) and for the deterrence explanation for conservatives' comparative unwillingness to help (and no support for the punitiveness hypothesis). Examining "both sides of the coin"—more positively and negatively valenced explanations for both liberals' and conservatives' behavior—provided a more complete understanding of the cognitive and motivational underpinnings of ideological differences.

Studying different explanations for ideological differences in willingness to help the personally responsible, however, is not the only research context in which a grid approach helps to advance knowledge. We turn next to an application of the grid approach to generate alternative hypotheses for understanding prejudice.

Applying the grid to ideological prejudice

As mentioned in the beginning of this chapter, theorists in political and social psychology have tended to argue that conservatives tend to be more prejudiced and discriminatory than liberals (see Sibley & Duckitt, 2008 for a meta-analysis). However, much of the research on this "prejudice gap" has focused on explaining why conservatives are more prejudiced than liberals, and not also trying to explain why liberals appear to be less prejudiced toward the same groups. Chambers, Schlenker, and Collisson's study (2013), however, was an exception, and approached this research topic from a strong inferences perspective by testing competing and ideologically balanced hypotheses. Although they did not explicitly construct their hypotheses in the grid format, we can easily adapt their theoretical rationales and study designs to see how their approach fit this strong inferences format, and therefore avoided the pitfalls outlined at the beginning of this chapter.

Explaining conservatives' prejudice toward low-status groups

The goal of the grid approach, again, is to generate equally plausible theoretical explanations for conservatives' prejudice that vary in normative implication. Chambers et al. (2013) theorized that one reason why conservatives are more prejudiced toward low-status groups than liberals is that conservatives are motivated to justify social hierarchies and are threatened by groups that might desire social change (i.e. low-status groups like African-Americans; Kay & Jost, 2003; Sidanius & Pratto, 2001). The system justification/social dominance hypothesis perspective suggests that conservatives, more than liberals, are motivated to see the social system as fair and, therefore, legitimize differences between high- and low-status groups. Because low-status groups often seek social change to better their circumstances, conservatives react to them with fear and hostility because these groups potentially threaten conservatives' social status. If the system justification hypothesis is true, conservatives should be similarly prejudiced toward all low-status groups, regardless of their perceived political affiliation (e.g. liberal and conservative African-Americans).

A more flattering explanation for the same prejudiced behavior, however, might be that conservatives are not threatened by groups who seek social change because it threatens conservatives' status, but instead might be prejudiced toward groups that threaten important conservative values (e.g. Chambers & Melnyk, 2006; Henry & Reyna, 2007). Instead of harboring negative feelings toward all low-status groups, conservatives may only be prejudiced against groups they perceive as violating their ideological values. Because many low-status groups tend to be liberal or at least support liberal policies that go against conservative values (e.g. ethnic minority groups often support social welfare programs and affirmative action), conservatives may only appear to be irrationally prejudiced toward low-status groups when, in fact, they are defending their ideological worldviews from perceived threats. If the (perhaps somewhat more flattering) selective prejudice hypothesis is true, conservatives should only show prejudice toward low-status groups that are perceived to be ideological worldview threats (e.g. obviously liberal African-Americans), rather than showing prejudice to all low-status groups (e.g. obviously conservative African-Americans) (see Figure 8.2).

	More Flattering	**Less Flattering**
Explaining Conservatives	Conservatives are prejudiced toward low-status groups whose values conflict with conservative values (e.g., liberal groups) [should only apply to liberal low-status groups]	Conservatives are prejudiced toward low-status groups because of perceived threats to social hierarchy [should apply to liberal and conservative low-status groups]
Explaining Liberals	Liberals show positive regard to low-status groups because of a desire for a more equal society [should apply to liberal and conservative low-status groups]	Liberals selectively show positive regard to low-status groups whose values fit with liberal values (e.g., liberal groups) [should only apply to liberal low-status groups]

FIGURE 8.2 Example grid approach explaining ideological differences in prejudice (see also Chambers et al., 2013). Highlighted cells indicated supported hypotheses.

Explaining liberals' positive regard toward low-status groups

Chambers et al. (2013) also theorized that liberals might be less prejudiced toward low-status groups than conservatives because liberals value equality and are more concerned with issues of social justice and reform than their conservative peers (e.g. Farwell & Weiner, 2000). Liberals might therefore be motivated to have higher esteem for low-status groups because helping these groups will facilitate a more egalitarian society (a core liberal value). If this comparatively flattering liberal egalitarian hypothesis is true, liberals should show similar positive regard toward all low-status groups, regardless of perceived political affiliation.

In contrast to the liberal egalitarian hypothesis, a relatively less flattering interpretation might be that liberals only display positive regard to low-status groups that are sympathetic to a liberal ideological worldview and are prepared to neglect needy groups who are unlikely to advance liberals' interests. If the somewhat cynical selective positive regard hypothesis is true, liberals should only show positive regard toward low-status groups that are perceived to have similar ideological values (e.g. obviously liberal African-Americans) and neglect those who do not (e.g. obviously conservative African-Americans) (see Figure 8.2).

Testing the ideological prejudice grid

Liberal and conservative participants across three studies were asked to give impression ratings of different target groups and individuals (e.g. African-Americans; Chambers et al., 2013). In support of the selective prejudice hypothesis, conservatives had less favorable impressions of a Black target when the target was portrayed as having liberal compared to conservative policy stances. Conservatives were therefore not blindly motivated to dislike any low-status group, but only disliked those whose ideological worldviews conflicted with their own. Similarly, in support of the selective positive regard hypothesis, liberals had more favorable impressions of a Black target when the target endorsed liberal policy stances compared to conservative policy stances. Liberals, therefore, were not motivated by strictly egalitarian motives to help the disadvantaged. Instead, liberals were only selectively motivated to help low-status groups whose ideological worldviews fit with their own. These results, along with many like them (e.g. Crawford & Pilanski, 2014; Wetherell, Brandt, & Reyna, 2013), suggest that motivations for conservative and liberal prejudice and intolerance are primarily driven by ideological worldview conflict, rather than one-sided ideological individual differences (e.g. conservative system justification or liberal egalitarianism).

In summary, the grid approach to hypothesis testing for ideological differences allows researchers to make strong inferences about when, why, and where liberals and conservatives behave the way that they do. Depending on context and theoretical perspective, researchers can come to vastly different conclusions about conservative and liberal behavior as a function of how they pose their research question. It is equally important to try to explain liberals' in addition to conservatives' thoughts, feelings, and behavior, and to at least attempt to balance ideological biases by making sure that one fully explores explanations that are equally likely to paint ideological motivations as normatively positive or negative. Failing this, one should at least consider positive and negative ways to frame any given finding. As the results above revealed, cynical explanations of liberals' motivations are equally as plausible as more cynical explanations for conservatives' motivations.

Conclusion

The goal of any field of inquiry is to advance knowledge. Testing hypotheses in some fields, however, is not very likely to be infected with ideological biases. Because political psychologists are themselves motivated reasoners when it comes to politicized topics, guarding against ideological bias is especially crucial to building a solid corpus of knowledge. Although many have documented actual and potential ways in which psychologists studying political issues may be biasing their research (e.g. Duarte et al., 2015; Inbar & Lammers, 2012; Jussim, Crawford, Anglin, Stevens, & Duarte, 2016; cf. Skitka, 2012), there is still a question of whether the reality of ideological bias matches possible perceptions of ideological bias in the field. The range of responses in the commentaries on Duarte et al. (2015) suggest that the match between the reality of bias and perception of bias might depend on who you ask. For example, more liberal researchers might perceive ideological bias to be less of a problem than it actually is because such bias reflects poorly on liberals. However, more conservative researchers might perceive ideological bias to be more of a problem than it actually is because a lot of the findings in social and political psychology have painted conservatives in a negative light. Regardless of which case it is, the best antidote to real or perceived bias is to design studies that conform to the grid approach—that is, research explicitly designed to consider whether there are plausible positive and negative explanations for both liberals' and conservatives' thoughts, feelings, and behaviors, and to test these possibilities using approaches that allow for strong inferences.

References

Altemeyer, B. (1981). *Right-wing authoritarianism*. Winnipeg: University of Manitoba Press.

Altemeyer, B. (2004). Highly dominating, highly authoritarian personalities. *The Journal of Social Psychology, 144*(4), 421–448.

Berkowitz, L., Corwin, R., & Heironimus, M. (1963). Film violence and subsequent aggressive tendencies. *Public Opinion Quarterly, 27*, 217–229.

Brandt, M. J., Reyna, C., Chambers, J. R., Crawford, J. T., & Wetherell, G. (2014). The ideological-conflict hypothesis: Intolerance among both liberals and conservatives. *Current Directions in Psychological Science, 23*(1), 27–34.

Chambers, J. R., & Melnyk, D. (2006). Why do I hate thee? Conflict misperceptions and intergroup mistrust. *Personality and Social Psychology Bulletin, 32*, 1295–1311.

Chambers, J. R., Schlenker, B. R., & Collisson, B. (2013). Ideology and prejudice: The role of value conflicts. *Psychological Science, 24*, 140–149.

Cohen, J. (1994). The earth is round ($p < .05$). *American Psychologist, 49*, 997–1003.

Conway, L. G., Gornick, L. J., Houck, S. C., Anderson, C., Stockert, J., Sessoms, D., & Mccue, K. (2015). Are conservatives really more simple-minded than liberals? The domain specificity of complex thinking. *Political Psychology, 37*(6), 777–798.

Crawford, J. T., & Pilanski, J. M. (2014). Political intolerance, right and left. *Political Psychology, 35*, 841–851.

Duarte, J. L., Crawford, J. T., Stern, C., Haidt, J., Jussim, L., & Tetlock, P. E. (2015). Political diversity will improve social psychological science. *Behavioral and Brain Sciences, 38*, e130.

Farwell, L., & Weiner, B. (2000). Bleeding hearts and the heartless: Popular perceptions of liberal and conservative ideologies. *Personality and Social Psychology Bulletin, 26*, 845–852.

Feshbach, S., & Singer, R. D. (1971). *Television and aggression: An experimental field study.* San Francisco, CA: Jossey-Bass.

Frenkel-Brunswik, E. (1949). Intolerance of ambiguity as emotional and perceptual personality variable. *Journal of Personality, 18*, 108–143.

Frimer, J. A., Gaucher, D., & Schaefer, N. K. (2014). Political conservatives' affinity for obedience to authority is loyal, not blind. *Personality and Social Psychology Bulletin, 40*(9), 1205–1214.

Frimer, J. A., Skitka, L. J., & Motyl, M. (2017). Liberals and conservatives are similarly motivated to avoid exposure to one another's opinions. *Journal of Experimental Social Psychology, 72*, 1–12.

Graham, J., Haidt, J., & Nosek, B. A. (2009). Liberals and conservatives rely on different sets of moral foundations. *Journal of Personality and Social Psychology, 96*(5), 1029–1046.

Henry, P. J., & Reyna, C. (2007). Value judgments: The impact of perceived value violations on American political attitudes. *Political Psychology, 28*, 273–298.

Inbar, Y. & Lammers, J. (2012). Political diversity in social and political psychology. *Perspectives on Psychological Science, 7*, 496–503.

Jencks, C. (1992). *Rethinking social policy: Race, poverty, and the underclass.* Cambridge, MA: Harvard University Press.

Jost, J. T., Glaser, J., Kruglanski, A. W., & Sulloway, F. J. (2003). Political conservatism as motivated social cognition. *Psychological Bulletin, 129*(3), 339–375.

Jussim, L., Crawford, J. T., Anglin, S. M., Stevens, S. T., & Duarte, J. L. (2016). Interpretations and methods: Towards a more effectively self-correcting social psychology. *Journal of Experimental Social Psychology, 66*, 116–133.

Kahneman, D. (2003). A perspective on judgment and choice: Mapping bounded rationality. *American Psychologist, 58*(9), 697–720.

Kay, A. C., & Jost, J. T. (2003). Complementary justice: Effects of "poor but happy" and "poor but honest" stereotype exemplars on system justification and implicit activation of the justice motive. *Journal of Personality and Social Psychology, 85*, 823–837.

Klayman, J., & Ha, Y. W. (1987). Confirmation, disconfirmation, and information in hypothesis testing. *Psychological Review, 94*(2), 211–228.

Kunda, Z. (1990). The case for motivated reasoning. *Psychological Bulletin, 108*(3), 480–498.

Langer, E. J. (1978). Rethinking the role of thought in social interaction. In J. Harvey, W. Ickes, & R. F. Kidd (Eds.), *New directions in attribution research* (Vol. 2). Hillsdale, NJ: Erlbaum.

McClelland, D. C. (1987). *Human motivation.* Cambridge, UK and New York, NY: Cambridge University Press.

McGuire, W. J. (1997). Creative hypothesis generating in psychology: Some useful heuristics. *Annual Review of Psychology, 48*, 1–30.

McGuire, W. J. (2004). A perspectivist approach to theory construction. *Personality and Social Psychology Review, 8*, 173–182.

Morgan, G. S., Mullen, E., & Skitka, L. J. (2010). When values and attributions collide: Liberals' and conservatives' values motivate attributions for alleged misdeeds. *Personality and Social Psychology Bulletin, 36*(9), 1241–1254.

Mullen, E., Bauman, C. W., & Skitka, L. J. (2003). Avoiding the pitfalls of a politicized psychology. *Analyses of Social Issues and Public Policy, 3*, 171–176.

Murray, C. (1984). *Losing ground: American social policy, 1950–1980.* New York, NY: Basic Books.

Platt, J. R. (1964). Strong inference. *Science, 146*(3642), 347–353.

Pratto, F., Sidanius, J., Stallworth, L. M., & Malle, B. F. (1994). Social dominance orientation: A personality variable predicting social and political attitudes. *Journal of Personality and Social Psychology, 67*(4), 741.

Rothman, S., & Lichter, S. R. (2008). The vanishing conservative: Is there a glass ceiling? In R. Maranto, R. E. Redding, & F. M. Hess (Eds.), *The politically correct university: Problems, scope, and reforms* (pp. 60–76) Washington, DC: AEI Press.

Sanitioso, R., Kunda, Z., & Fong, G. T. (1990). Motivated recruitment of autobiographical memories. *Journal of Personality and Social psychology, 59*(2), 229–241.

Sibley, C. G., & Duckitt, J. (2008). Personality and prejudice: A meta-analysis and theoretical review. *Personality and Social Psychology Review, 12*(3), 248–279.

Sidanius, J., & Pratto, F. (2001). *Social dominance: An intergroup theory of social hierarchy and oppression.* Cambridge, UK: Cambridge University Press.

Skitka, L. J. (2012). Multifaceted problems: Liberal bias and the need for scientific rigor in self-critical research. *Perspectives on Psychological Science, 7*, 508–511.

Skitka, L. J., & Tetlock, P. E. (1992). Allocating scarce resources: A contingency model of distributive justice. *Journal of Experimental Social Psychology, 28*, 33–37.

Skitka, L. J., & Tetlock, P. E. (1993). Providing public assistance: Cognitive and motivational processes underlying liberal and conservative policy preferences. *Journal of Personality and Social Psychology, 65*(6), 1205.

Stanovich, K. E., & West, R. F. (2000). Individual differences in reasoning: Implications for the rationality debate? *Behavioral and Brain Sciences, 23*(5), 645–665.

Tetlock, P. E. (1994). Political psychology of politicized psychology: Is the road to scientific hell paved with good moral intentions? *Political Psychology, 15*, 509–529.

Tetlock, P. E. & Mitchell, P. G. (1993). Liberal and conservative approaches to justice: Conflicting psychological portraits. In B. Mellers, & J. Baron (Eds.), *Psychological perspectives on justice.* Cambridge, UK: Cambridge University Press.

Washburn, A. N., Morgan, G. S., & Skitka, L. J. (2015). A checklist to facilitate objective hypothesis testing in social psychology research. *Behavioral and Brain Sciences, 38*, e161.

Wetherell, G. A., Brandt, M. J., & Reyna, C. (2013). Discrimination across the ideological divide: The role of perceptions of value violations and abstract values in discrimination by liberals and conservatives. *Social Psychological and Personality Science, 4*, 658–667.

THEME 5

People interpreting science

9

IN GENES WE TRUST

On the consequences of genetic essentialism

Anita Schmalor and Steven J. Heine

At the age of 31 years, Csanád Szegedi, a member of the European Parliament, converted to Orthodox Judaism (Puhl, 2014). What makes his transformation noteworthy is that he was elected as a member of the Jobbik party, an extremist anti-Semitic party (Gorondi, 2014). Why would Szegedi undergo such a radical transformation? The key fact in this case is this: Szegedi had recently learned that his maternal grandmother was Jewish (Gorondi, 2014). Szegedi wasn't so bothered that she had been raised Jewish – indeed, when he first learned of his grandmother's past, he thought she had been raised by Jewish stepparents. As he said, "I calmed down, because it's only the stepparents – they are not blood relations of mine" (Applebaum, 2013). But later, he learned that his maternal grandmother's biological parents were also Jewish, and thus Szegedi was Jewish by descent. This story highlights how discoveries about one's own biological ancestry can have profound personal implications.

Szegedi's story may be extreme, but the notion that people look to their genetic ancestors to understand themselves is commonly found. In recent years, it has become possible to learn about the likely geographic origins of one's ancestors through consumer genomics companies. One investigation of the reactions that people had to surprising information that they learned from these tests revealed that some people came to choose different ethnic identities when completing a census, joined new communities, cheered for different sports teams, and took up learning new languages (see Roth & Lyon, 2016). This suggests that people turn to genes as a means to understand themselves on a deeper level. The question that arises, then, is how does the pervasiveness of genetic information affect our psychology? This question has become more important in light of the rapid increase in genetics research over the last few decades, which is often covered extensively in the media (e.g. Heine, Dar-Nimrod, Cheung, & Proulx, 2017).

Psychological essentialism

Why did Szegedi change his identity when he learned about the origin of his genes? Or, more broadly speaking, why do people seem to view genes as holding the key to understanding themselves on a deeper level? To answer these questions, we need to take one step back and consider psychological essentialism. Psychological essentialism is the tendency for people to believe that natural kinds are as they are because of an underlying hidden essence (e.g. Gelman, 2003). For example, when people consider what is a bird, they tend not to conceive of its identity as being determined by its visible surface features; rather they imagine an internal force that makes it so. Even if a bird were to lose all of its feathers or was no longer able to fly, we would still think of it as a bird – its identity lies somewhere deep beneath all that we can see. Essentialism in a metaphysical sense is philosophically problematic (Medin & Ortony, 1989); however, psychological essentialism doesn't speak to whether essentialist thinking is the "right" way to view the world. It merely describes a deeply engrained psychological tendency to categorize certain entities. Psychological essentialism is a widespread tendency that has been identified in a highly diverse range of different cultures (Henrich, Heine, & Norenzayan, 2010).

Importantly, essences are presumed to have specific characteristics. Essences are thought to be the ultimate cause for a specific outcome (Keil, 1989; Rips, 1989). That is, the cat has a cat essence and it is this essence that makes the cat a cat. Essences are also thought to be stable over time (Keil, 1989; Rips, 1989). So, a cat will always remain a cat, and won't somehow turn into a dog, and the reason for this stability is its essence. Essences are also thought to be immutable. This means that they, and the characteristics they underlie, cannot change, even if superficial characteristics are altered. Essences are not only believed to underlie different species of animals but are also seen to underlie human groups (Rothbart & Taylor, 1992); they make the natural world seem as though it consists of homogeneous and discrete categories. Hence, when people view social groups as sharing an essence, they engage in more stereotypical thinking about those groups (e.g. Haslam, Bastian, Bain, & Kashima, 2006). Last, essences are natural kinds and so the outcomes they cause are perceived as natural (Dar-Nimrod & Heine, 2011). In sum, essences are viewed as being the ultimate cause for a specific outcome, are stable over time and immutable, are natural, and they carve the natural world into homogeneous and discrete categories.

But what exactly makes up an essence? People have a difficult time forming concrete mental representations of what essences actually are, so they instead turn to an essence placeholder to make the essence appear more concrete (Medin & Ortony, 1989). There are many kinds of placeholders that have been used throughout history. For example, in the Judeo-Christian religions, the soul is typically thought of as the locus of the essence, whereas a person's blood type – which is thought to influence personality traits according to Japanese folk psychology beliefs – represents an essence placeholder in Japan (Heine, 2017). However, the layperson's typical understanding of genes makes for a particularly apt essence placeholder.

Genetic essentialism

People's lay conception of genes overlaps a great deal with how they think of essences (Dar-Nimrod & Heine, 2011). That is, genes are understood as ultimate causes, immutable, homogeneous, discrete, and natural. Therefore, when people consider how genes might be relevant to a given trait or outcome, they come to think of these outcomes in more essentialist terms, which is called "genetic essentialism" (Dar Nimrod & Heine, 2011). Specifically, the outcome that is influenced by genes tends to be viewed as *determined* and *immutable*. For example, if someone believes that they have "the alcoholism gene," they will likely see themselves as destined to become an alcoholic. Furthermore, the gene for a specific outcome is seen as having a specific etiology (Meehl, 1977) and is seen as the *ultimate cause*. In the face of this, other potentially contributing factors such as the environment are discounted. The imagined gene can be seen as a diagnosis for the associated outcome. Hence, if someone finds out they don't have "the alcoholism gene," they may conclude that they can safely drink as much alcohol as they like. A third perception is that groups who share genes are considered as *homogeneous* (all members that share the same genes would share the same phenotypes) and *discrete* from other groups (who have different genes). Last, a genetic foundation for a certain outcome may be viewed as *natural*. This can lead to the naturalistic fallacy: the tendency to consider as morally good what is perceived to be natural (Frankena, 1939). In sum, because genes serve as a placeholder for essences, when people learn about relevant genes they start to think about essences (Heine, Dar-Nimrod, Cheung, & Proulx, 2017).

We call genetic essentialism a biased way of thinking and hence, we might question whether such thinking is actually rational. On one hand, there are some conditions, almost all of them are rare genetic diseases, in which a single genetic cause is deterministic, such as Huntington's disease. In these cases, there is a specific etiology for the disease, it is immutable and the outcome is determined, it makes people with the disease homogeneous and different from those without disease, and it is natural. These kinds of conditions can be largely understood in ways similar to essences.

However, the ways that genes influence phenotypes exist on a continuum. Direct and deterministic relations between genes and phenotypes anchor one end of the continuum, but these represent the exception and not the rule. The vast majority of diseases, traits, and psychological characteristics are the result of far more complex processes (Chabris, Lee, Cesarini, Benjamin, & Laibson, 2015). Typically, many genes are involved (sometimes hundreds or thousands), the genes interact with each other, their expression is governed by experiences, and epigenetic markers further influence their expression (Jablonka & Lamb, 2006). The relation between genes and phenotypes in these conditions is not at all direct or deterministic, and essentialist thinking about these cases is simply incorrect.

The first law of behavioral genetics states that (almost) all human conditions are heritable (Turkheimer, 2000), which means that genes are almost always relevant, even if only rarely in a deterministic way. At the same time, much research has revealed that the public's understanding of basic genetic science is limited (Condit, 2010). For example, one survey found that 76% of American adults wrongly believed that single genes are responsible for specific human behaviors (Christensen, Jayaratne, Roberts, Kardia, & Petty, 2010). However, this limited genetic literacy does not stop people from frequently talking about genes, such as when Donald Trump attributes his success to having "a certain gene[1]." When people are thinking about genes, they are often thinking about essences, and this can lead to faulty conclusions.

In the rest of this chapter, we will give a brief overview on how genetic essentialism influences people's perception of gender, race, sexual orientation, criminality, health, and obesity, and their implications. Finally, we will consider ways to reduce genetic essentialism.

Gender

The sex of a person is ultimately determined by their chromosomes. Gender, on the other hand, is partially socially constructed and encompasses both biological and social aspects, such as sex organs and social roles, respectively (Dar-Nimrod & Heine, 2011). Gender is viewed as an essence more than any other social category (e.g. Gelman & Taylor, 2000; Haslam, Rothschild, & Ernst, 2000). When gender is essentialized, people view the genders as more homogeneous and discrete from one another (Dar-Nimrod & Heine, 2011), perceive more sex differences (Keller, 2005), and view men and women as having more gender-stereotypical traits (Brescoll & LaFrance, 2004).

What happens if people are led to view gender differences to be the result of genes? Consider the case of gender differences in math performance (e.g. Miller & Halpern, 2014). In one set of studies, Dar-Nimrod and Heine (2006) assigned female study participants to read a fictitious news article that either claimed that men outperform women on math tests because of their genes or because of their early childhood experiences. Then, the participants completed a math test and their performance was compared with those assigned to control conditions. Those women who read about math genes showed evidence for stereotype threat, replicating past research (Spencer, Steele, & Quinn, 1999). In contrast, those who learned about environmental causes for sex differences in math showed no evidence for stereotype threat. This difference is especially noteworthy as both the gene and experience articles described the gender difference in math to be the identical magnitude (i.e. 5%, another fictitious claim). These findings suggest that if an environmental explanation (such as different experiences between men and women in this study) is made salient, people will hold less essentialist views of gender.

In sum, people tend to view gender in essentialized ways. When people conceive of gender as the product of genes, they tend to view gender differences as being caused by the underlying genes, as immutable, as creating homogeneous groups, and as natural. While there are mean differences between men and women in many traits and characteristics, most traits and characteristics are normally distributed, and the distributions of men and women largely overlap (e.g. height). But when gender is essentialized, people perceive these differences to be more problematic.

Race and ethnicity

Race and ethnicity are key social categories that people use for understanding others. While race and ethnicity may be meaningful categories, the question whether they have any biological basis is still debated. By and large, a majority of social scientists and biologists view race as socially constructed, rather than biologically based, as the genetic variability that lies between the continental races (4.3%) is a small fraction of the total genetic variability between individuals (e.g. Rosenberg et al., 2002; Templeton, 2013). Nonetheless, many people view different racial groups as biologically different (e.g. Gil-White, 2001; Wade, 2014).

When people think of race as the product of different genes, they are more likely to engage in stereotypical thinking and prejudice (e.g. Keller, 2005). For example, Jayaratne and colleagues (2006, 2009) found that people, who attributed racial differences in intelligence, aspirations, and violence more to genetic causes, were also higher in their endorsement of racist attitudes. Likewise, when Jewish and Arab participants in the United States learned that Jews and Arabs were genetically distinct, they were more willing to use physical aggression against an outgroup target than when they learned they were genetically similar (Kimel, Huesmann, Kunst, & Halperin, 2016). Moreover, people are more willing to view ethnic stereotypes to be a product of genetic differences when they learn that gene frequencies are distributed unevenly around the world compared with those who learned about the relative homogeneity of the human genome (Schmalor, Cheung, & Heine, 2017). These examples show that thinking about a genetic foundation of race leads people to an altered perception of reality. Different ethnic groups are viewed as homogeneous and discrete, and as having characteristics and traits that are immutable and as natural.

Sexual orientation

People's attitudes toward the acceptability of homosexuality vary tremendously. Curiously, a key variable that predicts one's attitudes toward homosexuality is what one perceives as its cause. Much research finds that people who view genes as underlying differences in sexual orientation tend to have more pro-gay attitudes than those who don't view genes as being involved (e.g. Hegarty & Pratto, 2001; Jayaratne et al., 2006). Given that these data are correlational, there are multiple interpretations of this relation. For example, it's possible that people turn to genetic accounts of sexual orientation to rationalize their support for gay rights. However, there have also been experiments that test how people react when they learn of a genetic cause for sexual orientation. These studies have found that people who read about genetic causes of sexual orientation report more support for gay rights than those who read about environmental causes (e.g. Frias-Navarro, Monterde-i-Bort, Pascual-Soler, & Badenes-Ribera, 2015). Perhaps the rapidly increasing support for gay rights is the product of the corresponding increase in people's beliefs that sexual orientation is innate (Heine, 2017). Interestingly, whereas perceived genetic causes of gender differences and ethnic differences are associated with less tolerance to those of different sexes and races, perceived genetic causes of sexual orientation have the opposite effect. Social conservatives often criticize gay men and lesbians because they perceive their sexual orientation to be "unnatural." Considering the role of genes in sexual orientation leads people to assume that an underlying gay essence renders different sexual orientation as natural, and therefore more acceptable (Dar-Nimrod & Heine, 2011). People's reactions to arguments about genetic bases of sexual orientation represent an interesting case, as the evidence regarding actual causes of sexual orientation continues to be debated. Sexual orientation is heritable (Bailey & Pillard, 1995), but the meaning of this is unclear as the first law of behavioral genetics reminds us that (almost) all human behavioral traits are heritable (Turkheimer, 2000). As of yet, there have been no single genes identified that predict sexual orientation although there is debate about the relevance of a region on the X chromosome for male sexual orientation (e.g. Sanders et al., 2015). The most direct evidence for a biological basis of homosexuality is an immune system response from mothers in which they produce anti-male antibodies in response to the male-specific antigens that are created by male fetuses. With each subsequent son, the number of these antibodies increases, and this has the effect of increasing the likelihood that the younger sons will become gay (Bogaert & Skorska, 2011).

Criminality

What causes the behavior of criminals? This is a key legal question, as perceptions of guilt hinge importantly on the concept of *mens rea*, which translates into a "guilty mind." However, much research reveals that discussions of the role of genes in criminal behavior can have a significant impact on the ways that people think about guilt and responsibility, even among legal professionals (Aspinwall, Brown, & Tabery, 2012; Berryessa, 2016).

Although thus far there have been no common genetic variants that have been found to have a large impact on the likelihood of criminal behavior (see Heine, 2017 for a review), people are influenced by the mere discussion of such kinds of genetic influences. For example, Cheung and Heine (2015) found that when people learned of a genetic predictor of violent behavior, they were more likely to endorse a diminished capacity defense compared with those who learned of an experiential cause of violence (also see Monterosso, Royzman, & Schwartz, 2005). Moreover, genetic causes, as opposed to experiential causes, are associated with a perception that the perpetrators have less control over their behavior (Dar-Nimrod, Heine, Cheung, & Schaller, 2011). On the other hand, genetic causes are thought to be associated with increased recidivism among convicted criminals (Cheung & Heine, 2015). The believed cause of criminal behavior can affect legal decision making. This shows that perception of reality (whether criminality is caused by genes) can have significant consequences.

Health

A key impetus of the genomics revolution is to study the ways that genes impact our health. However, much research points to an unintended consequence of this endeavor: Learning about genetic causes to health can change the very ways that we think about illness and health.

The ways that genetic attributions for health affect people's perceptions are most clearly evident in discussions of mental illness. On the one hand, genetic attributions for mental illness tend to be associated with increased sympathy and tolerance to those afflicted. The afflicted is viewed as having less control over their disease, and therefore is viewed as less blameworthy (e.g. Kvaale, Gottdiener, & Haslam, 2013). But the double-edged sword of genetic essentialism cuts both ways, and genetic attributions for mental illness can make people more pessimistic about one's prognosis (Phelan, Cruz–Rojas, & Reiff, 2002; Schnittker, 2008). Indeed, if the cause of the illness is perceived to lie in one's genes, and because one's genes aren't going to change, people are more likely to view the condition as chronic. Moreover, genetic attributions for mental illness can sharpen the line that distinguishes between the afflicted and the healthy, and it can thus further stigmatize those with the condition (Mehta & Farina, 1997). For example, research in schizophrenia finds that when people learn of genetic accounts of schizophrenia, they view people with the condition to be more dangerous (e.g. Kvaale et al., 2013). Furthermore, when people learn that a condition has a genetic basis, they are more likely to view a biologically grounded treatment, such as medications rather than psychotherapy, as the most effective way to treat the condition (Lebowitz & Ahn, 2014; Phelan, Yang, & Cruz-Rojas, 2006). In sum, the very way we conceive of mental illness, and the expectations that we have for those afflicted by them, hinges on whether we believe that genes are involved.

Obesity

Obesity is a highly moralized topic, and people are often prejudiced against obese people and blame them for their weight. However, when genes are brought into the discussion, obesity comes to be seen as more immutable and beyond one's control. For example, research finds that people are less likely to blame someone for overeating when a genetic cause, as compared to an environmental cause, was provided (Crandall, 1994; Monterosso et al., 2005). On the other hand, environmental explanations, such as the influence of friends and changing social norms, do not tend to reduce blame. Of course, a purely genetic account of obesity makes little sense considering that obesity rates have risen across the world in the past few decades (Organization for Economic Co-operation and Development, 2004).

However, believing that obesity is caused by genes can have other implications. Dar-Nimrod, Cheung, Ruby, and Heine (2014) exposed participants to information that either stated that (1) genes are a cause of obesity; (2) one's social networks are a cause of obesity; or (3) they read no information about obesity. Afterwards, participants were invited to evaluate the taste of some cookies. Those who had learned about a genetic cause to obesity ate more cookies than participants in the other two conditions. This suggests that people come to think of their own weight in more fatalistic terms, and, ironically, this belief itself may lead people to engage in behaviors that will increase their likelihood of becoming overweight. What people take to perceive as the reality of obesity can thus directly affect their health outcomes.

Eugenics

Arguably, the most problematic consequence of genetic essentialism is support for eugenics. When genes are perceived to be the ultimate cause of a certain outcome, then it follows that efforts to try to change that outcome should target the underlying genes. Eugenic ideas have been around at least as long as Plato; however, they achieved their high water mark in the early 20th century. During this time, eugenic ideas held popular support across the industrialized world; however, eugenics curried particular favor among geneticists. In the early 20th century, there was much overlap between genetics and eugenics to the point that the latter was often thought of as applied genetics (Paul, 1995). The links between the two fields were evident in 1916, when every member of the founding editorial board of the journal, *Genetics*, endorsed the eugenics movement (Ludmerer, 1972). Moreover, it was stated that half of academic biologists in Germany joined the Nazi party prior to the war, which was the largest representation of any professional group (Paul, 1995).

A key reason that the study of genetics and eugenics overlapped so much in the early 20th century was because many early geneticists favored simple Mendelian accounts of human traits, where each trait was seen to be matched with a corresponding gene (Heine, 2017). For example, the leading American eugenicist, Charles B. Davenport, argued that such human traits as feeble-mindedness, a love for the sea, nomadism, shiftlessness, and innate eroticism, were the product of single genes (Comfort, 2012; Kevles, 1985). If single genes really were the direct cause of human traits, then it would indeed be more straightforward to imagine efforts to change the future of humankind through controlled breeding. However, there are no single genes that can account for a large proportion of the variance for any human psychological traits. Rather, as the so-called "fourth law of behavioral genetics" puts it, human traits are the product of many genes that each contribute a very small amount (Chabris et al., 2015).

We investigated whether there was a relation between endorsing genetic essentialist views and support for eugenics policies. Indeed, the more that people believed genetic essentialist views, the more likely they were to endorse government policies to control breeding (Cheung, Schmalor, & Heine, 2017). The field of eugenics demonstrates that even the most horrific behaviors can be viewed as more or less justified based on what reality is believed to be.

Public communication

It is perhaps not surprising that genetically essentialist views are commonplace, when we consider that the media frequently oversimplifies genetics findings. For example, Conrad (2002) criticized the media for often describing genetics research using a one gene, one disease (OGOD) framework. Moreover, as in the rest of scientific research, studies that yield positive findings tend to get more media coverage than subsequent research that fails to replicate those findings. And failed replications are particularly common in genetics research (Faraone et al., 2008), likely because the effect sizes of particular genetic variants are extremely small.

But the media is not solely responsible for the oversimplification of genetics findings. Scientists compete for funding and media attention, and often make broader generalizations than are warranted. One study investigated the original articles from scientists and their respective media coverage and found that only a small proportion had been grossly exaggerated by the media outlets (Bubela & Caulfield, 2004). While scientists of all disciplines sometimes overclaim, the consequences may be more severe when genetics researchers do so, given people's essentialist tendencies (Dar-Nimrod & Heine, 2011).

Reducing genetic essentialism

We have argued that genetic essentialism is a biased way of thinking that often yields negative consequences. This raises an important question: Can genetic essentialism be reduced? Are there ways of presenting genetics information that won't lead people to become overly fatalistic?

It would seem that a first problem with essentialism is that people have overly simplistic notions about genetic causes. Perhaps this comes from a high school curriculum where genes are frequently described in Mendelian terms, with each gene being matched with a corresponding phenotype. These simplistic causal stories lend themselves well for the deterministic thinking associated with essentialism. But, as noted above, this kind of genetic cause is the exception, not the rule, and there are very few human traits that are Mendelian (Jablonka & Lamb, 2006). For example, there is only one Mendelian trait (whether your earwax is wet or dry) out of the 60+ traits covered by the largest consumer genomics company, 23andme (Heine, 2017). For the most part, identified Mendelian traits in humans are limited to rare genetic diseases. The vast majority of human traits are the product of many genes interacting with themselves, an individual's experiences over a developmental trajectory, and whose expressions are further influenced by epigenetic markers (Chabris et al., 2015). This suggests that a more realistic understanding of genetics, in all its intricate richness, should be less associated with essentialist thinking.

There is evidence that more complex genetic causal accounts are associated with less essentialist thinking. For example, we provided participants with a vignette that described the violent behavior of a suspect, as well as some supposed research that investigated the etiology of violent behavior – these etiologies varied by condition, and were entirely fictitious (Cheung et al., 2017). Participants were then asked to evaluate the appropriateness of a diminished capacity defense. Replicating past research (Cheung & Heine, 2015), those who read about a simple genetic cause felt the diminished capacity defense was far more appropriate than those who read about no causes, or about the environmental cause. On the other hand, those who read more complex accounts of how genes relate to phenotypes were less likely to use the diminished capacity defense. This suggests that learning about the vast complexity of genotype–phenotype relationships may help reduce genetic essentialism.

Further evidence that essentialism is reduced by complex causal accounts can be seen in terms of the impact of genetics education on essentialism. Research finds that people who have taken more genetic courses (or who answer more items correct on a test of genetic knowledge) tend to show weaker genetic essentialism (Cheung et al., 2017). One international comparison of primary and secondary school teachers revealed that more biological training was associated with less of a tendency to appeal to innate and essentialist understandings of group differences (Castéra & Clément, 2014). In particular, research has found that genetics education that focuses on the interactive role of genes and experiences leads to a less deterministic understanding of genetic causes in comparison to a traditional Mendelian curriculum (Radick, 2016). These findings highlight that the more that people understand how genes actually operate, in all their intricate richness, the less likely they are to be vulnerable to essentialism.

Conclusion

People want to understand the social worlds they live in. One way to make sense of human behavior and diverse ethnic groups is to invoke genetic explanations. While research consistently shows that individual genes rarely predict human traits (Chabris et al., 2015), lay people often think in terms of genes as determining life outcomes. Sometimes, essentialist thinking is associated with increased tolerance for others, as found in research on attitudes toward homosexuality, criminal behavior, and mental illness, whereas in other domains essentialist thinking can be associated with increased racism, sexism, and support for eugenics. Given that genes are involved in virtually all human traits (Turkheimer, 2000), it is important to understand when and how encounters with genetic ideas will lead to essentialist thinking.

Most research on genetic essentialism has been conducted in Western industrialized societies and it remains to be seen to what extent other cultures tend to think in genetic essentialist ways (Dar-Nimrod & Heine, 2011). Although psychological essentialism occurs in many different cultures (e.g. Gil-White, 2001), some studies suggest that other cultures may show genetic essentialism to a lesser degree. For example, East Asians are more likely than Westerners to consider the situational context in evaluating the behavior of others (e.g. Choi, Nisbett, & Norenzayan, 1999), and tend to have more incremental views of self (Heine et al., 2001). One study found that when Chinese made predictions about the future of a person, they were less likely to consider biological information than Canadians were (Lee, 2009). In addition, people of lower socioeconomic status are less likely to make dispositional attributions in comparison with those of higher status (Kraus, Piff, Mendoza-Denton, Rheinschmidt, & Kelter, 2012). Research on genetic essentialism in other cultural groups would certainly be informative.

Genetics research is undoubtedly important. It may help cure diseases, aid in the production of safe food, and increase the quality of life in a variety of ways. On the other hand, an oversimplified picture of how genes work not only leads to genetic essentialism with all its negative consequences but it may also reduce the political desire to change environmental factors in the pursuit of political goals. For example, if people believe that school performance is determined by one's genetic endowment, then they will not see the benefit of allocating funds toward improving the school performance of disadvantaged groups. Likewise, overly focusing on genetic causes may redirect research funding away from studying the key role that people's experiences can have on life outcomes. It is important to attend to all of the kinds of influences on our lives.

Note

1 Quote from CNN interview, February 11, 2010. Retrieved on May 31, 2017 from www.cnn.com/2010/SHOWBIZ/02/11/donald.trump.marriage.apprentice/.

References

Applebaum, A. (2013, November 11). Anti-semite and Jew. *The New Yorker.* www.newyorker.com/magazine/2013/11/11/anti-semite-and-jew.

Aspinwall, L. G., Brown, T. R., & Tabery, J. (2012). The double-edged sword: Does bio-mechanism increase or decrease judges' sentencing of psychopaths? *Science, 337*(6096), 846–849.

Bailey, J. M., & Pillard, R. C. (1995). Genetics of human sexual orientation. *Annual Review of Sex Research, 6,* 126–150.

Berryessa, C. M. (2016). Judges' views on evidence of genetic contributions to mental disorders in court. *The Journal of Forensic Psychiatry & Psychology, 27,* 586–600.

Bogaert, A. F., & Skorska, M. (2011). Sexual orientation, fraternal birth order, and the maternal immune hypothesis: A review. *Frontiers in Neuroendocrinology, 32,* 247–254.

Brescoll, V., & LaFrance, M. (2004). The correlates and consequences of newspaper reports of research on sex differences. *Psychological Science, 15,* 515–520.

Bubela, T. M., & Caulfield, T. A. (2004). Do the print media "hype" genetic research? A comparison of newspaper stories and peer-reviewed research papers. *Canadian Medical Association Journal, 170,* 1399–1407. PMid: 15111473.

Chabris, C. F., Lee, J. J., Cesarini, D., Benjamin, D. J., & Laibson, D. I. (2015). The fourth law of behavior genetics. *Current Directions in Psychological Science, 24*(4), 304–312.

Cheung, B. Y., & Heine, S. J. (2015). The double-edged sword of genetic accounts of criminality: Causal attributions from genetic ascriptions affect legal decision making. *Personality and Social Psychology Bulletin, 41*(12), 1723–1738.

Cheung, B. Y., Schmalor, A., & Heine, S. J. (2018). *On genetic essentialism: Eugenic implications, and mitigation.* University of British Columbia. Unpublished data.

Choi, I., Nisbett, R., & Norenzayan, A. (1999). Causal attribution across cultures: Variation and universality. *Psychological Bulletin, 125,* 47–63.

Christensen, K. D., Jayaratne, T., Roberts, J., Kardia, S., & Petty, E. (2010). Understandings of basic genetics in the United States: Results from a national survey of black and white men and women. *Public Health Genomics, 13*(7–8), 467–476.

Comfort, N. (2012). *The science of human perfection.* New Haven, CT: Yale University Press.

Condit, C. M. (2010). Public understandings of genetics and health. *Clinical Genetics, 77,* 1–9.

Conrad, P. (2002). Genetics and behavior in the news: Dilemmas of a rising paradigm. In J. S. Alper, C. Ard, A. Asch, J. Beckwith, P. Conrad & L. N. Geller (Eds.), *The double-edged helix: Social implications of genetics in a diverse society.* Baltimore, MD: Johns Hopkins University Press.

Crandall, C. S. (1994). Prejudice against fat people: Ideology and self-interest. *Journal of Personality and Social Psychology, 66,* 882–894.

Dar-Nimrod, I., Heine, S. J., ★Cheung, B. Y., & Schaller, M. (2011). Do scientific theories affect men's evaluations of sex crimes? *Aggressive Behavior, 37,* 440–449.

Dar-Nimrod, I., Cheung, B. Y., Ruby, M. B., & Heine, S. J. (2014). Can merely learning about obesity genes lead to weight gain? *Appetite, 81,* 269–276.

Dar-Nimrod, I., & Heine, S. J. (2006, October 20). Exposure to scientific theories affects women's math performance. *Science, 314,* 435.

Dar-Nimrod, I, & Heine, S. J. (2011). Genetic essentialism: On the deceptive determinism of DNA. *Psychological Bulletin, 137*(5), 800–818.

Faraone, S. V. et al. (2008). Editorial: The new neuropsychiatric genetics. *American Journal of Medical Genetics Part B (Neuropsychiatric Genetics), 147B,* 1–2.

Frankena, W. K. (1939). The naturalistic fallacy. *Mind, 48,* 464–477. http://mind.oxford journals.org/ doi:10.1093/mind/XLVIII.192.464

Frias-Navarro, D., Monterde-i-Bort, H., Pascual-Soler, M., & Badenes-Ribera, L. (2015). Etiology of homosexuality and attitudes toward same-sex parenting: A randomized study. *The Journal of Sex Research, 52*(2), 151–161.

Gelman, S. A. (2003). *The essential child: Origins of essentialism in everyday thought.* New York, NY: Oxford University Press.

Gelman, S. A., & Taylor, M. G. (2000). Gender essentialism in cognitive development. In P. H. Miller, & S. E. Kofsky (Eds.), *Toward a feminist developmental psychology* (pp. 169–190). Florence, KY: Taylor & Francis/Routledge.

Gil-White, F. (2001). Are ethnic groups biological "species" to the human brain? Essentialism in human cognition of some social groups. *Current Anthropology, 42,* 515–554.

Gorondi, P. (2014, June 10). Anti-Semitic, far-right politician's astonishing transformation after finding out he is a Jew. *National Post*. http://news.nationalpost.com/2014/06/10/anti-semitic-far-right-politicians-astonishing-transformation-after-finding-out-he-is-a-jew/.

Haslam, N., Bastian, B., Bain, P., & Kashima, Y. (2006). Psychological essentialism, implicit theories, and intergroup relations. *Group Processes and Intergroup Relations, 9*, 63–76.

Haslam, N., Rothschild, L., & Ernst, D. (2000). Essentialist beliefs about social categories. *British Journal of Social Psychology, 39*, 113–127.

Hegarty, P., & Pratto, F. (2001). Sexual orientation beliefs: Their relationship to antigay attitudes and biological determinist arguments. *Journal of Homosexuality, 41*, 121–135.

Heine, S. J. (2017). *DNA is not destiny: The remarkable, completely misunderstood relationship between you and your genes.* New York, NY: W. W. Norton & Company.

Heine, S. J., Dar-Nimrod, I., Cheung, B. Y., & Proulx, T. (2017). Essentially biased: Why people are fatalistic about genes. In J. Olson (Ed.), *Advances in experimental social psychology* (Vol. 55, pp. 137–192). Cambridge, MA: Academic Press.

Heine, S. J., Kitayama, S., Lehman, D. R., Takata, T., Ide, E., Leung, C., & Matsumoto, H. (2001). Divergent consequences of success and failure in Japan and North America: An investigation of self-improving motivations and malleable selves. *Journal of Personality and Social Psychology, 81*, 599–615.

Henrich, J., Heine, S. J., & Norenzayan, A. (2010). The weirdest people in the world. *Behavioral and Brain Sciences, 33*, 61–83.

Jablonka, E., & Lamb, M. J. (2006). *Evolution in four dimensions: Genetic, epigenetic, behavioral, and symbolic variation in the history of life.* Cambridge, MA: MIT Press.

Jayaratne, T. E., Gelman, S., Feldbaum, M., Sheldon, J., Petty, E., & Kardia, S. (2009). The perennial debate: Nature, nurture, or choice? Black and White Americans' explanations for individual differences. *Review of General Psychology, 13*, 24–33.

Jayaratne, T. E., Ybarra, O., Sheldon, J. P., Brown, T. N., Feldbaum, M., Pfeffer, C. A., & Petty, E. M., (2006). White Americans' genetic lay theories of race differences and sexual orientation: Their relationship with prejudice toward Blacks and gay men and lesbians. *Group Processes and Intergroup Relations, 9*, 77–94.

Keil, F. (1989). *Concepts, kinds, and cognitive development.* Cambridge, MA: MIT Press.

Keller, J. (2005). In genes we trust: The biological component of psychological essentialism and its relationship to mechanisms of motivated social cognition. *Journal of Personality and Social Psychology, 88*, 686–702.

Kevles, D. H. (1985). *In the name of eugenics: Genetics and the uses of human heredity.* Berkeley: University of California Press.

Kimel, S. Y., Huesmann, R., Kunst, J. R., & Halperin, E. (2016). Living in a genetic world: How learning about interethnic genetic similarities and differences affects peace and conflict. *Personality and Social Psychology Bulletin, 42*(5), 688–700.

Kraus, M. W., Piff, P. K., Mendoza-Denton, R., Rheinschmidt, M. L., & Kelter, D. (2012). Social class, solipsism, and contextualism: How the rich are different from the poor. *Psychological Review, 119*, 546–572.

Kvaale, E. P., Gottdiener, W. H., & Haslam, N. (2013). Biogenetic explanations and stigma: A meta-analytic review of associations among laypeople. *Social Science & Medicine, 96*, 95–103.

Lebowitz, M. S., & Ahn, W. -K. (2014). Effects of biological explanations for mental disorders on clinicians' empathy. *Proceedings of the National Academy of Sciences, 111*, 17786–17790.

Lee, A. (2009). *The book of life in the double helix: Cultural differences in biological beliefs.* Unpublished master's thesis, Queens University, Kingston, ON, Canada.

Ludmerer, K. M. (1972). *Genetics and American society: A historical appraisal* (p. 34). Baltimore, MD: Johns Hopkins University Press.

Medin, D. L., & Ortony, A. (1989). Comments on Part I: Psychological essentialism. In S. Vosniadou & A. Ortony (Eds.), *Similarity and analogical reasoning* (pp. 179–195). New York, NY: Cambridge University Press.

Meehl, P. E. (1977). Specific etiology and other forms of strong influence: Some quantitative meanings. *The Journal of Medicine and Philosophy, 2,* 33–53. Retrieved from http://jmp.oxfordjournals.org/.

Mehta, S., & Farina, A. (1997). Is being 'sick' really better? Effect of the disease view of mental disorder on stigma. *Journal of Social & Clinical Psychology, 16,* 405–419.

Miller, D. I., & Halpern, D. F. (2014). The new science of cognitive sex differences. *Trends in Cognitive Sciences, 18,* 37–45.

Monterosso, J., Royzman, E. B., & Schwartz, B. (2005). Explaining away responsibility: Effects of scientific explanation on perceived culpability. *Ethics and Behavior, 15,* 139–158.

Organisation for Economic Co-operation and Development. (2004, February 22). Health at a glance: OECD indicators 2003: Chart 8. Increasing obesity rates among the adult population in OECD countries. Retrieved May 24, 2017, from www.oecd.org/LongAbstract/0,2546,en_2649_201185_16361657_1_1_1_1,00.html.

Paul, D. B. (1995). *Controlling human heredity: 1865 to the present.* New York, NY: Humanity Books.

Phelan, J. C., Cruz-Rojas, R., & Reiff, M. (2002). Genes and stigma: The connection between perceived genetic etiology and attitudes and beliefs about mental illness. *Psychiatric Rehabilitation Skills, 6,* 159–185. Retrieved from http://journalseek.net/cgi bin/journalseek/journalsearch.cgi?field"issn&query"1097–3435.

Phelan, J. C., Yang, L. H., & Cruz-Rojas, Rr. (2006). Effects of attributing serious mental illnesses to genetic causes on orientations to treatment. *Psychiatric Services, 57,* 382–387.

Puhl, J. (2014, April 3). Metamorphosis: A Hungarian extremist explores his Jewish roots. *Der Spiegel.* www.spiegel.de/international/europe/a-hungarian-right-wing-extremist-explores-his-jewish-roots-a-962156.html.

Radick, G. (2016). Teach students the biology of their time. *Nature, 533,* 293.

Rips, L. I. (1989). Similarity, typicality, and categorization. In S. Vosniadou & A. Ortony (Eds.), *Similarity and analogical reasoning* (pp. 21–59). New York, NY: Cambridge University Press.

Rosenberg, N. A., Pritchard, J. K., Weber, J. L., Cann, H. M., Field, K. K., Zhivotovsky, L. A., & Feldman, M. A. (2002). Genetic structure of human populations. *Science, 298,* 2381–2385.

Roth, W. D., & Lyon, K. (2016). Genetic ancestry tests and race: Who takes them, why, and how do they affect racial identities? In K. Suzuki & D. von Vacano (Eds.), *Reconsidering Race: Cross-Disciplinary and Interdisciplinary Approaches.* New York, NY: Oxford University Press.

Rothbart, M., & Taylor, M. (1992). Category labels and social reality: Do we view social categories as natural kinds? In G. R. S. Semin & K. Fiedler (Eds.), *Language, interaction and social cognition* (pp. 11–36). Newbury Park, CA: Sage.

Sanders, A. R. et al. (2015). Genome-wide scan demonstrates significant linkage for male sexual orientation. *Psychological Medicine, 45,* 1379–1388.

Schmalor, A., Cheung, B. Y., & Heine, S. J. (2017). Genetic attributions and ethnic stereotypes. University of British Columbia. Unpublished data.

Schnittker, J. (2008). An uncertain revolution: Why the rise of a genetic model of mental illness has not increased tolerance. *Social Science & Medicine, 67*, 1370–1381.

Spencer, S. J., Steele, C. M., & Quinn, D. M. (1999). Stereotype threat and women's math performance. *Journal of Experimental Social Psychology, 35*, 4–28.

Templeton, A. R. (2013). Biological races in humans. *Studies in History and Philosophy of Science Part C: Studies in History and Philosophy of Biological and Biomedical Sciences, 44*, 262–271.

Turkheimer, E. (2000). Three laws of behavioral genetics and what they mean. *Current Directions in Psychological Science, 9*, 160–164.

Wade, N. (2014). *A troublesome inheritance.* New York, NY: Penguin Press.

10

POST-TRUTH, ANTI-TRUTH, AND CAN'T-HANDLE-THE-TRUTH

How responses to science are shaped by concerns about its impact

Robbie M. Sutton, Aino Petterson, and Bastiaan T. Rutjens

Introduction

People generally report positive attitudes to science and scientists (Gauchat, 2012). It is valued for the contribution that it makes to social, cultural, and economic progress. For many people, indeed, faith in science is akin to religious faith and may serve some of the same psychological functions (Rutjens, van Harreveld, & van der Pligt, 2013). Science is supported by investments of large sums of money; according to World Bank statistics, fully 2% of global gross domestic product (GDP) is spent on research and development, and the richer the country, the higher this proportion grows (The World Bank, 2018). But, paradoxically, science is also frequently opposed: scientific findings and conclusions are censored and suppressed, whereas scientists are silenced, harassed, surveilled, sanctioned, and even persecuted.

Examples abound. Columbia University now hosts a website containing multiple instances (since November 2016) in which authorities have censored, obstructed, or misrepresented scientific research – and where scientists have censored their own work or that of their colleagues (Columbia Law School, 2018). Just as happened with the election of Steven Harper in Canada (The Professional Institute of the Public Service of Canada, 2013), the censorial and obstructive policy position toward climate science in the United States seems to have stemmed from the election of Donald J. Trump and his appointment of Scott Pruitt, a vocal critic of climate science and frequent litigator against the Environmental Protection Agency (EPA) as the head of that same agency (Chiacu & Volcovici, 2017; McKie, 2017; Nuccitelli, 2017). Also in 2017, the Turkish government completely removed evolution from the curriculum of 9th graders, with the explicit aim of introducing a more "value-based curriculum" (Frayer & Saracoglu, 2017). In recent years, prominent scientists have complained about being targeted by online abuse, legal complaints, vexatious and repeated freedom of information requests, and dubious re-analyses of data designed to delay, censor, and alter the interpretation of published findings. These findings span not only climate change but also other controversial topics such as false memory and child abuse (Lewandowsky, Mann, Bauld, Hastings, & Loftus, 2013; Lewandowsky, Mann, Brown, & Friedman, 2016). Indeed, opposition to science is not the preserve of right-wing and religious groups. Whatever the scientific merits of Herrnstein and Murray's research on racial differences in IQ, it has been described in published academic papers as "crude and dangerous" (Gillborn, 2016, p. 365) and has been silenced by no-platform and other aggressive tactics on university campuses (Beinart, 2017), echoing the campus attacks on Edward O. Wilson in the 1960s (Wilson, 1995). Of course, the perception that scientific research can be dangerous and needs to be silenced and shut down is not new, and stems back (at least) to the persecution of Galileo Galilei, whose frank observations of planetary movements threatened the view that the earth is the center of the cosmos – and by implication, an entire edifice of theology and power (Dreger, 2015).

What explains this perennial opposition to science? There is surprisingly little research on this question, despite a long and strong tradition of research into motivated skepticism about scientific findings (for reviews, see Hornsey & Fielding, 2017; Rutjens, Heine, Sutton, & van Harreveld, 2018). There is an urgent need for such research because opposition to science threatens scientific, and therefore social and economic progress, and appears to be gathering pace in an era of declining support for democratic and enlightenment values. To be sure, motivated skepticism about science is an important phenomenon: for example, it causes people to leave themselves and their children unprotected from preventable diseases and encourages them to make personal and political choices that degrade the environment (Rutjens et al., 2018). But as much as motivated skepticism matters, it has no chance to operate when scientific advances are censored or prevented from happening in the first place. Nor, in this case, does anyone have the opportunity to make choices informed by their own reading of the evidence. Thus, people's preferences for policies that support versus oppose science may be at least as important as their attitudes toward science itself.

In this chapter, we outline some preliminary theoretical and empirical groundwork for the systematic study of opposition to science. Our core proposal is that people not only doubt the facts produced by some scientific investigations but that they also perceive them as a threat to collective interests. In turn, this perception motivates cognitive and behavioral responses that serve to neutralize the threat. Such responses include motivated skepticism since findings are less likely to have impact if they are not believed. They also include motivated opposition to science since findings are less likely to have impact if they remain obscure, are prevented from informing policy, or from happening at all.

Why science seems dangerous

We suggest that science seems dangerous because it is designed to disrupt the constraints of other methods of establishing and sharing knowledge. Communication is normally governed by conventions designed to preserve social relationships, including harmony and hierarchy. Although politeness takes different forms in different cultures, politeness itself is pancultural, and in every culture, it mandates that one should be more formal and less frank with strangers and social superiors (Brown & Gilman, 1960). One of the main aims of normal communication is to establish a common ground of understanding between communicators (Clark, 1992), and ultimately, a shared cultural reality within a cultural ingroup (Echterhoff, Higgins, & Levine, 2009). Thus, people tend to inhibit the expression of ideas that deviate from normative understandings of reality (e.g. Kashima, 2000a, 2000b; Toma & Butera, 2009) and react negatively when these ideas are shared too openly. For instance, Klar and Bilewicz (2017; see also Bilewicz, 2016) found that group members' belief in the accuracy of their ingroup's historical narrative motivates individuals to act as lay censors of historical accounts that run counter to this "official" account. People also inhibit other ideas out of paternalistic concern for the harm they may do to their audience. Thus, we are normally expected to refrain from telling people exactly what it is about their intellect, appearance, or character that we find unattractive. Hate speech is explicitly banned in many countries and frowned upon in most others. Research on the third-person effect (Davison, 1983) shows that in the domain of mass communication, people perceive that advertising, pornography, and propaganda may exert an undesirable influence on others, if not themselves. The more they perceive it to harm others, the more they support censorship of this material (Chung & Moon, 2016; Davison, 1983; Douglas & Sutton, 2004, 2008).

If normal human communication is polite and strategically economical with the truth, science in its ideal form is supposed to be impersonal and mercilessly frank. Put differently, perceptions of reality should be dictated by science in its ideal form, rather than perceptions of reality shaping which science to accept and which to reject. Results should be reported regardless of what people generally believe or prefer to believe, and no matter what their implications for social harmony and hierarchy. Instead of carefully editing their message to suit their own or others' interests, researchers hand over control of their message to the vicissitudes of their data. The studies they conduct are rolls of the dice, and like oracles or soothsayers (a Middle English term, first recorded in Kent, which means one who speaks the truth), they are formally obliged to convey the results.

Freeing science from the conventions of ordinary communication has been crucial to its success in freeing our understanding of the world from the shackles of prejudice and superstition. But science is not completely free, and its freedom is viewed with suspicion and resentment. Indeed, popular representations of science often cast it as dangerous, immoral, or pernicious (see Rutjens & Heine, 2016). Haynes (2003) examined cultural representations of scientists in Western literature and film, and identified several pernicious stereotypes. Frankenstein is an example of an "inhuman researcher" who puts aside normal human emotions such as empathy in the single-minded pursuit of knowledge and mastery of nature. In other works, scientists are represented as "foolish" and "helpless" – unduly ready to make far-reaching decisions on the basis of a few scientific observations and unable to predict or control their inventions. In *Jurassic Park*, genetically engineered dinosaurs run amok, much to the surprise and chagrin of the scientists who created them; in *Terminator*, the same is true of an artificially intelligent defense system that becomes sentient. Scientists are also sometimes represented straightforwardly as "mad, bad, and dangerous" (dangerous in particular still resonates with public opinion; Rutjens & Heine, 2016), like the nuclear scientist Dr Strangelove in Stanley Kubrick's film.

We suggest that motivated doubt and opposition to science are best understood within a *social functionalist* perspective on motivated cognition (Tetlock, 2002). This theoretical perspective, like other accounts of motivated cognition, assumes that when people think, feel, and act, they are pursuing goals – in other words, that human psychology should be understood in functionalist terms. However, other accounts of motivated cognition are concerned with essentially intrapsychic functions: people's thoughts, feelings, and actions are designed to make them feel better about themselves, that they are in control of the world, or that they have a stable working understanding of reality (Kruglanski, 1990; Kunda, 1990; Landau, Kay, & Whitson, 2015). Research on attitudes to science has, thus far, concerned itself largely with intrapsychic motives, for example on how people are skeptical of scientific research when it contradicts their beliefs about a topic (Lord, Ross, & Lepper, 1979) or threatens their self-image (Bastardi, Uhlmann, & Ross, 2011), their sense of personal optimism (Ditto & Lopez, 1992) or their moral (Colombo, Bucher, & Inbar, 2016) and ideological (Washburn & Skitka, 2017) convictions. In contrast, Tetlock's (2002) social functionalist account is concerned with the "social functions of thought," and posits that motivated cognition can be understood only in terms of the "embeddedness of human beings in relations with other people, institutions, and the broader political and cultural environment" [35: p. 452]. This perspective assumes that the pursuit of collective goals, including social order, requires people to think, feel, and act in certain ways – ways that enable them to cope effectively with the demands of living in complex interdependent collectives. These demands include the ability to hold others accountable for actions that may threaten collective interests, and to cope with being held accountable by others. Note that the distinction made between intrapsychic motives and Tetlock's social functionalist account is not definite since any ideological or morality-based motivations likely incorporate both (e.g. Washburn & Skitka, 2017), and these are often difficult to tease apart (Tetlock & Manstead, 1985). Nonetheless, most work on attitudes to science, and especially the classic work, was informed by cognitive consistency accounts of confirmation bias (e.g. Lord et al., 1979), with limited attention devoted to the wider social functions of this bias.

Within this overarching perspective, Tetlock (2002) proposed three theoretical models detailing ways in which social functionalism plays out. People function as *intuitive theologians*, defending sacred values such as shared moral foundations, ideological assumptions, and binding myths from ideas and evidence that contradict them. Data and ideas that contradict these sacred values, which might include egalitarian ideals about racial equality or fundamentalist beliefs about the incontrovertible truth of the Bible, are rejected. When people's concerns about the potential impact of research lead them to cast doubts on its veracity and to support censorship, they are acting as intuitive theologians. Second, people function as *intuitive prosecutors*, defending rules and regimes that they perceive as legitimate. This includes finding blame and supporting efforts to punish those who pose a threat to these regimes. When people oppose research by favoring censorship, defunding, and sanctions, they are acting as intuitive prosecutors. Third, when their own actions may be under the spotlight, they function as *intuitive politicians*, and think, feel, and act in ways that protect and enhance desired impressions of themselves. People may do this by appealing to cherry-picked scientific findings that support their chosen attitude or policy position while casting doubt on other findings.

Note that scientists and their work are not passive in these processes. Social functionalism is a ubiquitous feature of social cognition and motivation and is also displayed by scientists themselves. Researchers function as intuitive politicians when they selectively pursue research questions, choose methods, and report results to avoid controversy or accrue available rewards (Ioannidis, 2012; but see also Nosek et al., 2015). They act as intuitive prosecutors when they call out fellow researchers who produce work that they perceive as potentially harmful (e.g. Dominus, 2017). In such cases, the concern is generally not paternalistic concern for impacts on the public, or concern about dangerous technologies, but harms to the integrity of the scientific community and its members (e.g. the misdirection of theory and effort by inauthentic findings). They act as intuitive theologians when their moral and political preferences affect their selection of research questions, methods, analyses, and interpretations (Duarte et al., 2015; Jussim, Crawford, Anglin, Stevens, & Duarte, 2016). Indeed, Jussim, Stevens, and Honeycutt (2018; see also Stevens, Jussim, Anglin, & Honeycutt, 2018) argued that many questions concerning the accuracy of stereotypes remain unasked in part because researchers fear the negative impact that certain findings could have on stigmatized groups.

Impact, science skepticism, and censorial responses to science

Viewed from a social functionalist perspective, skepticism and opposition to research are motivated by concerns about the potential impact of scientific findings on collective interests. Studies should show, therefore, that this concern affects responses to scientific research over and above the effect of intrapsychic motivations such as the confirmation bias. We (Sutton, Lee, & Hartley, 2018) put this hypothesis to the test in the context of pregnant women's alcohol consumption during pregnancy. Although there is some evidence that high levels of prenatal alcohol exposure are associated with risks to children's cognitive development (Flak et al., 2014; but see also Henderson, Kesmodel, & Gray, 2007), meta-analytic studies have found no harmful effects of low or moderate levels (Flak et al., 2014; Henderson, Gray, & Brocklehurst, 2007). Some studies even show the opposite trend: children who have been exposed to low or moderate levels of alcohol during pregnancy demonstrate higher intelligence later compared to those who had no prenatal alcohol exposure (Humphriss, Hall, May, Zuccolo, & Macleod, 2013; Lewis et al., 2012). Nonetheless, public opinion flies in the face of this evidence: there appears to be a consensus that exposure to even small amounts of alcohol during pregnancy poses a risk to a child's cognitive development (Murphy, Sutton, Douglas, & McClellan, 2011).

As we shall see below, this might be understood partly as a result of biased and censorious coverage of relevant science in the media (Lowe, Lee, & Yardley, 2010), and in advice and communiques issued by official agencies who are explicitly concerned that women do not become confused about how much might be safe to consume (Gavaghan, 2009). Thus, the departure of public opinion from the evidence may not reflect the operation of psychological mechanisms. Sutton, Lee and Hartley (2018), however, also examined whether impact bias might motivate skepticism even when people are exposed to accurate coverage of scientific findings. We presented experimental groups of participants with the results of a (real) cohort study (Lewis et al., 2012) that found 8-year-old children had significantly higher IQs if their mothers had consumed low-to-moderate amounts of alcohol during pregnancy (vs. if they had abstained completely from alcohol). Control groups were presented with a fictional variant of the study in which milk, rather than alcohol, was the substance that mothers had consumed (Study 1), or in which the actual results of the study were reversed, indicating that children had lower IQs if their mothers drank moderately (Study 2).

Sutton, Lee, and Hartley (2018) found evidence of impact bias: as predicted, participants in the experimental groups systematically and consistently devalued the research. They perceived its methods and its results to be less reliable and convincing than did control participants. Crucially, participants also indicated that they thought the findings of the actual research (i.e. children whose mothers drank alcohol were more intelligent) would be bad for mothers, children, and society, whereas the fictional findings (drinking milk led to higher IQs or drinking alcohol lead to lower IQs) would be good for them (responses were significantly different from mid-point in contrasting directions). Results indicated that these perceptions of impact mediated the effect of the putative study results: participants saw the actual findings as more dangerous than the fictional findings, and subsequently were more skeptical of them. Perceptions of impact also appeared to mediate other interesting responses to the alcohol-during-pregnancy studies: people were less likely to interpret the actual effect in causal terms and were more likely to ascribe it to some confound (e.g. mothers who drank more were higher in socio-economic status – a finding actually observed in the original study by Lewis et al., 2012). These findings also held when prior beliefs about the effects of prenatal exposure to alcohol (or milk) on child IQ were adjusted for. These prior beliefs had a large effect consistent with the confirmation bias, but over and above this effect, perceptions of impact accounted for differential reactions to the research.

Sutton et al.'s (2018) findings also indicate that as we have proposed, people are also motivated to adopt obstructive, censorial, and even punitive responses to science that they perceive as dangerous. In these studies, participants opposed the funding, dissemination, and application of studies showing that alcohol may be associated with higher child IQ. They also tended to show some desire to see the scientists responsible for the research to be disciplined. In contrast, on the same measures, they supported the fictional studies in which drinking milk led to higher child IQ or drinking alcohol led to lower child IQ. Once more, these effects were mediated by the perceived impact of the research. Participants seemed motivated to protect society from dangerous scientific results by not only casting doubt on these results but also supporting measures to prevent similar results from seeing the light of day, including censorship and punishment of researchers.

Scientists are not merely censored by authorities but also censor their own work. This is especially apparent in studies that touch upon controversial topics such as climate change, where researchers are careful to manage their terminology and draw causal conclusions from their data to protect their funding (Hersher, 2017). Scientists report that fear of negative reactions both from the public and fellow researchers influence what they study and how they report findings (Kempner, Perlis, & Merz, 2005). Seen through Tetlock's (2002) social functionalist perspective, scientists therefore act as intuitive politicians, managing accountability demands by strategically presenting their work to the world.

Alcohol consumption during pregnancy is controversial topic surrounded, as we have seen, by concerns about the impact of the research. Lee, Sutton, and Hartley (2016) analyzed media coverage of Lewis et al.'s (2012) study into child intelligence and maternal drinking during pregnancy. Lee et al. (2016) found that the researchers played an important role in media misrepresentations of their work. One of its key and most incendiary findings – that mothers who drank some (vs. no) alcohol had more intelligent children – was reported in the article. However, Lewis et al. (2012) attributed this result to a socio-demographic confound (expectant mothers were less likely to abstain from alcohol if they were older, more educated, or higher income), despite running no analysis adjusting for this confound. More strikingly, the press release issued by the researchers' institution made no mention of this result (University of Bristol, 2012). Instead, it contained a quote from the senior researcher to the effect that the study's results gave grounds for women not to drink during pregnancy. Only a third of the subsequent media stories mentioned the empirical relationship between maternal drinking and child intelligence, and of those, two-thirds reversed the direction of the effect, stating that mothers who abstained had less intelligent children. A near-universal theme in the coverage was that women should abstain from alcohol. These misrepresentations were not entirely media inventions but could be traced back to the scientific paper and especially the press release. Scientists commonly complain that their work is misrepresented because of the sensationalism, political agenda, and scientific illiteracy of media outlets. The analysis by Lee et al. illustrates that scientists may also be involved in misrepresenting their work.

Participants' responses to the target studies presented by Sutton, Lee and Hartley (2018) reflect a consensus that if these studies lead pregnant women to drink alcohol, this would be a bad outcome. In contrast, the value attached to other impacts of research may differ markedly across participants, which is in line with more general notions derived from work on the ideological-conflict hypothesis (Brandt et al., 2014). Liberals, for example, are likely to loathe the idea that a scientific finding could lend support to the death penalty, or undermine permissive immigration policies by indicating that immigration undermines neighborhood cohesion. Conservatives, in contrast, are likely to view both of these outcomes rather favorably.

McConnell and Sutton (2018) tested this possibility and examined whether these politically loaded perceptions of impact also produce impact bias effects. Similar to Washburn and Skitka (2017; see also Kahan, 2013; Skitka & Washburn, 2016), they showed that participants on both sides of the left-right political spectrum were skeptical of research that contradicted their views. In line with Sutton, Lee and Hartley (2018), they showed that this effect was mediated by the perception that politically uncongenial findings could be harmful to society. Indeed, McConnell and Sutton (2018) observed the third-person effect in relation to politically uncongenial findings: liberals thought that conservative-friendly policies would have larger effects on others than themselves, and perceptions of impact on others, rather than the self, were related to skepticism. Furthermore, as observed by Sutton et al. (2018), McConnell and Sutton found that perceptions of harmful impacts also mediated between the political congeniality of research results and censorious and punitive responses to the research.

One limitation of these studies is that they use correlational methods to isolate the effects of perceived harmful consequences of research (impact bias) from effects of contradictions of prior beliefs (confirmation bias). It is possible, in principle, to manipulate perceived impact orthogonally to prior beliefs about a research topic. Campbell and Kay (2014) took such an approach in their study of politically motivated skepticism about climate science. It is well documented that conservatives tend to be more skeptical of climate science than liberals. This has been explained in terms of various motivations such as higher national- rather than global-level identification (Devine-Wright, Price, & Leviston, 2015), system justification (Hennes, Hampton, Ozgumus, & Hamor,

2018; see also Feygina, Jost, & Goldsmith, 2010), dominance motives (Jylhä, Cantal, Akrami, & Milfont, 2016), and endorsement of free-market ideology (Lewandowsky, Gignac, & Oberauer, 2013), but in line with the latter finding of Campbell and Kay (2014) suggested that it might be motivated by *solution aversion*: typically, measures proposed to mitigate climate change involve government intervention in the form of taxes and regulation. When Campbell and Kay (2014) presented free-market solutions to participants, in the form of private-sector innovations in energy technology, conservatives indicated no more skepticism about climate change than liberals. This finding indicates that concern about the policy impact of climate science motivates climate skepticism: people doubt climate science if it looks like it will lead to unwanted policy outcomes.

Scientific malpractice and conspiracy

In their social functionalist role as intuitive prosecutors, people are more punitive toward harmdoers whose actions are intentional. Indeed, people prefer to perceive harmdoing as intentional insofar as it enables collectives to exert control over negative outcomes by blaming, punishing, and incapacitating wrongdoers (McClure, Hilton, & Sutton, 2007). This suggests that findings that are seen as dangerous are more likely to be seen as the product of intentional wrongdoing, rather than an innocent mistake or incompetence. It also suggests that once represented as intentional wrongdoing, science is much more likely to be opposed.

We have obtained preliminary evidence for both of these suggestions. McConnell and Sutton (2018) found that people on both the left and right sides of the political spectrum tended to perceive ideologically uncongenial results as the product of a conspiracy by researchers. In another line of work, we (Sutton, Douglas, & Petterson, 2018) found that after adjusting for skepticism about climate change, belief in conspiracy theories about climate science (e.g. that scientists exaggerate the danger of climate science to secure funding) predicted support for the censorship, surveillance, and punishment of climate scientists. In a subsequent experiment, we found that experimentally exposing participants to these conspiracy theories increased their opposition to climate science on the same measures.

Conspiracy theories explain socially significant phenomena as the outcome of covert plots, generally orchestrated by powerful elites to serve their own interests (Douglas, Sutton, & Cichocka, 2017). Conspiracy theories surround several topics of scientific inquiry, most famously vaccination and climate change. Conspiracy theories are widespread in the general population, with over a third of Americans agreeing that "global warming is a hoax" in a recent survey (Jensen, 2013). Conspiracy theories about science are not a peculiarly American or conservative problem: Bessi et al. (2015) found that conspiracy content with anti-science messages was shared among Italian Facebook users about three times as often as scientific content. Their relation to skepticism about scientific research is well established and is likely bidirectional: implausible findings fuel conspiracy beliefs, and conspiracy beliefs fuel skepticism (Lewandowsky, Oberauer, & Gignac, 2013; see also Lewandowsky, Gignac, & Oberauer, 2013) while exposure to conspiracy theories has been found to reduce inclination to vaccinate one's children and mitigate climate change (Jolley & Douglas, 2014; van der Linden, 2015). However, conspiracy theories may also provide a powerful impetus to anti-science politics – beyond the tendency for political leaders and spokespeople to merely cast doubt on or ignore scientific findings.

Conclusion

In this chapter, we have reviewed anecdotal and empirical evidence that skepticism and efforts to suppress scientific findings are motivated by concerns about their societal impact. We have attempted to lay the groundwork for further theory and research by suggesting that these phenomena are best understood from a social functionalist perspective. In this perspective, people act, think, and feel not only to satisfy internal motivations such as cognitive consistency but also to achieve social objectives. Our recent work illustrates that these phenomena can be approached with established methods for studying support for censorship and motivated skepticism of science. Much more specific theoretical work is needed to uncover the specific mechanisms that lead scientific findings to be perceived as harmful. This work might draw on advances in moral reasoning and the perception of harm (Graham, Haidt, & Nosek, 2009; Gray, Schein, & Ward, 2014). A critical question is whether judgments of harmfulness may themselves be rationalizations of opposition to research that are motivated by other moral concerns, such as perceived purity violations (cf. Graham et al., 2009), or more parochial concerns such as the perceived interests of the self or a relevant ingroup. Another critical question is what (exactly) different types of scientific research is perceived to harm – an abstract conception such as society, or specific constituencies within society – and whether this affects the degree and form of opposition to science. Further theoretical work is also required to understand boundary conditions – notably, when people perceive scientific findings to have potentially dangerous impacts but nonetheless do not support efforts to suppress them or to punish researchers.

Science is routinely and quite appropriately judged according to the good that it can do us (Massey & Barreras, 2013). Funders consider not only the scientific but also the social and economic value of research. Ethics panels, before they approve research, weigh its scientific benefits against the potential harms to its participants. The phenomena we have examined in this chapter, however, are different. They pose a threat to the integrity of science, and – ironically – to its contribution to society. There is an urgent need for research to examine the apparently all-too-common perception that science is a danger that must be counteracted. As long as science is perceived as a danger, we are prone to letting belief systems and ideologies dictate how science is judged rather than letting science shape how we should perceive reality.

References

Bastardi, A., Uhlmann, E. L., & Ross, L. (2011). Wishful thinking: Belief, desire, and the motivated evaluation of scientific evidence. *Psychological Science, 22*(6), 731–732. doi:10.1177/0956797611406447.

Beinart, P. (2017, March 6). A violent attack on free speech at Middlebury. *The Atlantic.* Retrieved from www.theatlantic.com/politics/archive/2017/03/middlebury-free-speech-violence/518667/.

Bessi, A., Coletto, M., Davidescu, G. A., Scala, A., Caldarelli, G., & Quattrociocchi, W. (2015). Science vs conspiracy: Collective narratives in the age of misinformation. *PloS One, 10*(2), e0118093. doi:10.1371/journal.pone.0118093.

Bilewicz, M. (2016). The dark side of emotion regulation: Historical defensiveness as an obstacle in reconciliation. *Psychological Inquiry, 27*(2), 89–95. doi:10.1080/10478 40x.2016.1162130.

Brandt, M. J., Reyna, C., Chambers, J., Crawford, J., & Wetherell, G. (2014). The ideological-conflict hypothesis: Intolerance among both liberals and conservatives. *Current Directions in Psychological Science, 23*, 27–34.

Brown, R., & Gilman, A. (1960). The pronouns of power and solidarity. In T. A. Sebeok (Ed.), *Style in language* (pp. 253–276). Cambridge: MIT Press.

Campbell, T. H., & Kay, A. C. (2014). Solution aversion: On the relation between ideology and motivated disbelief. *Journal of Personality and Social psychology, 107*(5), 809–824. doi:10.1037/a0037963.

Chiacu, D., & Volcovici, V. (2017, March 19). EPA chief unconvinced on CO_2 link to global warming. *Reuters.* Retrieved from www.reuters.com/article/us-usa-epa-pruitt/epa-chief-unconvinced-on-co2-link-to-global-warming-idUSKBN16G1XX.

Chung, S., & Moon, S. I. (2016). Is the third-person effect real? A critical examination of rationales, testing methods, and previous findings of the third-person effect on censorship attitudes. *Human Communication Research, 42*(2), 312–337. doi:10.1111/hcre.12078.

Clark, H. H. (1992). *Arenas of language use.* Stanford, CA and Chicago, IL: Center for the Study of Language & Information.

Colombo, M., Bucher, L., & Inbar, Y. (2016). Explanatory judgment, moral offense and value-free science. *Review of Philosophy and Psychology, 7*(4), 743–763. doi:10.1007/s13164-015-0282-z.

Columbia Law School. Sabin Center for Climate Change Law. (2018). Silencing science tracker. Retrieved from http://columbiaclimatelaw.com/resources/silencing-science-tracker/about/.

Davison, W. P. (1983). The third-person effect in communication. *Public Opinion Quarterly, 47*(1), 1–15. doi:10.1086/268763.

Devine-Wright, P., Price, J., & Leviston, Z. (2015). My country or my planet? Exploring the influence of multiple place attachments and ideological beliefs upon climate change attitudes and opinions. *Global Environmental Change, 30*, 68–79. doi:10.1016/j.gloenvcha.2014.10.012.

Ditto, P. H., & Lopez, D. F. (1992). Motivated skepticism: Use of differential decision criteria for preferred and nonpreferred conclusions. *Journal of Personality and Social Psychology, 63*(4), 568. doi:10.1037/0022-3514.63.4.568.

Dominus, S. (2017, October 18). When the revolution came for Amy Cuddy. *The New York Times Magazine.* Retrieved from www.nytimes.com/2017/10/18/magazine/when-the-revolution-came-for-amy-cuddy.html.

Douglas, K. M., & Sutton, R. M. (2004). Right about others, wrong about ourselves? Actual and perceived self-other differences in resistance to persuasion. *British Journal of Social Psychology, 43*(4), 585–603. doi:10.1348/0144666042565416.

Douglas, K. M., & Sutton, R. M. (2008). The hidden impact of conspiracy theories: Perceived and actual influence of theories surrounding the death of Princess Diana. *The Journal of Social Psychology, 148*(2), 210–222. doi:10.3200/socp.148.2.210-222.

Douglas, K. M., Sutton, R. M., & Cichocka, A. (2017). The psychology of conspiracy theories. *Current Directions in Psychological Science, 26*(6), 538–542. doi:10.1177/096372 1417718261.

Dreger, A. (2015). *Galileo's middle finger: Heretics, activists and the search for justice in science.* New York, NY: Penguin Group.

Duarte, J. L., Crawford, J. T., Stern, C., Haidt, J., Jussim, L., & Tetlock, P. E. (2015). Political diversity will improve social psychological science. *Behavioral and Brain Sciences, 38*, 1–58. doi:10.1017/s0140525x14000430.

Echterhoff, G., Higgins, E. T., & Levine, J. M. (2009). Shared reality: Experiencing commonality with others' inner states about the world. *Perspectives on Psychological Science, 4*(5), 496–521. doi:10.1111/j.1745-6924.2009.01161.x.

Feygina, I., Jost, J. T., & Goldsmith, R. E. (2010). System justification, the denial of global warming, and the possibility of "system-sanctioned change". *Personality and Social Psychology Bulletin, 36*(3), 326–338. doi:10.1177/0146167209351435.

Flak, A. L., Su, S., Bertrand, J., Denny, C. H., Kesmodel, U. S., & Cogswell, M. E. (2014). The association of mild, moderate, and binge prenatal alcohol exposure and child neuropsychological outcomes: A meta-analysis. *Alcoholism: Clinical and Experimental Research, 38*(1), 214–226. doi:10.1111/acer.12214.

Frayer, L., & Saracoglu, G. (2017, August 20). In Turkey, schools will stop teaching evolution this fall. *National Public Radio.* Retrieved from www.npr.org/sections/paral lels/2017/08/20/540965889/in-turkey-schools-will-stop-teaching-evolution-this-fall.

Gauchat, G. (2012). Politicization of science in the public sphere: A study of public trust in the United States, 1974 to 2010. *American Sociological Review, 77*(2), 167–187. doi:10.1177/0003122412438225.

Gavaghan, C. (2009). "You can't handle the truth": Medical paternalism and prenatal alcohol use. *Journal of Medical Ethics, 35*(5), 300–303. doi:10.1136/jme.2008.028662.

Gillborn, D. (2016). Softly, softly: Genetics, intelligence and the hidden racism of the new geneism. *Journal of Education Policy, 31*(4), 365–388. doi:10.1080/02680939.2016.1139189.

Graham, J., Haidt, J., & Nosek, B. A. (2009). Liberals and conservatives rely on different sets of moral foundations. *Journal of Personality and Social Psychology, 96*(5), 1029. doi:10.1037/a0015141.

Gray, K., Schein, C., & Ward, A. F. (2014). The myth of harmless wrongs in moral cognition: Automatic dyadic completion from sin to suffering. *Journal of Experimental Psychology: General, 143*(4), 1600–1615.

Haynes, R. (2003). From alchemy to artificial intelligence: Stereotypes of the scientist in Western literature. *Public Understanding of Science, 12*(3), 243–253. doi:10.1177/ 0963662503123003.

Henderson, J., Gray, R., & Brocklehurst, P. (2007). Systematic review of effects of low–moderate prenatal alcohol exposure on pregnancy outcome. *BJOG: An International Journal of Obstetrics & Gynaecology, 114*(3), 243–252. doi:10.1111/j.1471-0528. 2006.01163.x.

Henderson, J., Kesmodel, U., & Gray, R. (2007). Systematic review of the fetal effects of prenatal binge-drinking. *Journal of Epidemiology and Community Health, 61*(12), 1069–1073. doi:10.1136/jech.2006.054213.

Hennes, E. J., Hampton, A. J., Ozgumus, E., & Hamori, T. J. (2018). System-level biases in the production and consumption of information: Implications for system resilience and radical change. In B. T. Rutjens, & M. J. Brandt (Eds.), *Belief systems and the perception of reality.* Oxon: Routledge.

Hersher, R. (2017, November 29). Climate scientists watch their words, hoping to stave off funding cuts. *National Public Radio.* Retrieved from www.npr.org/sections/thetwo-way/2017/11/29/564043596/climate-scientists-watch-their-words-hoping-to-stave-off-funding-cuts.

Hornsey, M. J., & Fielding, K. S. (2017). Attitude roots and Jiu Jitsu persuasion: Understanding and overcoming the motivated rejection of science. *American Psychologist, 72*(5), 459. doi:10.1037/a0040437.

Humphriss, R., Hall, A., May, M., Zuccolo, L., & Macleod, J. (2013). Prenatal alcohol exposure and childhood balance ability: Findings from a UK birth cohort study. *BMJ Open, 3*(6), e002718. doi:10.1136/bmjopen-2013-002718.

Ioannidis, J. P. A. (2012). Why science is not necessarily self-correcting. *Perspectives on Psychological Science, 7*(6), 645–654. doi:10.1177/1745691612464056.

Jensen, T. (2013, April 2). *Democrats and Republicans differ on conspiracy theory beliefs.* Retrieved from www.publicpolicypolling.com/polls/democrats-and-republicans-differ-on-conspiracy-theory-beliefs/.

Jolley, D., & Douglas, K. M. (2014). The social consequences of conspiracism: Exposure to conspiracy theories decreases intentions to engage in politics and to reduce one's carbon footprint. *British Journal of Psychology, 105*(1), 35–56. doi:10.1111/bjop.12018.

Jussim, L., Crawford, J. T., Anglin, S. M., Stevens, S. T., & Duarte, J. L. (2016). Interpretations and methods: Towards a more effectively self-correcting social psychology. *Journal of Experimental Social Psychology, 66*, 116–133. doi:10.1016/j.jesp.2015.10.003.

Jussim, L., Stevens, S. T., & Honeycutt, N. (2018). *Forbidden and unasked questions about stereotype accuracy.* Manuscript submitted for publication.

Jylhä, K. M., Cantal, C., Akrami, N., & Milfont, T. L. (2016). Denial of anthropogenic climate change: Social dominance orientation helps explain the conservative male effect in Brazil and Sweden. *Personality and Individual Differences, 98*, 184–187. doi:10.1016/j.paid.2016.04.020.

Kahan, D. M. (2013). Ideology, motivated reasoning, and cognitive reflection: An experimental study. *Judgment and Decision Making, 8*(4), 407–424. doi:10.2139/ssrn.2182588.

Kashima, Y. (2000a). Recovering Bartlett's social psychology of cultural dynamics. *European Journal of Social Psychology, 30*(3), 383–403. doi:10.1002/(SICI)1099-0992(200005/06)30:3<383::AID-EJSP996>3.0.CO;2-C.

Kashima, Y. (2000b). Maintaining cultural stereotypes in the serial reproduction of narratives. *Personality and Social Psychology Bulletin, 26*(5), 594–604. doi:10.1177/0146167200267007.

Kempner, J., Perlis, C. S., & Merz, J. F. (2005). Forbidden knowledge. *Science, 307*(5711), 854. doi:10.1126/science.1107576.

Klar, Y., & Bilewicz, M. (2017). From socially motivated lay historians to lay censors: Epistemic conformity and defensive group identification. *Memory Studies, 10*(3), 334–346. doi:10.1177/1750698017701616.

Kruglanski, A. W. (1990). Lay epistemic theory in social-cognitive psychology. *Psychological Inquiry, 1*(3), 181–197. doi:10.1207/s15327965pli0103_1.

Kunda, Z. (1990). The case for motivated reasoning. *Psychological Bulletin, 108*(3), 480–498. doi:10.1037/0033-2909.108.3.480.

Landau, M. J., Kay, A. C., & Whitson, J. A. (2015). Compensatory control and the appeal of a structured world. *Psychological Bulletin, 141*(3), 694.

Lee, E., Sutton, R. M., & Hartley, B. L. (2016). From scientific article to press release to media coverage: Advocating alcohol abstinence and democratising risk in a story about alcohol and pregnancy. *Health, Risk & Society, 18*(5–6), 247–269. doi:10.1080/13698575.2016.1229758.

Lewandowsky, S., Gignac, G. E., & Oberauer, K. (2013). The role of conspiracist ideation and worldviews in predicting rejection of science. *PLoS One, 8*(10), e75637. doi:10.1371/journal.pone.0075637.

Lewandowsky, S., Mann, M. E., Bauld, L., Hastings, G., & Loftus, E. F. (2013). The subterranean war on science. *APS Observer, 26*(9). Retrieved from www.psychological-science.org/observer/the-subterranean-war-on-science/comment-page-1.

Lewandowsky, S., Mann, M. E., Brown, N. J., & Friedman, H. (2016). Science and the public: Debate, denial, and skepticism. *Journal of Social and Political Psychology, 4*(2), 537–553. doi:10.5964/jspp.v4i2.604.

Lewandowsky, S., Oberauer, K., & Gignac, G. E. (2013). NASA faked the moon landing – therefore, (climate) science is a hoax: An anatomy of the motivated rejection of science. *Psychological Science, 24*(5), 622–633. doi:10.1177/0956797612457686.

Lewis, S. J., Zuccolo, L., Davey Smith, G., Macleod, J., Rodriguez, S., Draper, E. S., & ... Gray, R. (2012). Fetal alcohol exposure and IQ at age 8: Evidence from a population-based birth-cohort study. *PLoS One, 7*(11), e49407. doi:10.1371/journal.pone.0049407.

Lord, C. G., Ross, L., & Lepper, M. R. (1979). Biased assimilation and attitude polarization: The effects of prior theories on subsequently considered evidence. *Journal of Personality and Social Psychology, 37*(11), 2098–2109. doi:10.1037/0022-3514.37.11.2098.

Lowe, P., Lee, E., & Yardley, L. (2010). Under the influence? The construction of foetal alcohol syndrome in UK newspapers. *Sociological Research Online, 15*(4), 2. doi:10.5153/sro.2225.

Massey, S. G., & Barreras, R. E. (2013). Introducing "impact validity". *Journal of Social Issues, 69*(4), 615–632. doi:10.1111/josi.12032.

McClure, J., Hilton, D. J., & Sutton, R. M. (2007). Judgments of voluntary and physical causes in causal chains: Probabilistic and social functionalist criteria for attributions. *European Journal of Social Psychology, 37*(5), 879–901. doi:10.1002/ejsp.394.

McConnell, P. & Sutton, R. M. (2018). *The intolerable truth: Perceptions of malfeasance, harmful impact, and the desire to censor ideologically dissonant research findings.* Manuscript in preparation.

McKie, R. (2017, February 20). Scientists attack their 'muzzling' by government. *The Observer.* Retrieved from www.theguardian.com/science/2016/feb/20/scientists-attack-muzzling-government-state-funded-cabinet-office.

Murphy, A. O., Sutton, R. M., Douglas, K. M., & McClellan, L. M. (2011). Ambivalent sexism and the "do"s and "don't"s of pregnancy: Examining attitudes toward proscriptions and the women who flout them. *Personality and Individual Differences, 51*(7), 812–816. doi:10.1016/j.paid.2011.06.031.

Nosek, B. A., Alter, G., Banks, G. C., Borsboom, D., Bowman, S. D., Breckler, S. J., ... & Contestabile, M. (2015). Promoting an open research culture. *Science, 348*(6242), 1422–1425. doi:10.1126/science.aab2374.

Nuccitelli, D. (2017, January 31). Trump is copying the Bush censorship playbook. Scientists aren't standing for it. *The Guardian.* Retrieved from www.theguardian.com/environment/climate-consensus-97-per-cent/2017/jan/31/trumps-copying-the-bush-censorship-playbook-scientists-arent-standing-for-it.

The Professional Institute of the Public Service of Canada. (2013). Most federal scientists feel they can't speak out, even if public health and safety at risk, says new survey. Retrieved from www.pipsc.ca/portal/page/portal/website/issues/science/bigchill.

Rutjens, B. T., & Heine, S. J. (2016). The immoral landscape? Scientists are associated with violations of morality. *PLoS One, 11*(4), e0152798. doi:10.1371/journal.pone.0152798.

Rutjens, B. T., Heine, S. J., Sutton, R., & van Harreveld, F. (2018). Attitudes towards science. *Advances in Experimental Social Psychology, 57.* doi:10.1016/bs.aesp.2017.08.001.

Rutjens, B. T., van Harreveld, F., & van der Pligt, J. (2013). Step by step: Finding compensatory order in science. *Current Directions in Psychological Science, 22*(3), 250–255. doi:10.1177/0963721412469810.

Skitka, L. J., & Washburn, A. N. (2016). Are conservatives from Mars and liberals from Venus? Maybe not so much. In P. Valdesolo, & J. Graham (Eds.), *Social psychology of political polarization* (pp. 78–101). New York, NY: Routledge.

Stevens, S. T., Jussim, L., Anglin, S. M., & Honeycutt, N. (2018) Direct and indirect influences of political ideology on perceptions of scientific findings. In B. T. Rutjens, & M. J. Brandt (Eds.), *Belief systems and the perception of reality.* Oxon: Routledge.

Sutton, R. M., & Douglas, K. M. (2014). Examining the monological nature of conspiracy theories. In J. W. van Prooijen, & P. A. M. van Lange (Eds.), *Power, politics, and paranoia: Why people are suspicious of their leaders* (pp. 254–272). Cambridge: Cambridge University Press.

Sutton, R. M., Douglas, K. M., & Petterson, A. (2018). A tale of two conspiracies: Similarities and differences between conspiracy theories on either side of the climate debate. Manuscript in preparation.

Sutton, R. M., Lee, E., & Hartley, B. L. (2018). Could studies of drinking during pregnancy encourage drinking during pregnancy? Reactions to scientific research are shaped by concerns about its impact. Manuscript in preparation.

Tetlock, P. E. (2002). Social functionalist frameworks for judgment and choice: Intuitive politicians, theologians, and prosecutors. *Psychological Review, 109*(3), 451–471. doi:10.1037/0033-295x.109.3.451.

Tetlock, P. E., & Manstead, A. S. (1985). Impression management versus intrapsychic explanations in social psychology: A useful dichotomy? *Psychological Review, 92*(1), 59–77. doi:10.1037/0033-295X.92.1.59.

Toma, C., & Butera, F. (2009). Hidden profiles and concealed information: Strategic information sharing and use in group decision making. *Personality and Social Psychology Bulletin, 35*(6), 793–806. doi:10.1177/0146167209333176.

University of Bristol (2012). *Even moderate levels of drinking in pregnancy can affect a child's IQ* [Press release]. Retrieved from www.bristol.ac.uk/news/2012/8936.html.

van der Linden, S. (2015). The conspiracy-effect: Exposure to conspiracy theories (about global warming) decreases pro-social behavior and science acceptance. *Personality and Individual Differences, 87,* 171–173. doi:10.1016/j.paid.2015.07.045.

Washburn, A. N., & Skitka, L. J. (2017). Science denial across the political divide: Liberals and conservatives are similarly motivated to deny attitude-inconsistent science. *Social Psychological and Personality Science.* Advance online publication. doi:10. 1177/1948550617731500.

Wilson, E. O. (1995). Science and ideology. *Academic Questions, 8*(3), 73–81. doi:10.1007/bf02683222.

The World Bank. (2018). Graph illustration of research and development expenditure from 1996–2015. Retrieved from https://data.worldbank.org/indicator/GB.XPD.RSDV.GD.ZS.

INDEX

abortion rights 12
accuracy motivation 30
Aguilera, A. 103
Albers, C. J. 123
Altemeyer, R. A. 122
alternative facts 10–11
American national politics: factualization 14–19; morality and facts 10–11; moralization 11–14; political divide 22–3; socialization 19–22
anti-egalitarianism 48, 51
anti-elitism 84, 86–8
anti-pluralism 84–5, 88–9

Balcetis, E. 53
Bartlett, J. 89
belief bias 17
belief-driven processing 119
beliefs system, and reality perceptions 2
Berlusconi, Silvio 92
bias blind spots 30
Biden, Joe 13
"The Big Sort" (Bishop) 21
Bilewicz, M. 166
biomedical suffering construal 108; redemptive narratives vs. 109–11
Blanton, H. 126
Boehner, John 10
Brandt, M. J. 129
Breitborde, N. J. K. 103
Brexit 1
Brown, A. J. 124
Brown, R. 121

Brown v. Board of Education 35
Bruder, M. 87
Brulle, R. J. 34
Bush, George W. 36

Campbell, T. H. 171–2
capital punishment 15
Ceci, S. J. 68
Chambers, J. R. 50, 141
Cheung, B. Y. 154, 156
Clinton, Hillary 81
cognitive model: bottom-up influences 29–30; top-down influences 29–30
collectivist cultures, repressive suffering construal and 101–3
Collisson, B. 141
Conrad, P. 157
consequentialist reasoning 15
conspiracy theories 82, 172–3; see also populism
Crawford, J. T. 121, 129
criminality 154–5
cultural-existential psychology 98–9
cultural variation in suffering 99–101

Dar-Nimrod, I. 152, 156
Davenport, Charles B. 156
demographic gaps 122–3
deontological reasoning 14–15
direct and indirect influences 118
Dispensa, J. M. 34
distrust and conspiracy beliefs 86–7

Ditto, P. H. 17
diversity of political beliefs 128–9
Dunning, D. 53

Ecker, U. K. 36
egalitarian behavior 125
Ellemers, N. 123
Emotional Over-Involvement (EOI) of
    relatives 103
endorsement of free markets 124
ephemeral gain theory 85
essentialism: genetic 151–2, 157–8;
    psychological 150
eugenics 156–7
evidence of gender bias 67; incidental 72–3;
    methodological debate 69–70; mixed
    evidence 68–9; statistical criticism 70–2;
    structural 72–3; *see also* gender inequality
explanatory coherence model 14

factualization 14, 22; consequentialist
    justification 15; deontological
    justification 15; ideological reasoning
    17–19; motivated consequentialism
    16–17; motivated deontology 15–16
Fagerlin, A. 53
false beliefs 31
false consciousness 31
Farage, Nigel 84–5
Feckleton, R. P. 124
fostering independence 109
fourth law of behavioral genetics 156
Francis, Pope 92
F-Scale 120–1
Funder, D. C. 122

gender 152–3
gender inequality 4, 75n1; in academia
    65–6, 73–5; implicit bias 66–7; individual
    merit ideology 63–5; *see also* evidence of
    gender bias
genetic essentialism 151–2; reducing 157–8
Gignac, G. E. 124
Goh, J. X. 124
Gore, Al 10
grid approach 136–7; construction 138–9;
    ideological prejudice 143–4; negative
    test strategies 137; perspectivism 137–8;
    positive regard 143; prejudice 141–2;
    testing 140–1; unwillingness 139–40;
    willingness 140

Haines, E. L. 33
Hartley, B. L. 169–71
Haynes, R. 166

health 155
Heesacker, M. 50
Heine, S. J. 152, 154, 156
Hennes, E. P. 35
Hitler, Adolph 92
Hofstadter, R. 87, 89
Honeycutt, N. 168
Hulsizer, M. 53
humanism and normativism 103–7
hypothesis testing 119–20; *see also* grid
    approach

ideological differences 136, 141–4
ideological prejudice grid 143–4
ideological reasoning 17–19
ideological variables 87
ideology and inequality perceptions 47–8;
    differential exposure 51–2; ideologically
    motivated perceptions of inequality 54–5;
    implications of 56–8; motivated cognition
    53–4; social dominance orientation 50–2,
    54–6; strategic reporting 52–3
illegal immigration 13–13
Imhoff, R. 87
impact bias 5
Implicit Association Test (IAT) 125
implicit gender bias 66–7, 73–5
inaccurate beliefs 31
income inequality 50
individual merit ideology 63–5, 74
inequality perceptions 3, 48; ideological
    motivation 49–50; origins of 49; shaping
    ideology 56; *see also* ideology and
    inequality perceptions
information production and consumption
    29–31; system-level distortions of reality
    32–5
intergroup relations function of morality 13
intuitive politicians 168
intuitive prosecutors 168
intuitive theologians 168
issue moralization 11–12

Jaccard, J. 126
Jagel, K. 35
Jayaratne, T. E. 153
Jost, J. T. 31, 33, 35
Judis, J. B. 85
Jussim, L. 125–6, 168

Kay, A. C. 171–2
Klar, Y. 166
Kopelowicz, A. 103
Krouwel, A. P. M. 121
Kunda, Z. 30

Lee, E. 169–71
left-wing authoritarianism (LWA) 121–2
Lewandowsky, S. 36, 124
Liebold, J. M. 125
Liu, B. S. 17
Lopez, S. R. 103

McCauley, Clark 128
McConnell, A. R. 125
McConnell, P. 171, 172
Madden, K. 107
Maduro, Nicholas 83
Marietta, M. 12
Mashuri, A. 91
Melenchon, Jean-Luc 84
Merton, R. K. 127
Mertonian skepticism 127
Midlarsky, M. L. 85
Miller, C. 89
misperceptions of reality 35–7
Mitchell, G. 126
moral coherence process 14
moralization process 11, 22; see also political
    moralization
moral judgments 14
motivated cognition 4, 53–4
motivated consequentialism 16–17
motivated deontology 15–16
motivated reasoning 3, 32, 55, 119
Muller, J.-W. 83, 84
Munro, G. 53

Nan, X. 107
negative test strategies 137
neo-Popperian falsification 127–8
Nilsson, A. 105
normativism, humanism and 103–7
null hypothesis testing 119

Obama, Barack 1, 81
Obamacare 9
Oberauer, K. 124
obesity 155–6
O'Hara, B. 124
one gene, one disease (OGOD)
    framework 157
Oswald, F. L. 126

Paluck, E. L. 35
Paris Adult Theater I v. Slaton 33
personal moralization 12–13
perspectivism 137–8
p-hacking 119
Pilanski, J. M. 121
Platt, J. R. 4

political beliefs, diversity of 128–9
political confirmation bias 117
political moralization: consequences
    of 13–14; issue moralization 11–12;
    personal moralization 12–13
political psychology 134–6; grid approach
    (*see* grid approach); ideological
    differences 136; research 56–7
populism 4, 47; anti-elitism 86–8;
    anti-pluralism 88–9; and conspiracy
    theories 82; definition 83–6; threatened
    nationalism 90–1
positive regard, grid approach 143
positive test strategies 136
poverty 2
prejudice, grid approach 141–2
psychological essentialism 150
public communication 157

race and ethnicity 153
redemptive suffering construal 100–1;
    vs. biomedical narratives 109–11; and
    humanists 103–7; prompts 108
repressive suffering construal 100; and
    collectivist culture 101–3
right-wing authoritarianism (RWA) 87, 122
Ruby, M. B. 156
Rudner, R. 120, 129
Ruisch, B. C. 35

"sacred rhetoric" 12
sacred value protection model 13
Sanders, Bernie 10, 84
Scalise, Steve 9
Schlenker, B. R. 141
science: censorial responses 170–1; and danger
    166–8; impact to 168–72; malpractice and
    conspiracy 172–3; perennial opposition
    to 165; skepticism 168–72
scientific reasoning 23
SDO *see* social dominance
    orientation (SDO)
selective exposure 20–22
self-fulfilling prophecies 122–3
self-serving biases 31
sexual orientation 153–4
Shils, E. A. 121
Simpson, E. H. 123
skepticism: about climate change 32–4;
    Mertonian 127
Skitka, L. J. 139–41, 171
social dominance orientation (SDO) 50–2,
    54–6, 87
socialization 19, 22; selective exposure 20–2;
    similarity and group formation 19–20

social media studies 19–20
social psychology 1
Stevens, S. T. 168
Stone, W. F. 121, 122
strategic reporting 52–3
stress-related suffering 107–11
strong feelings of disgust 11
suffering perceptions 4, 97–8; cultural-
    existential psychology 98–9; cultural
    variation 99–101; redemptive suffering
    construals and humanists 103–7;
    repressive suffering construals and
    collectivist culture 101–3; stress-related
    107–11
Sutton, R. M. 169–72
Swan, L. K. 50
system justification 29, 31–5, 37
system-level distortions of reality:
    consumption of 32–4; production of
    34–5
system rejection 29, 37–8
Szegedi, Csanad 149, 150

Tang, D. T. 36
Tankard, M. E. 35
Taylor, S. 53

Tetlock, P. E. 126, 139–41, 167–8, 170
theoretical confirmation bias 117
threatened nationalism 85, 90–1
Tomkins, S. S. 101
transformation themes 109
Trump, Donald 81, 82, 84, 92, 152, 164
Twitter 21

UK Independence Party (UKIP) 81
unwillingness, grid approach
    139–40

value conflicts 2
value differences 2
van der Lee, R. 123
Van Prooijen, J.-W. 90–1, 121

Washburn, A. N. 171
weapons of mass destruction (WMDs) 36
Webb, T. J. 124
Wilders, Geert 85
Williams, W. M. 68
willingness, grid approach 140
Wilson, E. O. 165

Zaduqisti, E. 91